DISPUTE RESOLUTION

Negotiation, Mediation and Other Processes

Third Edition

Stephen B. Goldberg

Professor of Law, Northwestern University

Frank E.A. Sander

Bussey Professor, Harvard University

Nancy H. Rogers

Joseph S. Platt - Porter, Wright, Morris & Arthur

Professor of Law, Ohio State University

Copyright © 1999 by Stephen B. Goldberg, Frank E.A. Sander, and Nancy H. Rogers

All rights reserved
Printed in the United States of America

ISBN 0 - 7355 - 0442 - 3

This manual is made available as a courtesy to law teachers with the understanding that it will not be reproduced, quoted or cited, except as where indicated. In the event that anyone would like to cite the manual for thoughts drawn from it, a reference to the relevant page number of the materials text (with the formula "suggested by") may be appropriate.

                      Permissions
                      Aspen Law & Business
                      A Division of Aspen Publishers, Inc.
                      1185 Avenue of the Americas
                      New York, NY 10036

1 2 3 4 5

TABLE OF CONTENTS

Introduction	i
Sample Syllabi	v
Chapter 1. The Disputing Universe	1
Chapter 2. Negotiation	2
Questions 2.1 - 2.17	
Exercises 2.1 - 2.9	
Chapter 3. Mediation	46
Questions 3.1 - 3.27	
Exercises 3.1 - 3.9	
Chapter 4. Arbitration	81
Questions 4.1 - 4.10	
Chapter 5. Combining and Applying the Basic Processes	84
Questions 5.1 - 5.30	
Exercises 5.1 - 5.3	
Chapter 6. Courts and ADR	108
Questions 6.1 - 6.20	
Chapter 7. Confidentiality	116
Questions 7.1 - 7.16	
Chapter 8. Family Disputes	121
Questions 8.1 - 8.8	
Chapter 9. Public Disputes	126
Questions 9.1 - 9.9	
Exercises 9.1 - 9.2	
Chapter 10. International Disputes	139
Questions 10.1 - 10.4	
Exercises 10.1 - 10.2	
Chapter 11. The Future of ADR	165
Questions 11.1 - 11.7	
Chapter 12. Dispute Resolution Problems	167
Problems 12.1 - 12.16	

Introduction

As pointed out in the Preface to the text, this book can be used in a variety of ways–as a basis for class discussion of the conceptual issues raised by the excerpts, as a source for discussing the questions that appear throughout the book, as background reading for simulations or demonstrations, or in any combination of these. One suggestion for those teachers who intend to focus on the questions: We have found it useful to assign questions to teams of 3-4 students a week or two in advance of the class at which they are to be discussed. The team is responsible for turning in answers in time for them to be reproduced and distributed to the class 2-3 days before they are to be discussed. Those answers are then used as the starting-point for class discussion. This approach has produced both good answers and a high level of class discussion. A variant of this has been used by Professor Gerald Williams at Brigham Young Law School. He has assigned whole chapters, or parts of chapters, to such teams, with the team being responsible to submit an outline of the assigned material (including the questions) for subsequent class discussion.

We strongly recommend the use of the simulations included as exercises in Chapters 2, 3, 5, 9, and 10. We have found that students who have first-hand experience in ADR processes tend to appreciate their dynamics more than students whose knowledge comes exclusively from reading. Additional exercises can be obtained from the Case Clearinghouse at the Program on Negotiation, Pound Hall, Harvard Law School, Cambridge, Mass., 02138; the Clearinghouse has an extensive descriptive catalogue of its available offerings.

For each simulation included in this edition, there are general instructions in the text which contain information that is to be shared by all participants in the simulation. For most simulations, there is also confidential information, which is contained in this Teacher's Manual. The latter information should be reproduced and distributed to the student negotiator for whom it is intended, with strict instructions that it is not to be shown to the opposing negotiator. (In order to maintain the confidentiality of these materials, and preserve the value of the exercise for future students, many instructors collect the confidential information sheets at the end of the simulation.) We have also prepared teaching notes for each simulation, and these, too, are contained in this Teacher's Manual, following the confidential instructions for each exercise.

These exercises can be done either during class time or outside of class, depending on such factors as available class time and the ease with which students can meet outside of class. A good teaching device is to assign all negotiating groups except one to negotiate outside of class, then to have the remaining group negotiate the exercise in class, with the other students observing. As long as the negotiation does not go on too long (30-45 minutes maximum), the observers will be quite attentive, since they have recently struggled with the same exercise. An observation exercise such as this provides an excellent focal point for subsequent discussion of the exercise, since students can compare their negotiation approach and results with those of the demonstration group. A variant of this technique is to have two demonstration groups do the exercise; one group should remain outside while the other does its demo so as to get two independent cuts at the problem.. The discussion can then focus on the differences in the two approaches.

Another option available for Exercises 2.9, 3.1, 3.3, 3.9, 5.1, 5.2 and 5.3 is to assign them to be done outside of class and to show in class all or portions of the videotape of others doing the same exercise, stopping the tape to discuss how the students' technique differed from that viewed on the tape. This offers advantages in terms of control over presentation time, exposure to experienced practitioners, and uninhibited criticism of the techniques used by the videotaped practitioners.

Students can also gain practical knowledge of dispute resolution processes by watching professionals in action. Videotaped negotiations are available from Prof. Gerald R. Williams, Brigham Young University, J. Reuben Clark Law School, Provo, Utah, 84602. The National Institute for Dispute Resolution, 1527 New Hampshire Avenue, NW, Washington, D.C. 20036, has produced a set of 4 tapes of court-connected ADR processes (two on court-annexed arbitration, one on a court-referred mediation, and one of a summary jury trial). In 1991 West Publishing Company made available 4 videotapes produced by Prof. Leonard Riskin involving a dispute negotiation, a transnational negotiation, a mediation, and a meeting with client and opposing counsel to select an appropriate ADR process. Three of the exercises that are the basis of these tapes can be found in Chapters 2, 3 and 5 of our book.

Videotape demonstrations of both mediation and arbitration are also available from the various regional offices of the American Arbitration Association and a mini-trial and commercial mediation videotape is available from the CPR Institute for Dispute Resolution, 366 Madison Avenue, New York, N.Y., 10017. (The CPR tapes are reflected in Exercises 3.9 and 5.2). On occasion, the American Arbitration Association will arrange for students to observe an actual arbitration hearing. Observing actual negotiations or mediations is more difficult to accomplish, but may be possible for the determined student. Guest lecturers with practical experience are another means by which to provide students with a sense of the dynamics of dispute resolution. The local chapter of SPIDR (Society of Professionals in Dispute Resolution) should be able to assist you in finding speakers with experience in most fields; if not, try the national office of SPIDR, 1527 New Hampshire Avenue, NW, Washington, D.C. 20036, telephone 202-667-9700.

This book is designed for either a 2-hour or 3-hour one-semester course. In the former, it may not be possible to cover the entire book, although one of us (FS) has recently come close to doing so; his illustrative syllabus follows this Introduction. Obviously in a 30-hour course primary focus should be given to Chapters 1-5, with other chapters being worked in to suit the instructor's preferences. In the 3-hour course there should be ample time to cover all the materials. At least one of us (SBG) has been using more and more Questions and Exercises in teaching dispute resolution, and has recently begun offering students the option of having up to 2/3 of their final grade based upon these. Prof. Rogers uses the text to teach a Mediation Issues and Practice Seminar. A copy of her syllabus also follows the Introduction.

The problems contained in Chapter 12 are intended to provide the student with an opportunity to utilize, in a variety of contexts, the knowledge of dispute resolution processes he or she should have obtained from the preceding chapters. These problems might provide a useful focus for classes late in the semester; one or more of them might also be used as final examination questions.

The answers to the questions represent our best first efforts. We encourage suggestions for improvements in both the questions and the answers, so that these might be reflected in a subsequent edition.

> Stephen B. Goldberg
> Frank E.A. Sander
> Nancy H. Rogers

May, 1999

Sample Syllabus A

Alternative Methods of Dispute Resolution
Professor Sander
Tentative Outline

Sep. 13 - Introduction and Overview
Ass't: GSR* ch. 1.

Sep. 20 - Negotiation I
Ass't: GSR 17-76; Fisher, Ury and Patton
Getting to Yes (2d ed. 1991)
Problems: 2.2 (36), 2.4 and 2.5 (69),
2.6 and 2.7 (76), 2.9 and 2.10 (77).

Sep. 27 - Negotiation II
Ass't: GSR 76-99 and Jones negotiation (out of class)
Problems: 2.8 (76), 2.11 and 2.12 (77-78), 2.13,
2.14, 2.15, 2.16 and 2.17 (90-91).

Oct. 4 - Mediation I
Ass't: GSR 123-178 and Mediation Manual
Problems: 3.9 a.-d. (166).

Oct. 11 - Mediation II
Ass't: GSR 179-218 and 3 out-of-class mediations
Problems: 3.13 a.-f. (178-179).

Oct. 18 - Arbitration
Ass't: GSR ch. 4
Problems: 4.3 (244)**, 4.4, 4.7, 4.8 and 4.10 (268-269).

---

* Goldberg, Sander and Rogers, Dispute Resolution (3d ed. 1999).

** In lieu of doing a negotiation, point out the most significant issues for Appliances and the Consumers League, and how they might be resolved.

Oct. 25 - Combining and Applying the Basic Processes I
　　　　　　Ass't: GSR ch. 5 (271-311)
　　　　　　Problems: 5.1- 5.3 (278-279), 5.5 (286), 5.6,
　　　　　　　　5.8, 5.9-5.12 (313-313).

Nov. 1 - No class - flyout week.

Nov. 8 - Combining and Applying the Processes II
　　　　　　Ass't: GSR ch. 5 (316-357)
　　　　　　Problems: 5.15, 5.16, 5.18 (326-327), 5.20 (329),
　　　　　　　　5.23-5.26 (335-337), 5.29 (356).

Nov. 15 - Dispute Resolution and the Justice System
　　　　　　Ass't: GSR ch. 6
　　　　　　Problems: 6.3, 6.6 (383), 6.11-6.13, 6.15 (401-404).

Nov. 22 - Family Disputes
　　　　　　Ass't: GSR ch. 8
　　　　　　Problems: 8.4 a.-e., 8.5-8.9 (479-481).

Nov. 29 - Public Disputes
　　　　　　Ass't: GSR ch. 9
　　　　　　Problems: 9.2-9.5 (492-494), 9.7, 9.8 (504-505).

Dec. 6 - The Future of ADR
　　　　　　Ass't: GSR ch. 11
　　　　　　Problems: 11.1-11.5 (572-574).

FS Note: Sometimes we do simulations in class,
　　　　　　and sometimes we have special guests,
　　　　　as discussed in the Introduction to the
　　　　　Teacher's Manual.

Sample Syllabus B

Prof. Nancy Rogers

Prof. Laura Williams

MEDIATION ISSUES SEMINAR/CLINIC

I. COURSE OVERVIEW

This course is designed both to help you develop mediation skills and to examine legal, ethical, and policy issues that arise in the use of mediation. You will act as mediators in Small Claims Court and write and present seminar papers.

We have scheduled most of the class hours and the bulk of required reading for the first five weeks of the semester. By front-loading, we can get you ready to mediate at the court beginning on September 17. Also, we can discuss the law-related issues enough so that you can pick a seminar paper topic by September 21.

Extended mediation skills training classes will be held on three evenings from 6:00 to 9:30: Monday, August 31; Thursday, September 3; and Wednesday, September 9. At these training classes, we have arranged for one experienced mediator to assist each group of three students. We have canceled some classes in anticipation of these evening hours of class and your time at Small Claims Court.

At the first class session, you may sign up for a time to mediate at the Small Claims Court. Each student will mediate seven times, for about three hours each time, during the course of the semester. A number of you will mediate on Thursday evenings, but other times are available as well. Professor Williams will observe some of your mediation sessions and discuss them with you.

II. COURSE REQUIREMENTS

The course requirements are: (1) a rough draft, oral presentation, and final draft of a seminar paper, (2) three hours per week for seven weeks acting as mediators, and (3) prepared class participation. The course grade will be based on the following:

Class preparation, participation, and court mediation	35%
Seminar paper	65%

The seminar paper should be a well-documented legal research paper. Although there are no page minimums or maximums, our expectation is about 30 pages of text. Notes may be placed either as footnotes or endnotes.

The paper deadlines are as follows:

> Topic submitted for approval by September 21.
> Outline submitted by October 2.
> Rough draft (4 copies) submitted by November 2.
> Final paper submitted by December 18.

Please submit written assignments to our floor secretary, Ms. Trina Lott, in Room 215.

III. REACHING US

Please contact Professor Williams first about your mediation sessions. Her office is Room 208 and her phone is 688-3539. She will check the voice mail on her office phone twice per day. If you cannot reach Professor Williams and are unable to arrive on time for a mediation session, you may call Marlena Holman of the Small Claims Division of the Court at 645-8576. Please contact Professor Rogers first about seminar paper questions. Her office is Room 214 and her phone is 292-4223. She will check her office voice mail twice per day. You may also reach her by email, rogers.23@osu.edu.

IV. ASSIGNMENT SCHEDULE

The course text is STEPHEN B. GOLDBERG, FRANK E.A. SANDER, AND NANCY H. ROGERS, DISPUTE RESOLUTION: NEGOTIATION, MEDIATION, AND OTHER PROCESSES, THIRD EDITION (1999).

August 24   **Negotiation for mediators, Part 1**
Goldberg, Sander & Rogers, Text pp. 17-23, 36-49

August 25   **Negotiation for mediators, Part 2; Basic Mediation Techniques, Part 1**
Text pp. 49-60, 91-99, 123-133

August 31   **10:00 to noon Basic Mediation Techniques, Part 2**
No new reading

                6:00 to 9:30 p.m. Mediation Training, Part 1. Room 245
No new reading. Pizza will be served. (This is how I will use the royalties that I will receive as a result of your buying the text that I co-authored.)

September 1   **Workshop on Selecting Paper Topics; Mediation distinguished from other processes, history, current applications; Public Policy Concerns**
Text pp. 3-12; 171-179

Note: In class on September 1, role play instructions will be distributed. Please find two people to play the parts of the two disputing people in the role play while you mediate. Make an audiotape of this mediation. If you need to borrow a tape recorder, see Professor Williams. Listen to the audiotape and make notes about what skills you want to work on particularly during you mediation sessions at the court. Please turn in the tape and your notes to Ms. Trina Lott, Room 215, by September 8 (or bring them to class on that date).

September 3 6:00 to 9:30 p.m. Mediation Training, Part 2. Room 245
Re-read Text pp. 123-134.
Guest mediator: David Doyle, Tenth District Court of Appeals
Subs will be served.

September 8 **Mandatory mediation/ Pressures to settle**
Text pp.363-411
<u>**TAPES DUE:**</u> **Turn in tapes of the Fender-Bender exercise and make appointment to meet with Prof. Williams to discuss the tape.**

September 9 6:00 to 9:30 p.m. Mediation Training, Part 3. Room 251
Again, pizza. Guest mediator: William L. Clark

September 15 Mediation techniques, a few more points; Drafting mediated agreements; Meeting with Marlena Holman from Small Claims Court
Text pp. 134-162 (prepare answers to the questions interspersed throughout the transcript of the mediation); N. Rogers & C. McEwen, <u>Mediation: Law, Policy, Practice, Second Edition</u>, 39-47 (1994).

September 21 No class; <u>PAPER TOPIC DUE</u>
Two or three sentences, handwritten or typed, is fine. I ask you to submit the topic for two reasons. One is to be certain that the topic will require the use of legal research and analysis (not just a report on an interesting new mediation program, for example). The second reason is to avoid a situation in which two students take the same approach to the same topic.

September 22 Regulating mediation, Part 1
Text pp. 184-206

September 29 Regulating mediation, Part 2
No new reading

October 2 <u>**PAPER OUTLINE DUE.**</u>
This can be 1-3 pages, with questions, and may be either handwritten or typed.

October 6 **Confidentiality**
Text pp. 419-445

October 20 **Confidentiality (continued)**
No new reading

October 27 **Representing a client in mediation**
Text pp. 316-337

November 2   **ROUGH DRAFT DUE**
Please turn in four copies to Ms. Trina Lott in Room 215. One copy will be given to the student assigned to be your primary questioner. One copy will be put on reserve in the library. The other two copies are for the two of us. Please retain a copy for yourself. The rough draft should have footnotes or endnotes but these can be in rough form, e.g., "Riskin, Wash. U. article."

November 3 Mediation and legal ethics; Mediating criminal disputes
Text pp. 206-218; handouts on mediation and domestic violence

November 10 Mediating disputes involving inter-ethnic and other differences
Text pp. 167-171, 554-560

November 17 Dealing with impasse
Text pp. 162-164. Guest mediator: James A. Readey

November 23   Paper presentations

November 24   Paper presentations

December 1   Paper presentations

December 2   Paper presentations

December 18 SEMINAR PAPERS DUE
Please turn in a single copy to Ms. Lott in Room 215. Retain a copy for yourself.

CHAPTER 1 - THE DISPUTING UNIVERSE

The material contained in Chapter 1 can be dealt with in at least two ways. One possibility is to focus class discussion on particular portions of the chapter, such as the goals of the alternatives movement or the cautions and concerns raised by the chapter-ending questions. Another approach is to plunge the students at once into practical problems of dispute resolution. This can be done by assigning Chapter 1 to be read in advance of the first class, and asking each student to describe briefly a recent dispute in which he or she was involved, including how that dispute was resolved, and how, in light of Chapter 1, it might have been handled differently. This requires students to apply what they have read about the various processes, and demonstrates at once that the subject matter of the course is not abstract theory, but a very real search for what works. The discussion of what works can then be tempered by bringing in the chapter-ending cautions and concerns to demonstrate that the search for processes that effectively resolve disputes is not the only concern of the course. Rather, broad-ranging questions concerning the future of the alternatives movement and its implications for society must also be considered. A third approach used by one of the authors (FS) is to assign Chapter 1 for reading prior to class, and spend the first hour exploring with the students the "ADR Map" (i.e., obtaining a macro picture of the dispute resolution universe). In the second hour the students then get their first exposure to "getting the feel" of alternative processes by working through, in triads, a very simple divorce or small-claims-type case, first with the neutral acting as arbitrator, and then with the neutral acting as mediator. The resulting discussion is often very rich in revealing the students' perceptions of the important differences between these 2 basic processes.

CHAPTER 2 - NEGOTIATION

A. Questions

2.1   Beginning a long-term relationship, in which decisions must be made jointly, by using a distributional or competitive bargaining strategy would not seem wise. This strategy consists, in essence, of deceiving the other party about what one really wants, and why, in order to obtain a desired result. Initially this approach makes it less likely that the parties will achieve a mutually satisfactory outcome. Here, for example, as a compromise between a spring wedding and a fall wedding, the couple is to have a summer wedding, which neither wants. While the example may be exaggerated, the point is clear. Moreover, if the deception is discovered, it could have a harmful effect on the relationship. Both these points have obvious applicability beyond the context of this question.

2.2   While the straightforward nature of this approach is appealing, it is apt to be counter-productive. The negotiator who takes this approach gives the other negotiator no opportunity to participate in the terms of the bargain other than by accepting or declining the terms offered. This may be so damaging to the other negotiator's self-image or to his image vis-a-vis his client or constituents that it will be difficult to accept. Thus, a negotiator should consider carefully the effect of this approach on an opposing negotiator before using it. See Raiffa (1982: 48) (more often than not this strategy antagonizes the other party); cf. NLRB v. General Electric Co., 418 F.2d 736 (2nd Cir., 1969) (use of this strategy by an employer violates the National Labor Relations Act, in part because it deprives the union of any meaningful opportunity to bargain on behalf of its membership.) Query the extent to which the psychological fall-out of this approach is affected by the reasonableness of the offer? (The question assumes that the negotiator has been authorized by her client to take this approach to negotiation. If not, and immediate disclosure of the client's reservation price results in a less satisfactory outcome for the client than would be expected if the lawyer had pursued a more conventional approach, it is arguable that the lawyer has breached her duty of zealous representation.)

2.3   One problem with using the Tit-for-Tat strategy in face-to-face negotiations is that a strategy of punishing one's opponent for varying from a value-creating approach may lead to retaliation based on emotions that the computer does not possess. Your opponent may feel that his value-claiming approach was justified by his legitimate fears that you would engage in value
claiming first, so that you were wrong to punish him, and he will react by continuing in a value claiming mode regardless of what you do thereafter. This is not to say that the version of Tit Tat referred to by Lax and Sebenius (p. 51) as a "conditionally open" strategy is not a sound means by which to manage the tension between creating and claiming value, but that it must be employed with careful attention to the psychological make up of the opposing negotiator. See also A Note on "Tit-Tat", in R. Fisher and S. Brown, Getting Together 197 (1988).

The dynamics of the Prisoner's Dilemma, and the effects of various approaches to that dilemma, are nicely illustrated by Exercise 2.4 (Pepulator Pricing).

2.4   Following the Lax and Sebenius analysis of bargaining power, the U.S. position in negotiations of this type would appear to suffer from two defects. First, while the U.S. has enormous power to inflict harm on hostage takers or the countries that sponsor their activities, it has been unwilling to exercise that power because of fear that to do so might threaten the lives of the hostages and because identifying the sponsoring countries is often difficult. There is also the constraint that mounting a military attack against a sponsor nation, even if identified, would do harm to many innocent persons within that country. In light of these constraints, it is unlikely that anything can be done to increase the credibility of forcible U.S. response to hostage taking.

Another reason for U.S. lack of power in these negotiations, also suggested by Lax and Sebenius, is the control by the U.S. of substantial assets, both political and economic, which it has occasionally used in exchange for hostage release. In this respect, the U.S. is in a position not unlike that of the wealthy parents of a kidnapped child. And, just as Lax and Sebenius suggest that the parents' bargaining power would increase if their assets were impounded, so, too, the U.S. bargaining power would increase if it credibly vowed to make no concessions -- political, economic or other -- to hostage takers. As a political matter, however, such a position may be so difficult to sustain that the strongest practical position would be a vow to take no action as a result of the hostage taking that the U.S. would not have been willing to take had there been no hostage taking.

2.5   While it is unquestionably true that the negotiator with less bargaining power ought not follow a competitive, value-claiming approach, since she is likely to do quite poorly, the opposite is not at all clear. The negotiator with greater bargaining power is subject to at least two constraints in seeking to take advantage of that strength through the use of a competitive, value
claiming approach. First, if the relationship is a continuing one, and there is a possibility that the balance of power may shift in the future, the temporarily stronger party may not want to establish the precedent that such strength is to be used to the greatest extent possible. Even in the absence of a continuing relationship, the stronger party may have moral or ethical qualms about taking full advantage of that strength vis-a-vis a weaker opponent.

2.6   The risk is that the attorney may focus overmuch on the client's legal rights and her prospects of prevailing in litigation, ignoring or placing insufficient weight on the client's interests, the problem that underlies the dispute. If the attorney has a thorough understanding of interest-based or principled negotiation, this risk is reduced. It is also reduced if the client is present at the negotiation, but that may create other problems. See question 2.7.

2.7   (a) The clients' presence would probably increase the possibility of an integrative solution based on the parties' broader business dealings. At the same time, the parties will want to assess carefully what is likely to occur through legal proceedings if they do not settle, and thus the lawyers' presence may be important as well. On balance, the best approach might be to include both lawyers and clients. At the same time, there are disadvantages to this approach. The use of lawyers increases the costs of the negotiations. The presence of clients may result in disclosures that harm the negotiating posture. Further, the added people will make the discussions more complex and thus extend them. See generally, Riskin, 1991.

(b)   This example is taken from the Knebel and Clay excerpt at pp. 134-159 in which both lawyers and clients attend a mediation. There, the emotional exchange between clients, culminating in an apology, may have been a necessary precursor to serious negotiations about a plan for the future. In an interpersonal dispute, this argues for the presence of clients. Some students may contend that clients should be excluded in emotional disputes, so that cooler heads may negotiate. But the clients may be unwilling to accept a settlement recommended by their
lawyers if their anger has not been vented. Client attendance also permits immediate discussion of settlements based on future business interests.

If the clients attend, the lawyers may play a mediating role when emotions erupt. In addition, the presence of lawyers arguably makes the parties feel that they can agree without fear that they are foregoing better opportunities available through litigation. Further, developing the outlines of the settlement may require substantive legal expertise.

(c)   This situation resembles (b) because it involves an interpersonal relationship and the possibility of an integrative solution. This argues in favor of the presence of clients. However, if the battered spouse feels frightened, agreement, or at least a lasting agreement, seems less likely with the clients present. Thus, lawyer-to-lawyer negotiations, with the client available for consultation, may offer more advantages. Of course, the lawyer for the victim is unlikely to agree to negotiations with only the clients present, as this may place the client in physical danger.

(d) Here there may be little distinction between lawyer and client representatives in terms of negotiating ability or emotional investment. When the ability to predict the likely alternative to settlement is more of an issue, negotiations between lawyers may be more efficient.

2.8 This question raises the problem, adverted to by Rubin and Sander, of conflicting interests between principal and agent. Here, the principal appears to care only about the outcome of the negotiation, viewing it as a one shot deal. Conversely, the attorney cares about his reputation within the community. Presumably he does not want to be known as the lawyer who
participated in tricking Art Chicago into giving up a Gaugin for a fraction of its value.

In seeking a way out of this dilemma, the attorney may seek to persuade the client that it is not in the client's best interests to engage in the negotiations without first notifying Art Chicago of his advisor's views regarding the identity of the artist. If the client is a frequent purchaser of art, the willingness of other dealers and museums to deal with him, at least without painstaking precautions, may diminish sharply once it is known he has purchased this painting for a fraction of its value from an unsuspecting seller.

It is possible that the client will be dissuaded by such advice. In that event, counsel must either follow his client's instructions or withdraw from the negotiations, as it is clear that he cannot both represent the client and seek to further his interests at the expense of the client's interests. It is equally clear that counsel is under no ethical obligation to disclose the true value of the painting. See ABA Model Rules of Professional Conduct, Rule 4.1 at pp. 86 - 87.

2.9 Advantages - Negotiation (if it results in settlement) is likely to be faster and less expensive than adjudication. It permits the parties to take account more fully of circumstances that are peculiar to them and to fashion an agreement that meets their needs. While much depends on the circumstances of the particular case, negotiation is not as likely to create or exacerbate personal antagonisms as is adjudication.

Disadvantages - A party with a strong claim of legal right, but lacking in funds and sophistication, may do less well in negotiation than in adjudication. This is qualified, however, by the fact that a lack of funds and sophistication is also a handicap in litigation. Still, the public nature of the adjudication process may make it a better bet for a party in this situation. Adjudication may also be preferable to negotiation when a definitive ruling is important for precedent-setting purposes, when it is desirable that the moral force of the law be invoked in support of a particular outcome, or when blame needs to be attached. Finally, adjudication may be preferable when internal disagreement or conflict of interest within one of the disputing entities makes a negotiated agreement difficult; having the adjudicator as a scapegoat will often resolve internal disagreements.

2.10 One obvious settlement is to split the difference between the two offers, and propose a settlement at $9,500. A more creative approach would be for defendant to offer plaintiff a new car that sells for $16,000 at a price of $4,000. Assuming that a car that retails for $16,000 costs defendant $8,000 this would reduce defendant's out-of-pocket loss to $4,000, less than it had offered plaintiff in cash. Similarly, plaintiff would have a new car, which would otherwise cost him $16,000, for only $4,000, effectively receiving $12,000 in settlement. Thus, both parties are better off than at their last offers, and the case should settle if this suggestion is made. (This approach is obviously more appealing to defendant if the new car market is stagnant, so that he is not losing profit in addition to out-of-pocket costs.)

The purpose of this question is primarily to demonstrate that an exclusive focus on rights, i.e. the anticipated outcome at trial, will frequently preclude a settlement that might be achieved by examining the underlying interests of the parties. Here, plaintiff's interest is in having a new car to replace the car that was destroyed; defendant's interest is in minimizing its settlement costs. Both of those interests are furthered by the proposed settlement.

2.11   The maximum potential gain of $75,000 per year will accrue to the student if she can discourage Smith from making any use of the Burger Master franchise. This might be accomplished by persuading Smith that the student is going to operate her Best Burger restaurant regardless of what Smith does, so that Smith will be faced with the certainty of losing $25,000 per year as long as he operates his restaurant. The student who chooses this course runs the risk, however, that Smith will not be persuaded, but will believe that if he does operate, the student either will not do so, or will eventually be forced to withdraw. Under this scenario, each will lose $25,000 per year for the indefinite future. A final alternative is for the two franchise owners to form a partnership. They might agree, for example, that only one of the franchises would be operated, that they would jointly absorb the $50,000 cost of the other, and, after that expense is met, would share the $75,000 per year in profits, each netting $37,500.

In view of these alternatives, the student must decide whether to adopt a cooperative or a competitive approach to the negotiations. In making that decision, the real life negotiator would undoubtedly be influenced by her personality (would she be comfortable attempting to force Smith out of business?), her prospects of success (can Smith be persuaded to withdraw?), the financial resources of each (who could better withstand a $25,000 annual loss until the other withdrew?), and the effect of a competitive approach on any long term relationship the parties might have. In this problem, the latter might be quite important, as a competitive business relationship would be likely to have a negative effect on the neighborhood and family relationship of Smith and the student.

2.12   The purpose of this question is to encourage students to discuss the issue, not to suggest any particular answer. One means of stimulating such discussion is to show a videotape entitled Women Negotiate, produced by Professor Deborah Kolb, Simmons College Graduate School of Management, and the Program on Negotiation, Harvard Law School, and distributed by the Program on Negotiation.

2.13   The first part of this question forces the student to examine his personal ethical standards in this situation. The second part, which puts the student into the attorney's role, will be particularly difficult for those students who, representing themselves, would disclose. For, it is clear, the Model Rules impose no duty of disclosure in this situation. Indeed, the attorney's duty of zealous representation might be violated by disclosure. Does it matter, in either context, that the adverse information would be readily available if the buyers made suitable inquiry?

2.14   Once again, students must examine their own ethical standards in negotiation, then determine whether they would be willing to follow a different standard when acting on behalf of a client. For, whatever the student would do as an individual, there is clearly no ethical obligation on an attorney to decline to enter into a contract because it is unfair to the other party. If the contract were so unfair as to be unconscionable, the client runs the risk that it will be voided if challenged in court, but, as long as the client is advised of that fact, it raises issues for the client, not the attorney.

2.15   Since non-disclosure assists the client in committing a fraudulent act, disclosure would appear required by Rule 4.1 unless disclosure is prohibited by Rule 1.6. That Rule precludes the lawyer from revealing information relating to representation of a client, with certain exceptions, the only one of which is arguably relevant in this situation being that contained in Rule 1.6(b)

A lawyer may reveal such information to the extent the lawyer reasonably believes necessary:

(1) to prevent the client from committing a criminal act that the lawyer believes is likely to result in imminent death or substantial bodily harm.

Since the proposed fraud in this situation does not satisfy the criteria of Rule 1.6(b)(1), disclosure appears forbidden. However, Rule 1.2(d) provides that "a lawyer shall not ... assist a client in conduct that the lawyer knows is .... fraudulent," and Rule 1. 16(b)(1) permits the lawyer to withdraw from representing a client if "the client persists in a course of action involving the lawyer's services that the lawyer reasonably believes is ... fraudulent". Even after withdrawal, however, the lawyer cannot disclose a client's confidences that are protected by Rule 1.6. Thus the lawyer may be able to withdraw, but not to disclose.

2.16   Arguably the writer is under no duty to disclose because the information is as accessible to the potential purchasers as to the seller. Even if the writer would commit fraud by nondisclosure the attorney cannot disclose for the same reasons set out in the answer to Question 2.15. Nor is it relevant that the attorney's knowledge in this situation does not come from the client, since the confidentiality rule applies to all information relating to the representation, whatever its source.

2.17   In this situation, the seller's agent has not misrepresented the price her principal will accept, as did the agent in Shell's example, but has misrepresented her authority to accept that price. While reservation prices are not material as a matter of law, so that a misrepresentation concerning the acceptability of an offer is not fraudulent, there is not a similar exception for a misrepresentation concerning authority.

If the seller was to respond, "my authority is my business, but I will tell you right now that $11,000 is unacceptable," she would have both protected her bargaining position and avoided making a fraudulent misrepresentation.

B.   EXERCISES

The negotiation exercises contained on pages 99-117 of the text are intended to illustrate some of the problems described in the readings. For example, the decision whether to follow a cooperative or competitive negotiation strategy, which is treated in a number of excerpts, is presented by Exercise 2.4, Pepulator Pricing. The advantage of looking beyond positions to determine underlying interests is implicit in Exercise s 2.1, Texoil; 2.2, Nam Choi; and 2.3, Star. Exercise 2.5, Too Old to Rock and Roll presents the negotiators with a wide variety of objective criteria of the type that Fisher and Ury believe are of more value in negotiations than does Professor White. Too Old also introduces some of the issues, both tactical and ethical, that are presented when an attorney negotiates on behalf of a client. Exercise 2.6, Colonial Confectioners, raises still more of the ethical issues that can arise when lawyers negotiate, and encourages students to compare their negotiating behavior with the strictures of the Model Rules of Professional Conduct.

Exercise 2.7, Rapid Printing v. Scott Computers, and Exercise 2.8, FG & T Tower, are more complex than the others, though some of the issues are similar. Rapid v. Scott is intended to emphasize the elusiveness of the concept of bargaining power and to provide practice in reaching integrative outcomes. It was designed to be done jointly by law students playing the role of lawyers, and management students playing the role of business executives, and to provide each with experience negotiating in a lawyer-client relationship. FG&T Tower introduces the students to multilateral negotiations through an exercise in coalition-building.

Confidential instructions for each exercise (except Pepulator which has none) follow. Each exercise is followed by teaching notes, and preceded, where necessary, by instructions on how to conduct the exercise.

EXERCISE 2.1:   TEXOIL

Confidential Information for
Service Station Owner

It is imperative that you complete this sale promptly. You and your spouse have been working 60 hours per week for the last five years in order to save up enough money to realize your life's dream, which is to sail around the world. You are close to realizing that dream. You have purchased a boat and have begun to fit it out for a two-year around-the-world cruise. In order to pay the first installment on the boat, you sold your apartment and you and your spouse are now living in a small rental apartment near the service station. It is not very pleasant there and you are anxious to leave and begin your trip as soon as possible. In addition, you are both nearly 50 years old and you want to take this trip while you are still young enough to enjoy it.

You estimate your expenses for the trip as follows. First, you owe another $75,000 on the boat, which must be paid in full before you leave. To get the boat ready to sail will cost another $25,000. You anticipate that your personal living expenses, food, clothing, etc., will come to approximately $60,000 over the two years and that you must set aside at least $25,000 for boat repairs in case of damage. These are really minimum estimates and you cannot shave anything off them.

Additionally, you are convinced that you must have at least $50,000 in the bank for your return, since you are not at all sure what you will do on your return. Your spouse is on the edge of a nervous depression, and the doctor has told him/her that he/she cannot in the future work at a service station. Additionally, the life of the independent service station owner is becoming more and more difficult. Competition is increasing, there are constant price wars, and charges seem to go up and up. For all these reasons, you think it is crucial that you have $50,000 in reserve for your return so that you can explore various possibilities of earning a living. (It is possible that you will be able to sell the boat on your return, but that is so "iffy" that you cannot calculate income from such a sale in determining the amount you must have available on your return.) In sum, then, you must receive at least $235,000 from this sale.

You think that you can justify a $235,000 selling price. You paid $50,000 thirteen years ago for the property on which the station is located, and property values in the area have doubled since then. The cost of building the station was $75,000, and, based on what other station owners have told you, and what you have read in trade journals, building an equivalent station today would cost at least $150,000. Since it would cost Texoil approximately $250,000 to buy land in the area, and build a new station, your asking price of $235,000 is entirely reasonable.

Your ads to sell the service station have been running for about two months, without leading to any really attractive proposition.

Most of the big oil companies have looked at your service station, but the best offer you have received so far is $175,000 from British Petroleum, which would very much like to have a station in this area. The talks with them are continuing, but the likelihood that they are going to increase their offer is very slim in light of the firmness that they indicated at your last meeting.

All things considered, it appears that Texoil provides your only real opportunity to complete the sale at a price that will enable you to fulfill your life's dream. They know the property, they appear interested, and they have often said that they thought sales could be increased with a more aggressive marketing approach. You hope that that will lead them to make a substantial offer. If it does not, that's an end to your dreams.

EXERCISE 2.1:   TEXOIL

Confidential Information for Texoil Senior Vice President of Operations

Texoil has recently begun a five-year plan of increasing its service station ownership, and it hopes to add a minimum of 100 stations during those five years. Thus, it is very interested in purchasing this station. It is a shame that the operator is leaving, as he/she has been an excellent manager and Texoil needs good managers as it expands, but his/her leaving presents Texoil with an opportunity which it wants to take advantage of.

It is not easy, particularly in this area, to find good service stations for sale. Texoil is convinced that this is an excellent opportunity. The station is well situated, and is faced with comparatively little competition compared to other stations the company operates. The cost of purchasing land and building a similar service station in this area would exceed $250,000. However, a new station would have more modern equipment, and be capable of generating additional income. Hence, you are not authorized to pay more than $200,000 for this station.

You would not normally be dealing with a matter involving this little money, but you had other business in the Los Angeles area, so agreed to handle these negotiations on behalf of Texoil

EXERCISE 2.1:   TEXOIL

Teaching Notes

Texoil is intended to demonstrate that in some circumstances going beyond positions to explore interests will make it possible to reach an agreement that otherwise would not be possible.

In this exercise, the service station owner is told that he/she must receive at least $235,000 from the sale of the service station. This sum includes a $50,000 reserve for living expenses while he/she searches for employment on returning from the voyage. Texoil, however, is instructed that it can pay no more than $200,000 for the station. Thus, if the parties stick to their positions, they will reach impasse, as many students do.

If, however, each negotiator examines his/her interests, a deal is possible. If the service station owner is guaranteed employment as a manager or consultant by Texoil on his/her return, he/she does not need the $50,000 reserve. Thus, he/she could settle for $185,000, well within the Texoil limit. Nor is this agreement inconsistent with the owner's reasons for selling the station, all of which are tied to problems of being an independent service station owner.

To be sure, the Texoil negotiator is not explicitly authorized to enter into such an agreement, and some Texoil negotiators will say that they did not consider it for that reason. Still, Texoil's interest in adding good managers as it expands is so clearly furthered by this agreement that at least it should be entered into subject to approval of higher management.

In sum, creative negotiators who are focusing on interests may be able to find a mutually satisfactory agreement here, while positional negotiators cannot.

EXERCISE 2.2: NAM CHOI v. AUSTIN UNIVERSITY MEDICAL SCHOOL

Confidential Information for Attorney for Austin University

Your research on this case indicates that the crucial question, if this matter is litigated, will be whether Austin University Medical School has made reasonable accommodations necessary to satisfy the legitimate interests of both Nam Choi and the Medical School.

You are persuaded that the Medical School has satisfied its obligation in this respect through its provision of counseling, tutors, note-takers, and taped lectures. Thus you believe that the Medical School would prevail in litigation. Still, the Dean does not want to litigate. She wants a prompt settlement of this matter. Both local and national newspapers are having a field day portraying the Medical School as heartless, and the Dean wants that publicity to end as soon as possible. She also wants favorable publicity for the School's affirmative action program, not the unfavorable publicity generated by this suit.

As for the terms of a settlement, the Dean is willing to pay up to $75,000 to get Nam Choi to drop his suit. What the Dean will not do is to allow Nam Choi to take any different type examination than is taken by all other Austin students. She fears that any relaxation in test methods or graduation standards to benefit Nam Choi would affect the School's ability to attract quality students, as well as infuriate alumni and other major donors, whose financial support is necessary for the Medical School to retain its outstanding teaching and research faculty.

This will be your first meeting with the attorney for Nam Choi, and you are confident that with the funds you have to settle this case, you should be able to do so rather easily. (Annual tuition at Austin University Medical School is $25,000, and Nam Choi paid that amount for each of the two years he was at the School. While he undoubtedly has incurred some expenses in connection with the suit he filed, those expenses cannot be much in excess of $25,000
$30,000.)

EXERCISE 2.2: NAM CHOI v. AUSTIN UNIVERSITY MEDICAL SCHOOL

Confidential Information for Attorney for Ted Nam Choi

Ted Nam Choi has had his heart set on helping others in the Asian-American community. It is for that reason that he went to medical school. His parents have fully supported him, both emotionally and financially. Annual tuition at Austin University Medical School is $25,000, and Ted's parents have paid Ted's tuition for each of his two years at Austin, taking a $60,000 mortgage on their home to do so. Additionally, Ted's father, the proprietor of a small garage, has borrowed another $25,000 to pay your fees and expenses for the litigation to date.

The litigation has been an enormous strain on his family. Privately, Ted's father has suggested that to you the whole thing may not be worth the trouble. His view is that the case should be settled if the School will repay Ted's school and litigation expenses to date.

You have suggested to Ted that the Medical School might be willing to enter into a cash settlement that would enable him to repay his parents, but Ted has rejected this suggestion. As he put it, "It is not only my parents I must repay, but the entire Asian-American community that helped us so much when we came to this country. How do I accomplish that goal by walking away from this litigation?"

You have done considerable research on this case, and it is clear that, if the matter is litigated, the crucial question will be whether Austin University has made reasonable accommodations necessary to satisfy the legitimate interests of both Nam Choi and the Medical School.

You are certain that the Medical School has not satisfied its obligation in this respect. None of the assistance the School provided has any relationship to Ted's psychological problem. The only accommodation that would be reasonable would be to allow Ted to take a different type of examination, not multiple-choice. Yet the Medical School has so far refused to make that accommodation.

In view of the School's failure to make a reasonable accommodation that would satisfy Ted's legitimate interests, you believe that Ted will prevail if the case is litigated.

EXERCISE 2.2:   NAM CHOI v. AUSTIN UNIVERSITY MEDICAL SCHOOL

Teaching Notes

This exercise is similar to Texoil (Exercise 2.1), as it too demonstrates that at times an interest-based approach is necessary to reach agreement. The difference between the two exercises is that Texoil takes place in the context of negotiating an agreement, while Nam Choi consists of attempting to settle pending litigation.

In this exercise, a resolution is impossible as long as the attorneys focus on rights, since each is convinced that he/she will prevail if the matter goes to litigation. Each, however, is instructed by his/her client that the client does not want to litigate, but wants to settle.

One obvious approach to a settlement will be financial, but that will not work, since the plaintiff will not accept a financial settlement. (The plaintiffs father, who is financing the litigation, would settle for money, but he is not the client.)

The parties can reach a settlement, however, by focussing on their respective interests.
Ted's primary interest is in helping others in the Asian-American community. He went to medical school, not because he had a burning desire to become a doctor, but so he could be of service to his community. That opens up the possibility of a settlement pursuant to which he could be of service to his community in some way other than as a doctor.

In such a settlement, the School would repay Ted for some or all of his education and litigation expenses. Additionally, the Dean would agree to assist Ted in entering another helping profession. The Dean might even arrange his acceptance into a less demanding Austin University program, e.g. as a medical assistant. This type of settlement would satisfy both Ted's interest in being of service to his community, and the Deans interest in favorable publicity for the School's affirmative action program.

It is not clear whether Ted's interest is in personally helping the Cambodian community or whether indirect help might also serve his purposes. If the latter, then some settlement looking to the establishment of a scholarship (perhaps in his name) for the Cambodian community might also meet his goals, perhaps even more lastingly so. Such a solution also illustrates pie enlarging since the cost to Austin is clearly less than the value to Ted. Of course such a proposition might have to be combined with some financial repayment to Ted.

Another possible settlement would be for Ted to transfer to a foreign medical school with a different approach to testing. Inasmuch, however, as he could not practice in the U. S. without passing U. S. Medical Boards, which are multiple choice, that settlement would not appear to satisfy his interest in helping the Asian-American community.

Readmission to Austin University Medical School would appear to be the least satisfactory settlement, since the Dean will not agree to allow Ted to take exams that are not multiple choice. Even if she would, the Medical Boards are multiple choice, and Ted would surely fail those. Thus, re-admission would lead only to failure on Ted's part, and that would not further the interests of Ted or the Dean.

EXERCISE 2.3:   STAR

Confidential Information for Pacific Records' Representative

You are a vice president of marketing and public relations for Pacific Records. You and everyone else at Pacific Records are excited about the comeback of STAR. The time seems to be just right for the return of their brand of music, and it appears that any album by them, if properly marketed, will be a big seller. Still, you are doubtful that the group will be able to remain intact. Sarren's agent, Ted Gerard, recently told you and Paul Pack that Sarren contracted AIDS while in prison, and the best medical advice is that he will be able to continue working for another year at most. Thus, you would like to get a STAR album recorded and released as soon as possible.

Your marketing experts tell you that a STAR CD released within the next two months could easily top 1,000,000 copies sold. At the standard CD price of $15.00, that would amount to at least $15,000,000 gross. Your profit margin is difficult to anticipate with accuracy because of substantial variance in production expenses, promotion costs, etc., but you would hope to net $3,000,000, exclusive of what you must pay Heffen to allow Robin to record for Pacific.

Paul Pack, the president of Pacific Records, very much wants a STAR album for the Pacific label. In order to get Heffen's agreement to Robin recording for Pacific, you are authorized to offer Heffen up to $1,500,000.00.

It is possible that Heffen will not allow Robin to appear on the Pacific label, but will insist that Pacific allow Sarren, Trace, and Arthurs to appear on the Heffen label. Pack has told you that despite his public statements to the contrary, he will accept such an arrangement, though only as a last resort, and then only if Pacific receives a guaranteed payment of $1,500,000, regardless of sales. Pack has little confidence in Heffen's marketing ability, and will not accept a royalty arrangement tied to sales. In addition, Pack insists on total artistic control over the CD, regardless of which label it is on. Pack is convinced that he understands the STAR sound better than anyone else in the business, and wants a chance to demonstrate that to the public.

Pack has told you that these negotiations with Heffen are among the most important he has ever been involved in, and that he is not participating in them only because he is so emotionally involved, and because Pack does not think he could negotiate calmly with Heffen, whom he dislikes intensely. Many years ago, Pack and Heffen shared artistic control over a record, and their styles clashed so drastically that the record was a disaster. As a result, Pack would never work with Heffen again, though Pack would be delighted if he had the opportunity to show how superior his style is to that of Heffen. At the moment, however, Pack is most concerned that if Pacific and Heffen do not reach agreement, no STAR album will be released. Accordingly, Pack has authorized you to agree to whatever is commercially and artistically reasonable, subject only to the limitations he has imposed on you.

EXERCISE 2.3:   STAR

Confidential Information for Heffen Records' Representative

You are a young protégé of Helene Heffen, having become Heffen's executive assistant after seven years under her employ. Heffen believes that a STAR album should do quite well, selling up to 750,000 copies if it is handled right. Heffen also believes that a follow-up album, if released in the next 12-18 months, will be a smash hit, probably selling in excess of 1,500,000 copies.

Heffen Records would expect to sell a STAR CD at the standard CD price of $15.00. If 750,000 copies were sold, that would amount to $11.25 million gross; if 1,500,000 copies were sold, that would amount to $22.5 million gross. While profit margins are difficult to anticipate with accuracy because of substantial variance in production costs, promotion expenses, etc., Heffen would hope to net approximately 25% of the expected gross, exclusive of what she must pay Pacific to allow Sarren, Trace, and Arthurs to record for Heffen.

Heffen expects that Pacific will demand a high price for allowing Sarren, Trace and Arthurs to appear on a Heffen release, and has authorized you to offer up to 10% of her anticipated gross, but only if it is absolutely necessary to reach agreement.

It is also possible that Pacific will not allow Sarren, Trace and Arthurs to appear on the Heffen label, but will insist that Heffen allow Robin to appear on the Pacific label. Despite her public statements to the contrary, Heffen has told you that she will accept such an arrangement, but only as a last resort, and then only if Heffen Records receives at least $1,000,000. In addition, Heffen insists on total artistic control over the album, regardless of which label it is made on. Heffen is convinced that she understands the STAR sound better than anyone else in the business, and wants a chance to demonstrate that to the public.

Heffen has told you that she attaches great importance to these negotiations, and that she would be handling them if it were not for the personal antipathy that exists between her and Pack. Many years ago, they were co-artistic directors of a record, and their styles so clashed that the record was a disaster. As a result, Heffen would never work with Pack again, though Heffen would be delighted at the opportunity to show how superior the Heffen style is to that of Pack. At the moment, however, Heffen is most concerned that if an agreement is not reached, no STAR album will be released, which would be an artistic and financial tragedy. Accordingly, Heffen has authorized you to do whatever is commercially and artistically reasonable to get a contract with Pacific, subject only to the limitations she has imposed on you.

EXERCISE 2.3:   STAR

Teaching Notes

1.   Why did some of you reach impasse?

Each principal wanted total artistic control

2. How were others able to break that impasse?

Multi-record deal

3. How do you get to that agreement? How can you justify it in light of your principal's position?

Interest of each is in showing he/she best understands STAR sound -- having each control one/more records gives him/her a chance to show that -- so furthers interests of both

4. If you are going to make more than one record, which company will make first?

Must be Pacific

Two reasons:

> (1) Pacific not sure there will be a second album

(2) Heffen doesn't want first; and would offer only $1.12M for Saffen, Trace, and Arthurs, while Pacific would insist on $1.5M. Thus, no deal possible by which Heffen would make first album, Pacific second album

Does (1) raise any ethical issues?

How deal with?

5. In resolving ethical issues in negotiation, must consider:

Legal requirements

Industry/contextual standards

> Trust: impact on your success as negotiator

Personal moral/ethical standards

6. Once you reached agreement on who was going to make the STAR CD (or CDs), you had to deal with the issue of compensation for the use of the artists under contract to the other Company. How did you do so?

Let's look first at how much Heffen paid Pacific for use of Sarren, Trace and Arthurs

Maximum Heffen will pay is 10% of anticipated gross; for CD #2 (which is what Heffen wants), that is $2.25M. Since Pacific will accept $1.5M, there is zone of agreement between $1.5M and $2.25M

Most successful Heffen will pay $1.5M; least successful will pay $2.25M

Most successful Pacific will get $2.25M; least successful will get $1.5M

Look at different results -- ask lowest and highest paying Heffen, "What was your opening offer? Why?"

Ask Pacific who received most and least, "What was your initial demand? Why?"

OR

Look at how much Pacific paid Heffen for use of Robin

Should be between $1M (minimum Heffen will accept) and $1.5M (maximum Pacific will pay)

Look at different results asks Pacific: "What was your opening offer? Why?"

Ask Heffen, "What was your initial demand? Why?"

7. Raiffa points out in "The Art and Science of Negotiation," that there is research evidence that:

Outcome of most distributive negotiations is about midway between initial credible offers

What does that suggest as to how you determine your initial offer or demand in a distributive negotiation?

8. Next question on a distributive negotiation is who should go first?

What do you think? (Ultimately makes no difference as long as you don't get anchored)

9. These questions -- who goes first, and where to begin -- are relevant in a distributive negotiation that is competitive in nature -- where you want to get as much as possible for yourself, leave as little as possible for the other side.

Is there another approach to a distributive negotiation?

Fairness

If that is your goal (when might it be?), how determine fair outcome?

Objective criteria

10. Whatever your approach to negotiating price or other quantitative outcomes, you should recognize that many negotiations have two distinct aspects to them -- part is/may be value-creating. One example is the negotiation here to get one/more STAR records made

Once value is created, next question is how it is to be shared

In some negotiations, that is the only question -- how much will buyer pay seller?

11. Some principles are the same in integrative and in distributive bargaining

Focus on problem, not people

Know your BATNA

12. Other principles may be different in distributive negotiations than in integrative

negotiations, depending on your goal --

If your goal is to share gains fairly:

Search for objective criteria of fairness

If your goal is to get the best possible deal:

Start as high (or low) as you can justify

Give ground grudgingly

By reducing amount of concessions, signal that you are approaching your limit

EXERCISE 2 4:   PEPULATOR PRICING

Teaching Instructions

1.   Divide the class into groups of 12 people (or fewer, but at least 6) to play independent games.

Within Each Game

2.   Divide the players into two groups with an equal number of persons in each. One group will represent Consolidated Pepulator, the other will represent Pulsar Pepulator. Set the groups in different rooms so that they cannot see or hear each other. The teams should be told not to communicate with each other except when and in the manner instructed.

3.   Distribute the Pepulator Pricing Exercise and Score Sheet to each person and allow time for everyone to read it. Explain that as indicated there will be eight rounds of decision making, and that the choice of price should be made round by round, since each decision is a separate one frequently dependent upon past choices as well as being interdependent upon the choice of the opposing team. Note that profit will be cumulative throughout the game.

4.   Give each team 10 minutes to organize itself.

5.   Announce the beginning of Round 1, instructing each team that it has three minutes to reach a confidential pricing decision for the first month. At the end of the round, ask each team to write its price on a piece of paper and collect these sheets as nearly simultaneously as possible.

6.   Deliver each team's choice to the opposing team and record the resulting price and profits on your own tally sheet.

7.   Conduct Rounds 2 and 3 in the same manner.

8.   Before beginning Round 4, announce that the election of a new, even more pro-business administration means that 1) profit figures for this month will be doubled, and 2) that there will be a five minute period during which a representative of each side will be able to meet with a representative from the other side without fear of antitrust liability or prosecution. Any such meeting must be private and limited to the two representatives.

9. Before the meeting of the two representatives, give each team five minutes to plan for the meeting and select a representative.

10. At the end of the meeting of the two representatives, they return to their groups. Each group is allowed five minutes to confer with its representative and select a price for Round 4.

11. Rounds 5 and 6 proceed in the same manner as Rounds 1-3.

12. Before the beginning of Round 7, announce that extraordinary market conditions mean that profit figures for the next two rounds will be quadrupled. Also, a five minute private conference between representatives of each team (as in Round 4) will be allowed before Round 7, but not before Round 8.

13. Each group is allowed a five minute planning period before and after the private meeting.

14. Proceed with Round 7 and Round 8. Prepare the final point total.

(Some instructors end the exercise here. Others continue, after a discussion of the exercise to this point, with an additional four rounds. Instructions for those who wish to continue follow.)

15. Announce that the exercise will now continue with an additional four rounds. The teams will be the same as in Rounds 1-8 and each team will begin Round 9 with the cumulative total profit it amassed in Part I.

16. Distribute Score Sheets for Round 9-12

17. Send each team back to the location where it made pricing decisions in Part I. Allow no communication between teams as they return to their "headquarters."

18. Announce the beginning of Round 9, instructing each team that the rules are the same as in Round 1.

19. Conduct Rounds 9 and 10 in the same manner as Round 1. Announce and post team pricing choices and record resulting profits on a large tally sheet.

20. Before beginning Round 11, announce that extraordinary market conditions will mean that profit figures for the next two rounds will be quintupled for the firm with the largest profit or if the two firms have equal profits. Also, a conference as in Round 4 will be allowed before Round 11, but not before Round 12.

21. Allow a third private conference of up to three minutes. Proceed with Round 11 and 12. Prepare final point totals and subtotals for Part II.

EXERCISE 2.4:   PEPULATOR PRICING

Teaching Notes

As previously noted, the central purpose of this exercise is to demonstrate that negotiations can frequently be approached from either a cooperative or a competitive perspective, and that, at least under some circumstances, a cooperative strategy may be more productive for all parties. Thus, in this exercise, if the two groups cooperate by remaining in the $30 - $30 mode throughout, each team will have a profit of $1,650,000 ($2,640,000 if the exercise continues for 12 rounds). If the two groups have sought to undercut each other in order to maximize their profits, it is likely that neither will have a profit in excess of that which could have been attained through cooperation.

Other issues which are likely to arise in discussing this exercise are the effect of the duration of a relationship on the parties' negotiating strategy, the difficulty of insuring promise keeping or trustworthy conduct, the significance of the identity of a group's bargaining representative, and dealing with intra-group disagreement. If the opinions of women students are not heeded in the intra-group decision-making process, or women are not selected as group representatives in proportion to their number, the effect of gender on negotiating behavior may also be raised.

Questions that can be used to elicit a discussion of these issues include: What was each group's strategy? Did it remain consistent or change? If it changed, what caused it to do so?

Would you have acted differently if there were no eight - month (or 12 - month) end to the exercise, but it were going to continue indefinitely? Do you think that your experience in this negotiation will affect your interaction in future exercises? (This question frequently leads to some painful introspection by members of groups that engaged in efforts to undercut, particularly after a promise to the contrary, as they realize that their short-term "victory" may have had negative long-term effects on their reputation for trustworthiness.)

Was everyone in each group agreed on every choice? If not, how did you resolve disagreements? Who did you select to represent you? Why? What interpretation did you place on the other side's selection of a representative?

If you continue with Rounds 9 - 12 after a class discussion of the issues raised by Rounds 1 - 8, your questions might focus on the differences, if any, in negotiating behavior between Rounds 1 - 8 and 9 - 12. Did the in-class discussion after Rounds 1 - 8 affect the subsequent negotiations? Why?

EXERCISE 2.5:   TOO OLD TO ROCK AND ROLL

Confidential Information for Jerry McCarthy

   Your career is fading fast and you need either to make a comeback or to retire. You don't want to quit. STORMIN' is the best comeback vehicle you have seen in years. YOU WANT THE ROLE.

   Your new lawyer will be negotiating with SST, but you have doubts. Your last lawyer pushed so hard for a big fee that you lost a chance to be on the 1998 Legends of Rockdom tour. To you the job is more important than the size of the fee. Nonetheless, you will have an enormous amount of work to do to get ready for opening night. You can do it, because you are an experienced professional, and a quick study, but not many others can master a role as quickly as you can. Thus, for reasons of pride, reputation, and your value to future productions, you would be disappointed if you did not receive at least $150,000.

   Remember that SST has a good record for sending productions to Broadway. Having seen the script and score, you think STORMIN' has the potential to be a movie as well.

   You pay your lawyer 15% of your fees up to $100,000; you pay 30% of amounts in excess of $100,000.

EXERCISE 2.5: TOO OLD TO ROCK AND ROLL

Confidential Information for Jerry's Attorney

You are an associate at a large entertainment law firm. This is your first negotiating assignment for the firm. You believe you have been given Jerry McCarthy's account because the firm's bigwigs think Jerry is all washed up, and they might as well give the account to someone new.

If you make a lot of money for Jerry, you think your stock at the firm will rise dramatically, and many of its clients will want you to work for them.

Your firm has a standard deal with its clients. It gets 15% of fees up to $100,000 per job; it gets 30% of amounts in excess of $100,000.

Exact figures describing SST's operations are unknown, since it is privately owned, but you know it is profitable. You also know that name stars in other musicals in big markets (outside of New York) have been getting about $10,000 per performance (about $160,000 for sixteen shows). In addition, one of your firm's other clients received $150,000 last year to star in SST's yearly musical, a revival of "Cabaret."

You believe that SST will be in serious difficulty if it cannot sign Jerry promptly. He is ideal for the role, and SST has little time to seek someone else. Under these circumstances, you intend to try for $200,000, and hope to get at least $180,000.

EXERCISE 2.5: TOO OLD TO ROCK AND ROLL

Confidential Information for Director of STORMIN'

The story being given out that Tiny Turner quit STORMIN' over artistic differences with you is absolutely correct. The two of you simply had different visions of the character of Colonel Plotter, and you are happy to be rid of Turner.

You really want Jerry McCarthy for the role of Colonel Plotter. There's no one else out there who's right for it. Plus, you know that you can work with Jerry, because you did so the first time Jerry appeared with SST.

You have regularly produced artistic and financial success for SST, typically being the director of three of SST's six yearly shows. You really believe in STORMIN' as a piece of commercial theater, and think it has a very good shot at going to Broadway.

If SST cancels the show now, you will still get $50,000. That is only half what you will make if the show is actually produced, and peanuts compared to what the director will make if STORMIN' goes to Broadway and is successful. You have a shot at that job only if you direct the show's first production.

For all these reasons, you want the Business Manager to pay whatever is necessary to get Jerry.

You have been involved in negotiations with actors before, but only when the SST business manager was representing SST, not when a lawyer was doing so. You are concerned that the lawyer will be overly concerned with the salary aspects of the negotiations, and will not realize how crucial it is for SST to get Jerry for this role. In meeting with the lawyer prior to the negotiations, you must make this point clear.

You must also be willing to speak up at the negotiations if you think that there is a risk that the lawyer will lose Jerry.

EXERCISE 2.5:   TOO OLD TO ROCK AND ROLL

Confidential Information for SST Attorney

SST is a new client with your firm. In addition to being a fairly good-sized client for your small firm, having SST as a client will be a great asset in your firm's attempt to expand into entertainment law. Therefore you would very much like to make a favorable impression on the SST management during this negotiation.

SST is under pressure to hire Jerry McCarthy for the role of Colonel Plotter. The Director wants Jerry. The chief outside financial backer of STORMIN' has said she will pull her support for the show if a big name star isn't found soon. This will mean SST will have to fold the show and interrupt its tradition of a yearly musical. If SST folds the show now, it stands to lose about $250,000 in pre-production costs and penalties.

SST is a for-profit corporation, and it is profitable. It's that way largely because it does not willingly put on a show it knows will lose money. The current financial situation is this:

If SST fills the house to 75% of capacity (i.e., sells an average of 3,000 tickets a night) it breaks even before paying Colonel Plotter. Every penny of Jerry's fee to be Plotter has to come out of ticket sales in excess of 75%, or else the show loses money.

Since SST has averaged 90% of available seats sold over the past five years, it is moderately confident it will be OK. However, advance sales are below normal, and the loss of Tiny Turner will probably slow things further. Season ticket sales this year are down to only 40% of the house. Given all of this, SST would like to bring Jerry McCarthy on board for under $120,000.

SST had agreed to pay Tiny Turner $170,000 for the Colonel Plotter role. Last year SST paid $150,000 to the star of its yearly musical, "Cabaret." Other established stars are getting $10,000 per performance in major musicals in large markets outside of New York, (i.e., about $160,000 for sixteen shows.) SST is paying its two new stars, the romantic leads in STORMIN', $94,000 for sixteen shows.

On the upside, if SST puts on this production, it will then control all stage rights to STORMIN' for three years. This means that if it's a hit, SST gets to take it to Broadway or at least to sell the rights to Broadway producers. If SST cancels the show, stage rights for the next three years revert to the authors. SST does not control movie rights to the show.

EXERCISE 2.5:   TOO OLD TO ROCK AND ROLL

Teaching Notes

There are a great number of objective criteria that can be relied on by the negotiators in this case, and their attempt to persuade the other party that those criteria should have a substantial effect on the terms of the contract can lead to an interesting discussion of the effect of objective criteria on outcome, contrasting the views of White with those of Fisher & Ury. Additionally, each team has a dreadful BATNA (for Jerry, not getting the part; for SST, canceling the scheduled musical), leading to a discussion of the comparative effect of objective criteria and BATNA on outcome, as well as a discussion of the importance of determining both one's own BATNA and that of the other party.

The lawyer-client aspect of the exercise provides a basis from which to explore such questions as whether or not a client should be present at a negotiation such as this, and, if so, what role the client should play. The exercise is also constructed to create a conflict of interest between the lawyer and the client on each team (Jerry's lawyer has a greater interest in a high salary than does Jerry; the SST lawyer has a greater interest in a low salary than does the SST director). Thus, some discussion about recognizing and dealing with conflicts of interest is appropriate.

Some suggested questions to raise those issues are: What salary did Jerry initially propose? What salary did SST propose? How did each attempt to justify its proposal? (These questions can open up not only a discussion of objective criteria, but also of how to select an opening position, and the effect of one's opening on outcome. See Raiffa, p. 33.) Did any of the comparative salary figures (objective criteria) lead to or strongly influence the terms of the agreement? What else influenced the terms of the agreement? What were the comparative influence of objective criteria and the BATNA of each party?

Did you determine your BATNA and that of the other side prior to negotiating? What were they?

Did having your client present help you or hurt you in the negotiations? How?

Did you discuss with your client prior to the negotiation which of you would do the actual negotiating? Whether the client should answer questions from the other side? How you would deal with new information or offers?

How did Jerry and the director like having someone else negotiate for them? Were they troubled at any point? Was there anything they would have had the lawyer do differently?

Did the lawyer on either side perceive any potential lawyer-client conflict of interest? If so, how did the lawyer handle that potential conflict?

EXERCISE 2.6:   COLONIAL CONFECTIONERS, INC.

Confidential Information for J. M. Cublier
Colonial Confectioners' Attorney

Your client, Colonial Confectioners, is owned entirely by Tom Rampal, the 75-year-old president and chief executive officer of Colonial. The company was founded in 1897 by Tom Rampal's grandfather, and has been in continuous operation in a one-story building on the same site, on what is now the edge of downtown Salem, since then.

Two days ago, you were visited by Mr. Rampal. He told you that he had just received a phone call from an attorney named J. Lawrence, who said that he/she had a client who was interested in purchasing Colonial Confectioners. Mr. Rampal told Lawrence that he would be interested in whatever Lawrence had to say, but that he was leaving the country for a long
planned vacation with his wife. Accordingly, he directed Lawrence to contact you with his/her proposition.

According to Mr. Rampal, he is quite interested in selling Colonial. He had hoped to pass the business on to one of his children, but none of them is interested in the candy business. Still, he wants to see the business continue, partly out of respect for his grandfather and father, and partly out of concern for his 200 employees, many of who have been working for Colonial their entire lives. Thus, he would be very reluctant to sell to someone who is not in the candy business.

There is, however, one complicating factor. Rampal has a trustworthy friend in the Mayor's office who has given him confidential information that the Salem Housing Authority has decided to take by eminent domain, for the purpose of erecting public housing, a ten-block area that will include the block on which Colonial is located. When that happens, which will probably be in 2 - 3 years, Rampal would have to move the business, and he feels he is too old to do that. A taking by eminent domain will also result in a rock bottom price, which Rampal estimates at $5-6 million. From this perspective, the ideal purchaser would be someone who was unaware of the planned taking, but who would respond to it by moving the business elsewhere. As far as price is concerned, Mr. Rampal tells you that he would sell for $7.5 million to any purchaser in the candy business, but would insist on twice that amount from any purchaser who wanted to use the site for some other purpose (a real possibility, in view of the way in which downtown Salem has been expanding). Finally, Mr. Rampal tells you that on instructions from his wife, who does not want her long-awaited European vacation ruined by constant telephone negotiations, you are authorized to complete a sale without further communication with him.

When he talked to J. Lawrence, the attorney who called him, Mr. Rampal arranged a meeting between the two of you to discuss Lawrence's proposal. You should now prepare for that meeting.

EXERCISE 2.6:					COLONIAL CONFECTIONERS, INC.

Confidential Information for J. Lawrence
Delta Development Co.'s Attorney

Your client, Delta Development Co., has been quietly searching for some time in the hope of finding a suitable site near downtown Salem on which to erect a high-rise office building. Delta was ready to make an offer on one site approximately a year ago, but learned that the Salem Housing Authority was also interested in the site. Concerned about the possibility of a taking by eminent domain, Delta backed off without making an offer. Since then the demand for office space in downtown Salem has increased, and Delta, convinced that a well-managed building would be extremely profitable, has continued its search for a suitable site.

Approximately two weeks ago, you received a call from Tanya Gordon, president of Delta, telling you that she had found what appeared to be an ideal site for Delta's planned building. The site is on the edge of downtown Salem, and is presently occupied by a one
story candy factory, Colonial Confectioners, Inc. The factory was built about the turn of the century, and has been in continuous operation since then. The building would have to be demolished, but after that the site would be sufficiently large to support a 65-story building.

Ms. Gordon told you that neither the building nor the site is listed for sale. She was told by a friend, however, that Tom Rampal, the sole owner of Colonial, has been talking about retirement, and might be interested in selling. According to her friend, Rampal is quite anxious to see the business, to which he has devoted his life, continued, and would probably sell only to someone who was interested in continuing in the candy business. Ms. Gordon tells you that she regards that as sentimental poppycock, that she has no intention of operating a candy company, but that she does want to purchase the site. She tells you that in order to assist in completing the purchase, she has set up a shell corporation called Tanya's Candies, Inc., and you are free to approach Rampal on behalf of that company if you think it will help. In any event, she has authorized you to approach Mr. Rampal, and to offer him up to $10,000,000 for his business, including the factory and the site. She warns you, however, that if Rampal learns who really wants to buy the business

and why, his price, even if he would sell, is apt to be prohibitively great. In addition, she does not want the word to get out that Delta is searching
for a development site in downtown Salem, since that would drive up the price of other sites as well. Hence, under no conditions are you free to disclose Delta's intended use for the property.

Two days ago, you called Mr. Rampal, and told him that you had a client who was interested in purchasing his business. He expressed great interest, but said that he was about to leave the country for a long-planned vacation with his wife. Accordingly, he arranged for you to meet with his lawyer, J. M. Cublier, to discuss your client's proposal. You should now prepare for that meeting.

EXERCISE 2.6:   COLONIAL CONFECTIONERS, INC.

Teaching Notes

In this exercise, an agreement is possible only if neither negotiator discloses to the other the damaging information in its possession. If Colonial's attorney discloses the planned taking by eminent domain, Delta should not purchase; if Delta's attorney discloses that Delta will not operate a candy company, Colonial's minimum sales price will be $15,000,000, higher than the $10,000,000 Delta's attorney is authorized to offer. Conversely, if neither discloses, each will have entered into an agreement that neither would have entered into had it known all the facts.

As a result, the exercise should stimulate discussion of the attorney's obligation to be truthful in statements to others and to disclose damaging information to others. These issues can be treated not only in the context of Rule 4.1 of the Model Rules of Professional Conduct, but of whether that rules is sufficiently broad.

The questions that will trigger a discussion of these issues are rather straightforward. Is Lawrence free to advise Colonial that he/she is negotiating on behalf of Tanya's Candies, Inc., without revealing who owns Tanya's? Is Lawrence obliged to disclose the planned use of the building if Cublier has told Lawrence of Colonial's interest in keeping the business operating? If Cublier asks directly what Delta (or Tanya's Candies) plans to do with the building, is Lawrence then obliged to disclose Delta's plans? Is Cublier obliged to disclose the planned taking of the building by eminent domain? Suppose Lawrence asks directly whether Cublier knows of any eminent domain plans for the site; must Cublier disclose under those circumstances?

If some students conclude that neither attorney is under a duty to disclose damaging information absent a direct question to which the only alternatives are disclosure or lying, the instructor can ask whether that is a satisfactory state of affairs. Is the student satisfied at entering a profession in which one is free to mislead by silence, even on crucial matters? If not, what should be the lawyer's obligation of disclosure?

EXERCISE 2.7:   RAPID PRINTING CO. V. SCOTT COMPUTERS, INC.

Teaching Instructions

This exercise was designed to provide law and management students with experience negotiating jointly in the roles of lawyer and business person respectively. Thus, we recommend that if possible each negotiating team be composed of one law student and one management student. However, if that is not feasible, the exercise is still worth doing with law students playing all roles.

Divide the students into groups of four. Within each group, there are two 2-person teams -- a lawyer and a CEO representing Rapid, and a lawyer and a CEO representing Scott. The students should be advised that considerable preparation is necessary in advance of the actual negotiation. In particular, the lawyer and the client should meet for a pre-negotiation strategy session. As this tends to be a fairly lengthy negotiation, we normally do it outside of class. If it is done in class, approximately two hours should be allowed. Another one and one-half to two hours is generally required for post-negotiation discussion of the exercise.

EXERCISE 2.7:   RAPID PRINTING CO. V. SCOTT COMPUTERS, INC.

Confidential Information for
B.R. Brown, President, Rapid Printing

You are President and Chairman of the Board of Rapid Printing Co. Rapid is a comparatively small company specializing in business forms and multi-page documents, for example, journals and reports. Rapid's gross income for fiscal year 1997, was $1,777,000.

Late in 1996, Dee Williams, Rapid's Vice President for Operations, came to you with an idea that would provide Rapid with a substantial competitive edge in the printing industry. Williams' idea was to develop a computer system that would provide for remote computerized composition through portable terminals placed at customers' locations.

While other printing concerns were in the process of moving to computerized composition, to your knowledge and Williams', none of your competitors currently had a system with portable terminals.

You asked Williams what equipment Rapid would need to carry out his plan, and he told you that the best approach would be to lease a new mainframe computer, terminals and phototypesetter. While your knowledge of the technical aspects of computers was (and is) limited, you had great confidence in Williams, who had been responsible for selecting Rapid's existing business computer and had done the programming for it. Thus, you authorized him to request proposals from various computer companies to provide the system to carry out his plan.

From time to time over the next few months, Williams reported that he was in touch with various computer companies, and hoped soon to determine which system would best carry out his plans. In early February,1997, he told you that he had sent out requests for proposals to several companies, including Scott. Then, in late February, Williams told you that he had completed his investigation and recommended that Rapid lease the equipment it needed form Scott.

Scott is a large computer company with gross income in 1997 of $339,000,000. Scott equipment is widely used in the printing industry and you had no hesitancy about doing business with them.

Indeed, you thought that if Scott could provide a system that met Williams' requirements, the chances were excellent that the system would give you the competitive edge you needed to move into the forefront of the printing industry. You were, however, troubled by the lease charges of $102,192 a year, which were far more expensive than you had imagined they would be. Indeed, Rapid would be pushed to its financial limit to meet those charges.

You then discussed the matter at length with Williams. He agreed that the lease price was higher than he had anticipated, but told you that the Scott system was the only one in which he had total confidence. He also told you that he was concerned that if Rapid did not act promptly to carry out his plans, others in the industry would beat Rapid to the punch, and Rapid would lose the competitive advantage it would otherwise enjoy. You thought about the matter some more,
reexamined Rapid's financial condition, and ultimately decided that while you would be taking a very substantial financial risk, the potential gains justified doing so. Accordingly, on March 27, 1997, you signed

a lease agreement with Scott covering computer, terminals, phototypesetter, and all the software necessary to carry out Williams's plan.

In May 1997, the Scott equipment began to arrive. In July 1997, it was fully installed. It soon developed, however, that the Scott system was incapable of computerized composition because it lacked an appropriate application program. At that point, a dispute developed between Williams and Scott concerning the failure of the system to operate as planned. According to Williams, who has worked for you for many years, and in whom you have complete confidence, the Scott sales representative with whom he had dealt, June Robertson, had promised him that if Rapid leased Scott hardware, Scott would provide Rapid, at no additional charge, with Print Rite.

According to Williams, when he expressed doubt that Print Rite was sufficiently user friendly to be feasible for use by Rapid's customers, Robertson assured him both that it was, and that Scott was in the process of developing a successor to Print Rite, which should be available soon, and which would be more user-friendly than Print-Rite. Robertson also told Williams that if Rapid started with Print-Rite, the transition to a second generation Scott program would be comparatively simple. Williams decided, under all the circumstances, that Print-Rite would serve Rapid's needs, and told Robertson that he would recommend that Rapid select Scott.

Robertson's story was that she had offered Print-Rite to Williams for $1,750 per month, but Williams declined, saying that Print-Rite was not sufficiently user-friendly, that he did not want to wait for Scott to develop a second generation program, and that he would write the composition program for the new system himself. Thus, Scott took the position that it had contracted only to provide hardware and an operating system, and that the application programs were the responsibility of Rapid. Scott also demanded that Rapid begin immediately making payments under the lease.

When negotiations between Williams and Slade Gorton, Scott's Vice President for Sales, concerning Scott's obligation to provide Print-Rite broke down in February, 1998, you called Christian, Ingrid & O'Berne, and asked them to look into the matter with a view to filing a law suit against Scott. You told Lane Christian that in view of Rapid's precarious financial position, you would only be able to engage the firm on a contingent fee basis (1/3 of any recovery from Scott, plus costs). Christian agreed to represent Rapid on those terms. About one month ago, in April 1998, Christian filed, on Rapid's behalf, a complaint against Scott seeking over $5,000,000 in damages, primarily representing profits lost as result of the failure of the Scott system to operate as promised. So far, no other printing company has yet been able to implement the remote computerized system Williams conceived. You have heard rumors, however, that one or two are very close.

Christian called you yesterday to tell you that he had received a phone call from Gil Santina, who represents Scott, suggesting that Santina and S. S. Scott, Scott's President and C.E.O., meet with Christian and you to see if you can work out a settlement of the dispute between you. Christian agreed to such a meeting, subject to your approval. You agreed, and you and Christian are now to meet to plan for next week's meeting with Scott and Santina.

The importance of the pending dispute with Scott (and thus of this meeting) can hardly be overestimated. If Rapid must make the payments which the lease with Scott calls for, and the proposed system is not generating the anticipated profits, bankruptcy for Rapid within a year is almost a certainty, as Rapid has a heavy debt load. Furthermore, a judgment against Rapid for the amounts due under the lease would unquestionably lead to its bankruptcy. On the other hand, if Rapid is successful in litigation against Scott, or if, somehow, Williams' envisioned system can be made to operate successfully, the financial stability of Rapid will be assured for the foreseeable future. You estimate that Williams' system, if functioning properly, should generate $1,000,000 per year in profits for the next five years, before the competition catches up. (It was on the basis of that estimate that you sued Scott for $5,000,000.)

(Reminder: For purposes of this exercise, it is now May, 1998.)

EXERCISE 2.4:   RAPID PRINTING CO. v. SCOTT COMPUTERS, INC.

Confidential Information for Lane Christian
Counsel for Rapid Printing

You are the senior partner in Christian, Ingrid & O'Berne, a six-person law firm in Deerfield, Illiana. Your firm has represented Rapid Printing Co. from time to time, but they are a small company (gross income for fiscal year 1997 of $1,770,000), and you have never had a retainer from them.

Your initial involvement in Rapid's dispute with Scott Computers occurred in February 1998, when Brown called to tell you that Rapid had signed a contract with Scott, and that a serious problem had arisen under the contract. Brown asked you to come out the next day to meet with him/her and Dee Williams, Rapid's Vice President for Operations, and its key person in the deal with Scott. You did, and they told you the following.

Williams' primary background is in the printing business, but is also a self-taught computer expert. Indeed, from 1986 - 1996 he did all the programming for the computer used by Rapid to handle business and financial matters. In 1996, he became interested in developing a computer system that would provide for remote computerized composition through portable terminals placed at Rapid's customers' locations.

In January, 1997, Brown gave Williams the go-ahead to explore his idea with various computer companies. Williams did so, sending a request for proposal to about ten companies, including Scott. Each of those companies responded, and Williams met with representatives of each. It soon became apparent to Williams that the proposal presented by Scott came closest to fitting his specifications. Williams became particularly interested in the Scott system when the Scott representative with whom he dealt, June Robertson, told him that if Rapid leased Scott hardware, Scott would provide Rapid, at no additional charge, with a Scott program known as Print-Rite. According to Williams, when he expressed doubt that Print-Rite was sufficiently user
friendly to be feasible for use by Rapid's customers, Robertson assured him both that it was, and that Scott was in the process of developing a successor to Print-Rite, which should be available soon, and which would be more user-friendly than Print-Rite. Robertson also told Williams that if Rapid started with Print-Rite, the transition to a second generation Scott program would be comparatively simple. Williams decided, under all the circumstances, that Print-Rite would serve Rapid's needs, and told Robertson that he would recommend that Rapid select Scott.

Once the Scott contract was signed, all went smoothly during the installation stage from May, 1997, through July 1997. When the Scott hardware was fully installed, however, it developed that it was incapable of computerized composition because it lacked an appropriate application program. At that point, a dispute developed between Rapid and Scott concerning whose responsibility it was to provide the application program that should make the system function as intended. According to Rapid, the responsibility was Scott's, and Rapid had understood that Scott would fulfill that responsibility by providing Print-Rite. According to Scott, it had contracted only to provide hardware and operating systems, not application programs. The responsibility for developing application programs rested on Rapid, not Scott.

Robertson's story was that she had offered Print-Rite to Williams for $1,750 per month, but Williams declined, saying that Print-Rite was not sufficiently user-friendly, that he did not want to wait for Scott to develop a better program, and that he intended to write the application program himself. Williams denied this, saying that he knew that writing a program of that complexity was beyond his ability. Scott demanded that Rapid begin making the payments due under the contract and Rapid refused. Negotiations between them broke down in February, 1998, and that's when Brown called you.

Brown told you, after he and Williams had given you all the foregoing information, that he/she wanted your firm to represent Rapid in this matter, and to file a law suit against Scott to recover the profits lost by Rapid as a result of Scott's failure to provide the services it had promised. Brown estimated those lost profits at $5,000,000. Brown also told you, however, that the failure of the computer system to function as anticipated had left Rapid in a very precarious financial position. Indeed, if Rapid had to make the payments called for under the lease with Scott, bankruptcy within a year would be almost a certainty. Thus, Brown requested that you handle this matter on a contingent fee basis, consisting of 1/3 of any recovery from Scott, plus costs. You were initially reluctant to take the case on a contingency, as it did not look very promising, but business has been slow recently, so you agreed to do so. In April, 1998, you prepared and filed a complaint against Scott.

Yesterday, about four weeks after the complaint was filed, you received a telephone call from Gil Santina, a senior partner in Santina and Jakes, which represents Scott. Santina suggested that the two of you, together with your clients, meet to discuss this matter. Santina said that he/she thought it was essentially a frivolous lawsuit, but that Scott's policy was to attempt to settle promptly all litigation, and he/she was complying with that policy. When you asked Santina why he/she thought the suit was frivolous, Santina told you that it was clear, particularly after talking with Robertson, that the suit was a product of Williams' efforts to get himself out of an embarrassing position. As Santina saw it, Williams, a self-taught computer expert, knows less than he thinks he does. Williams planned to write the application program but over-estimated his ability to do so. When he found that writing the program was beyond his capacity, he invented a story about having been promised an application program by Robertson. He did so in an effort to cover himself in what would otherwise be an extremely embarrassing and financially difficult situation. If the case were to go to trial, Scott would prove precisely that. Scott intended, moreover, unless this matter were promptly settled, to bring a counter-claim against Rapid for $510,960, the full amount due under the lease.

After talking to Brown, you called Santina and told him/her that you and Brown would be pleased to meet. Santina said that Scott's president, S. S. Scott, would also be at the meeting, which you scheduled for next week. You and Brown are now to meet to make your plans for next week's meeting with Santina and Scott.

You are not very optimistic, based upon your research and analysis, of Rapid's chances of prevailing in its suit against Scott, or if Scott sues Rapid for the amount due under the lease. Despite Brown's confidence in Williams, the chances are slim, based on the evidence, that a jury will believe Williams' testimony that Robertson promised to provide Print-Rite at no cost. Williams' RFP makes no reference to application programs. He is sophisticated in the computer world, wrote a detailed RFP, and his failure to request proposals for application programs strongly suggests that he was not seeking application programs. Furthermore, not only does the RFP not refer to application programs, neither does the contract. If the jury does not believe Williams, not only will Rapid's suit fail, but Scott will necessarily be found to have fully performed its part of the lease. Thus, Rapid will have breached the contract in its failure to make the payments called for.

(Reminder: For purposes of this exercise, it is now May, 1998.)

EXERCISE 2.7:   RAPID PRINTING CO. V. SCOTT COMPUTERS, INC.

Confidential Information for S.S. Scott
CEO Scott Computers

You are the President and Chief Executive Officer of Scott Computers, Inc., a large company engaged in the manufacturing, selling, and leasing of computers and associated software. Scott's gross income for fiscal 1997 was $339 million.

Your company is involved in a lawsuit filed by Rapid Printing Company, seeking $5,000,000 in damages. Rapid is a comparatively small, but highly regarded printing company specializing in business forms, multi-page documents, journals and reports. Rapid's gross income for fiscal year 1997 was $1,770,000. The facts, as they have been reported to you by Slade Gorton, Scott's Vice President for Sales, and Gil Santina of Santina & Jakes, which frequently represents Scott in litigation, are these:

In February, 1997, Dee Williams, Rapid's Vice President for Operations, telephoned Scott to request that a salesperson call upon him. In response to Williams' request, Scott salesperson June Robertson met with Williams. At this meeting, a general discussion took place concerning Rapid's desire to acquire computer equipment that would provide for remote computerized composition through portable terminals placed at Rapid's customers' locations. With such a system, customers could transmit data directly to Rapid in typeset-ready format, enabling Rapid to perform its composition functions faster and more accurately than its competitors, none of whom possessed a computer system such as that envisioned by Williams.

At the close of this meeting, Williams told Robertson that he would send a written request for a proposal, which he then did. That written request was limited solely to hardware, and contained no reference to software. Williams and Robertson then had a series of meetings in which they discussed Rapid's computer needs and Scott's capacity to satisfy those needs. In the course of these meetings, Rapid's needs for software were discussed, but those discussions were limited to operating programs and did not include applications programs.

At one point Robertson told Williams about Print-Rite, an application program developed by Scott for use in the printing industry that Rapid could rent for $1,750 per month. Williams expressed doubt that Print-Rite was sufficiently user-friendly to be used by Rapid's customers, and Robertson told him that Scott was in the process of developing a successor to Print
Rite, which should be available soon, and which would be more user-friendly. Robertson also told Williams that if Rapid started with Print-Rite, the transition to a second generation Scott program would be comparatively simple. Williams' response was that he did not want to wait for Scott to develop a better program, that he had been writing programs for Rapid for years, and that he would write the application program for the new system himself. After this, there was no further discussion of application programs. Thereafter, in March, 1997, Rapid and Scott entered into a contract enumerating the specific items of hardware and operating systems to be leased by Scott to Rapid. No reference was made in that contract to any application software.

In July 1997, the Scott hardware was fully installed at Rapid. It soon developed, however, that the system was incapable of computerized composition because it lacked an appropriate application program; At that point, a dispute developed between Rapid and Scott concerning whose responsibility it was to provide an application program. According to Rapid, June Robertson had promised Williams that Scott would provide Rapid with Print
Rite at no cost if Rapid would lease Scott hardware. Robertson denied having promised to provide Print-Rite, asserting that when she sought to interest Williams in leasing Print-Rite, he said he was not interested, since he planned to program the new system himself. Scott took the position that it had fully performed its obligations under the lease and demanded that Rapid begin making payments. Rapid refused, and the matter

was turned over to Scott's legal department, which, in turn, engaged Santina & Jakes to institute proceedings against Rapid for the full amount due and owing under the lease.

In April 1998, before Santina & Jakes could act, Rapid brought suit against Scott, claiming that Scott had defrauded Rapid, and had breached its contract with Rapid, by promising Print-Rite and not making it available. Rapid sought approximately $5,000,000 in damages from Scott, claiming that it lost profits in that amount as a result of the failure of the new system to operate as planned.

While you have no reason to doubt that Rapid would earn approximately $5,000,000 in profits if its remote computerized system were the first in the printing industry, you are convinced that Rapid's factual allegations against Scott have no basis whatsoever. You are also certain that a counter-claim by Scott for the approximately $500,000 due it under the lease would be sustained. Not only is there no reference in the lease to Scott providing Print-Rite at no charge but Robertson would have had no authority to promise to provide it at no charge. Print-Rite was available at that time at a lease price of $1,750 per month and Robertson could not have waived that charge. Indeed, Scott had been having such problems with Print-Rite that at the time of Robertson's meetings with Williams, Scott was losing money on Print-Rite, even at $1,750 per month. The problem with Print-Rite was that it required an operator to be a sophisticated computer programmer and a knowledgeable typesetter. The complexities of the program made it difficult to train operators, who then continued to have problems with the program even after extensive training. With customer service costs skyrocketing, Scott took Print-Rite off the market in March, 1998.

About two years ago, Scott research and development personnel began work on an application program for the printing industry to replace Print-Rite. Known as SCPPI (Scott Composition Program for the Printing Industry), this new program, designed to be user-friendly like the Macintosh, is a potential source of great profits. However, it has not yet undergone field development and is not available commercially.

It is Slade Gorton's view, based primarily on what Robertson told him, that Williams concocted his story out of whole cloth in an effort to extricate himself from an embarrassing and financially difficult position. Williams did plan to provide a composition program for the system he had designed, but overestimated his abilities, and found that he was incapable of writing a program of that complexity. Rather than admit his error and lease the Print-Rite program, which would have added very considerably to the lease cost, Williams fabricated his story about having been promised Print-Rite at no charge.

Despite the seemingly straight-forward nature of the legal issues presented by this case, the business considerations are somewhat more complex. Even if you could persuade Rapid to drop its claims against Scott, Rapid would still owe Scott over $500,000. You have learned recently that Rapid's financial position is not as good as thought when the lease was signed. Unless its proposed new system is operational, Rapid probably cannot meet its obligations under the lease, and a judgment against it would almost surely put it into bankruptcy. It is clear that Scott would spend more to obtain such a judgment than it would recover. (Gil Santina has estimated trial costs at a minimum of $50,000 assuming a two-week trial, billing at the firm's normal rate of $200 per hour for partners and $100 per hour for associates.) On the other hand, you do not want companies that do business with Scott to think that they can breach leases with impunity. Furthermore, the computer leasing market is currently quite weak and there is no likelihood of Scott being able to recoup its losses on the Rapid lease by immediately leasing the equipment involved to some other company.

Scott's policy is to attempt to resolve all disputes short of litigation. In pursuance of that policy, Gil Santina and you are to meet next week (approximately four weeks after Rapids complaint was filed) with B.R. Brown, President of Rapid, and Lane Christian, Rapid's lawyer, You are now to meet with Santina to make your plans for next week's meeting with Brown and Christian.

(Reminder: For purposes of this exercise, it is now May, 1998.)

EXERCISE 2.7:   RAPID PRINTING CO. V. SCOTT COMPUTERS, INC.

Confidential Information for Gil Santina
Counsel for Scott Computers. Inc.

You are the senior partner in Santina & Jakes, a 12-person law firm in Deerfield, Illinois. From time to time, your firm represents Scott Computers, Inc., in litigation, but you are not on a retainer. Business conditions have been somewhat depressed in Deerfield lately, with the result that your billings have not been as high as you would like. Thus, you were delighted to be asked to represent Scott in this case, which appears headed for trial, and in which your firm's billings should be well in excess of $50,000. (You estimate a two-week trial at your normal billing rates of $200 per hour for partners, $100 per hour for associates.) Scott is a large company engaged in the manufacturing, selling, leasing of computers and associated software. Scott's gross income for 1997 was $339 million.

Your firm was asked to represent Scott in collecting approximately $500,000 which Rapid Printing Company owed Scott pursuant to a computer lease. You were preparing to file a complaint against Rapid for that amount when, in April, 1998, Rapid brought suit against Scott, claiming that Scott breached its contract with Rapid, and had defrauded Rapid. Rapid seeks approximately $5,000,000 in damages from Scott, claiming that it lost profits in that amount as a result of Scott's fraud and breach of contract. The events which led to this dispute, as they were reported to you by Slade Gorton, Scott's Vice President for Sales, and June Robertson, a Scott salesperson, were these:

In February,1997, Dee Williams, Rapid's Vice President for operations, telephoned Scott to request that a salesperson call upon him. In response to Williams' request, Scott salesperson June Robertson met with Williams. At this meeting, a general discussion took place concerning Rapid's desire to acquire computer equipment that would provide for remote computerized composition through portable terminals placed at Rapid's customers' locations. With such a system, customers could transmit data directly to Rapid in typeset-ready format, enabling Rapid to perform its printing functions faster and more accurately than its competitors, none of whom possessed a computer system such as envisioned by Williams.

At the close of this meeting, Williams told Robertson that he would send a written request for a proposal, which he then did. That written request was limited solely to hardware, and contained no reference to software. Williams and Robertson then had a series of meetings in which they discussed Rapid's computer needs and Scott's capacity to satisfy those needs. In the course of these meetings, Rapid's needs for software were discussed, but those discussions were limited to operating programs, and did not include application programs. At one point Robertson told Williams about Print-Rite, an application program developed by Scott for use in the printing industry, which Rapid could rent for $1,750 per month. Williams expressed doubt that Print
Rite was sufficiently user-friendly to be used by Rapid's customers, and Robertson told him that Scott was in the process of developing a successor to Print-Rite, which should be available soon, and which would be user-friendlier. Robertson also told Williams that if Rapid started with Print-Rite, the transition to a second generation Scott program would be comparatively simple. Williams' response was that he did not want to wait for Scott to develop a better program, that he had been writing programs for Rapid for years, and that he would write the application program for the new system himself. After this, there was no further discussion of application programs.

In late February 1997, Williams requested that Robertson have a contract drawn up, enumerating the specific items of hardware and operating systems to be leased by Scott to Rapid. Pursuant to this request, a version of Scott's form contract was drafted by Scott and sent to Williams for his signature. No reference was made in that contract to any application software. Thereafter, in late March, 1997 Rapid signed, without change, the contract Scott had sent it in February.

In July 1997, the Scott system was fully installed at Rapid. It soon developed, however, that the Scott system was incapable of computerized composition because it lacked an appropriate application program. At that point, a dispute developed between Rapid and Scott concerning whose responsibility it was to provide an application program. According to Rapid, June Robertson had promised Williams that Scott would provide Rapid with Print-Rite at no cost if Rapid would lease Scott hardware. Robertson denied having promised to provide Print-Rite, asserting that when she sought to interest Williams in leasing Print-Rite, he said he was not interested, since he planned to program the new system himself. Scott took the position that it had fully performed its obligations under the lease and demanded that Rapid begin making payments. Rapid refused, and the matter was turned over to Scott's legal department, which, in turn, engaged Santina & Jakes to institute proceedings against Rapid for the full amount due and owing under the lease.

In April, 1998, before Santina & Jakes could act, Rapid brought suit against Scott, claiming that Scott had defrauded Rapid, and had breached its contract with Rapid by promising Print-Rite and not making it available. Rapid sought approximately $5,000,000 in damages from Scott, claiming that it lost profits in that amount as a result of the failure of the new system to operate as planned.

Gorton told you that he has no doubt that Rapid would earn approximately $5,000,000 in profits if its remote computerized composition system were the first in the printing industry. However, he claims that Rapid's factual allegations against Scott have no basis whatsoever. Not only is there no reference in the lease to Scott providing Print-Rite at no charge, but Robertson would have had no authority to promise to provide it at no charge. Print-Rite was available at that time at a lease price of $1,750 per month, and Robertson could not have waived that charge. Indeed, Scott had been having such problems with Print-Rite that at the time of Robertson's meetings with Williams, Scott was losing money on Print-Rite, even at $1,750 per month. The problem with Print-Rite was that it required an operator to be a sophisticated computer programmer and a knowledgeable typesetter. The complexities of the program made it difficult to train operators, who then continued to have problems with the program even after extensive training. With customer service costs skyrocketing, Scott took Print-Rite off the market in March, 1998.

It is Gorton's view, based primarily on what Robertson told him, that Williams concocted his story out of whole cloth in an effort to extricate himself from an embarrassing and financially difficult position. Williams did plan to provide an application program for the system he had designed, but overestimated his abilities, and found that he was incapable of writing a program of that complexity. Rather than admit his error and lease the Print-Rite program, which would have added very considerably to the lease cots, Williams fabricated his story about having been promised Print-Rite at no charge.

It is Scott's policy to make a serious effort to resolve disputes without resort to litigation. Pursuant to that policy, you telephoned Lane Christian, senior partner in Christian, Ingrid & O'Berne, which is representing Rapid in this matter, to arrange a meeting to discuss settlement possibilities. In the course of that call, you let Christian know precisely how weak you think Rapid's position in this matter is, and how certain you are that a counter-claim by Scott for the full amount due it under the lease will be successful. Thus, it should be clear to Rapid that while Scott initiated settlement discussions, it did not do so out of any sense of weakness. Quite to the contrary, you would relish going to trial in this case, as you see a certain victory.

Subsequent to your phone call, Christian called you back and agreed to a meeting next week at which Christian and B.R. Brown, Rapid's President, are to meet with you and S.S. Scott, President and Chief Executive Officer of Scott Computers. In preparation for that meeting, which will take place approximately one month after Rapid's complaint was filed, you are now to meet with S.S. Scott.

(Reminder: For purposes of this exercise, it is now May, 1998.)

EXERCISE 2.7: RAPID PRINTING CO. V. SCOTT COMPUTERS, INC.

Teaching Notes

Introduction

This exercise was designed to stimulate discussion of three elements of the lawyer-client relationship: Under what circumstances does a manager need legal representation? What should be the role of the lawyer and the manager in designing a negotiation strategy and in implementing it? What conflicts of interest exist between lawyer and client, and how might they be managed?

The exercise also illustrates how the dynamics of the power relationship between disputants can shift when the dispute is moved into a legal setting. Rapid v. Scott is designed so that one party has both legal and financial strength, but such power does not result in bargaining strength.

The exercise is appropriate for law and business students who have had negotiations training that emphasizes techniques useful for reaching integrative solutions. The exercise can be used with other student groups, but some of the interesting dynamics of the exercise are unlikely to materialize. For example, management students who are untrained in negotiations are likely to give their lawyers a free hand in designing and implementing the negotiating strategy.

It is important for the instructors to decide in advance how the groups will report their results. We think joint class time is too valuable to be used having each group report their results orally. We suggest the groups be asked to turn in a results sheet indicating roles, names, and terms of settlement or final offers at the point of impasse, in advance of class. These results sheets can then be photocopied and distributed to the students at the outset of the debriefing. Requiring that the results be turned in prior to the joint debriefing also helps the instructors plan their line of questioning.

Debriefing

These suggestions for debriefing are organized around a set of questions for the instructors to pose to students. The principles and concepts underlying the questions are discussed in the response guidelines following each question. Since there are likely to be two instructors, a law professor and a management professor, we strongly recommend that the instructors meet ahead of time and agree as to who is to pose what question and who is to make what type of comments. We have found that whereas law and management students are interested in the other instructor's perspective, when it comes to being critical of the students' actions in this exercise, criticism is more acceptable when it comes from their own instructor. Question I. Ask the students to read over the results.

Most of the settlements are likely to be some kind of joint venture between Scott and Rapid. This is because Scott is, in many ways, in a position of overwhelming strength vis-a-vis Rapid. Scott has enormous resources and a legal position that appears unassailable. Even if Rapid could prevail on a breach of contract theory, the contract expressly bars recovery for consequential damages, which would include lost profits, and such clauses have been upheld (see Garden State Food Distributors, Inc. v. Sperry Rand Corp., 512 F.

Supp. 975 (D.N.J. 1982)). Thus, if Rapid is to recover lost profits, it must do so on a fraud theory. It is difficult, however, to see how Rapid could prevail on such a theory (or, indeed, on a breach of contract theory). The essence of Rapid's fraud case is that Robertson promised to provide the Print-Rite application program at no charge, had no intention of fulfilling that promise, and that that promise was crucial to Rapid entering into a contract with Scott. But, as Scott points out:

a. Williams' RFP makes no reference to application programs. He is sophisticated in the computer world, wrote a detailed RFP, and his failure to request proposals for application programs strongly suggests that he was not seeking application programs.

b. Neither the RFP nor the contract refer to application programs. Furthermore, the last paragraph of the contract provides that it constitutes the entire agreement between the parties, and supersedes all prior proposals, representations and agreements between the parties.

c. Robertson could have no motive for falsely representing that Scott would provide Print-Rite at no charge. Scott would not, in fact, do so, Williams would soon discover that, and Robertson would be in serious trouble. Thus, it is wholly unlikely that Robertson made the alleged false representations. It is much more likely that, as Scott alleges, Williams' overconfidence in his programming ability led him to believe that he could write an application program for the system he devised. When he discovered that he could not do so, he tried to extricate himself from his difficulties by fabricating the claim that Robertson had promised to provide Print-Rite at no charge.

In sum, Rapid has very little chance of prevailing either on a fraud theory (Robertson promised Williams Print-Rite at no charge, knowing that Scott would not carry out that promise) or on a breach of contract theory (Scott contracted to provide Rapid with Print-Rite at no charge, and did not carry out that promise). Scott, then, has every chance of prevailing on its claim that it provided Rapid with everything it contracted to provide, and Rapid is in breach by failing to meet its financial obligations under the contract.

Despite Scott's strong legal position and financial resources, which would appear to provide it with great bargaining power vis-a-vis Rapid, Rapid's very weakness provides it with bargaining strength. If the parties do not come to a mutually acceptable settlement and the case is litigated, a judgment in Scott's favor will provide Scott with nothing more than a claim against a bankrupt company, since execution of such a judgment would put Rapid into bankruptcy. This would serve Scott's interest in demonstrating that its leases cannot be breached with impunity, but at the not inconsiderable cost of $50,000 in attorney's fees. Scott would also be left holding computer equipment that it could not easily lease to anyone else.

While litigation would be expensive and of little value to Scott, it would be disastrous for Rapid which would likely be forced into bankruptcy. Thus, the challenge presented by this exercise is to find an integrative solution that furthers both parties' interests more than the litigation alternative. Many negotiating groups will devise such a solution.

The key to an integrative solution lies in Scott's possession of SCPPI, which has the potential to make Rapid's remote computerized composition plan functional. For, if Rapid is first in the printing industry with remote composition capacity, Rapid will earn enormous profits by virtue of its industry leadership. Rapid and Scott, if they can get beyond the legal issues, are likely to explore the possibility of a settlement agreement that would provide for some type of joint venture for the development of SCPPI. This agreement should also deal with the risks and uncertainties that have attended the development of SCPPI to date.

Scott's interest in entering such an agreement is twofold. First, it is unlikely to be able to collect on a judgment against Rapid. Second, sooner or later, Scott would probably have to enter into a joint venture with a printing company in order to have a field site for testing and refining SCPPI. While Scott could enter into a joint venture with any printing company for the development of SCPPI and its application to remote, computerized composition, there are a number of reasons why Rapid is an attractive partner. First, Rapid will go into bankruptcy if it has to pay the Scott lease without receiving the efficiencies and increase in business that the remote computerized composition system was anticipated to bring. Second, though Rapid is a relatively small company, it is highly regarded as an innovator in the printing industry. It also has customers whose printing needs are simple enough, e.g., no colored catalogs, that remote composition is feasible. Finally, since Rapid will go into bankruptcy if no settlement is reached with Scott, Scott should be able to negotiate a joint venture with Rapid on terms desirable to Scott. If Scott were to set up a joint venture with another printing company, that printer would be in a better position than Rapid to demand that Scott share the profits from SCPPI.

In order for such a joint venture to be reached:

a. Scott must disclose to Santina the weak financial position of Rapid, and the fact that a judgment against Rapid would be useless. Scott must also disclose to Santina the existence of SCPPI, of which Santina knows nothing. (If Santina is performing capably, he/she will ferret out this information, even if it is not volunteered by Scott.)

b. Scott and Santina must recognize the advantage of a settlement along these lines to a "victory" in court. This requires that the potential conflict of interest between Scott and Santina be resolved in Scott's favor. (See response to question 7).

c. Scott and Santina must disclose the existence of SCPPI to Brown and Christian.

d. Brown and Christian must recognize the weakness of their legal position. (This is primarily Christian's responsibility.) In doing so, they must give up their hopes for a $5,000,000 judgment in favor of a settlement that will promise no immediate financial gain to Rapid. This requires that the conflict of interest between Christian and Rapid be recognized and resolved in Rapid's favor. (See response to question 7.)

e. Brown and Christian must also recognize that since no other printing company has successfully developed Williams' idea (which Brown knows), this settlement has great potential gains for Rapid.

f. It is possible that Scott and Santina will not see the possibility of an integrative settlement along the lines here set out, but Christian and Brown, by good questioning and imagination, could see and develop it. This would, of course, require that Scott and Santina display imagination and good judgment in working out the settlement.

Question 2. Pick one or more groups that reached a joint venture settlement. Ask the students in those groups to explain the process by which they reached their agreement. Several useful questions are:

a. Who first proposed the joint venture? Why?
b. What was the reaction of the other party? Why?

These questions should elicit an analysis similar to that in the introduction to these debriefing notes. In brief:

Scott must see that the company's interests will be furthered less by a "victory" in court than by a sound business deal.

Santina must recognize the strength of Scott's legal position, as well as the point that Scott's interests will be furthered less by winning in court than by a sound business deal.

Brown must be capable of recognizing that a judge or jury may not believe Williams, whom he/she believes to be telling the truth, and therefore be willing to give up a chance for a multi-million dollar verdict, i.e., "victory", in favor of a mutually advantageous settlement.

Christian must recognize the weakness of Rapid's legal position and, if necessary, convince Brown that the chance of a multi-million dollar verdict is less advantageous than a favorable settlement.

Question 3. Why are there so many different types of joint venture agreements?

The terms of the joint venture agreements are likely to vary widely depending on the students' creativity and their perceptions of their bargaining power.

Question 4. Which of the joint venture agreements are best? This question leads students into a discussion of the criteria for evaluating potential settlements. They should be able to generate several, including:

a. Distributive justice - both parties think the settlement is fair, are satisfied with the settlement.

b. Completeness - the settlement spells out the role of each party in the settlement, e.g., who will do what and when, and addresses how problems generated in the future joint development of SCPPI will be handled.

Both of these criteria are important if future litigation is to be avoided.

Question 5. (Assuming some teams reached an impasse) Why did you not reach an agreement?

The reasons for impasse typically include:

Scott's failure to recognize that the company's interests will be furthered less by victory in court than by a sound business deal with Rapid. Alternatively, Scott may be unwilling to enter into a business deal with Rapid because of distrust of Brown or Williams, or a belief that Rapid is poorly managed.

Santina's desire to take the case to court in order to meet his/her firm's financial interests. (More about this in response to question 7.)

Brown's inability to accept the weakness of Rapid's legal position. Alternatively, Brown, trading on Rapid's poor financial condition, may demand more than Scott is willing to give in a joint venture.

Christian's failure to recognize Rapid's weak legal position, inability to convince Rapid of its weak legal position, or desire to take the case to court in order to further his/her firm's financial interests. (More about this in response to question 7.)

Question 6. What alternatives are available to groups that reached an impasse?

This question stimulates discussion about alternative third party dispute resolution procedures. If the negotiations are not successful, the parties should consider whether they want their dispute resolved in court or through some alternative method of dispute resolution. Among the alternatives that should be considered in this case are mediation, arbitration, and the mini-trial.

The advantage of arbitration over court adjudication would be that it would probably be speedier (unless the local courts have no appreciable backlog in civil cases), and could be less expensive (unless the parties provide for an arbitration procedure that essentially copies court procedure). Additionally, the parties could select an arbitrator with experience in computer-related disputes, instead of having to accept whichever judge was assigned to the case (though that may not be so important in this case, since it appears to turn on a question of credibility). Finally, if secrecy is important to the parties, their arbitration proceedings could be kept wholly private, except to the extent that subsequent judicial proceedings are necessary to enforce the arbitrator's award. (If that were to happen, the potential time and cost advantages of arbitration would also be lost.)

The advantage of mediation or a mini-trial over either court adjudication or arbitration in this case is that the adjudicative process (which characterizes arbitration as well as court adjudication) tends to provide "all-or-nothing" results, rather than a mutually acceptable outcome. In this case, for example, the outcome of either arbitration or court adjudication is likely to be a judgment against Rapid for $500,000, a result which furthers the interests of neither Rapid nor Scott. The goal of either mediation or a mini-trial, however, would be to assist Rapid and Scott to find an outcome that met both their interests.

As between mediation and a mini-trial, one might argue that the mini-trial is better suited to this case. There is a factual dispute at the heart of the conflict. (Did Robertson promise Williams that Scott would provide Rapid with Print-Rite at no charge?) Mediation does not provide for the formal presentation of proofs and arguments to a decision-maker, and may not be as successful in resolving factual disputes as the mini-trial, which does so provide. On the other hand, a mediator might seek to minimize the significance of the factual conflict by pointing out to Scott that even if it prevailed on the factual issue, the most it could get would be a useless judgment against Rapid. Thus, the mediator could point out to Scott that it would be better off to seek a mutually acceptable outcome than to attempt to prevail on the factual issue. While Scott should accept this reasoning, Rapid would be less likely to do so, since a judgment in its favor could lead to a substantial recovery (unless Rapid could be persuaded either that it was unlikely to prevail on the factual issue or that the gains of a long-term association with Scott to develop a computerized remote composition system were greater than the gains of even successful litigation). If Rapid wanted a means by which to compare its evidence on the factual dispute with Scott's evidence, a creative mediator might set up a mini-trial on that issue. Then, with the evidence all in (and pointing strongly in Scott's favor), the mediator should be able to guide the parties to an integrative solution.2

7a. Were there conflicts of interest between Rapid and its lawyer, Christian?

   b. Were there conflicts of interest between Scott and its lawyer, Santina?

   c. How and at what stage of the negotiation were these conflicts of interest resolved?

There is a conflict of interest between Rapid and its lawyer, Christian. Since Christian is being paid on a contingency basis, any settlement that does not involve Scott paying money to Rapid will create problems in determining Christian's fee, even though such a settlement might be in Rapid's best interest.

2As must be obvious, this question is susceptible of meaningful discussion only after students have read Chapters 3 - 5.

There is a similar, albeit perhaps lesser, conflict of interest between Santina and Scott. Since Santina is being paid on an hourly basis (and business is slow), a settlement short of trial, however good it may be for Scott, cuts against Santina's financial interests.

Lawyer-client teams vary dramatically in terms of when these issues are addressed. In some teams, either lawyer or client will raise the conflict of interest problem in the strategy session and negotiate a new fee arrangement before a strategy is developed. In other teams, the fee arrangement is renegotiated between lawyer and client after they determine that their negotiating strategy will result in the lawyer receiving little or no compensation for services. Some management students, while clearly seeing the conflict of interest, are unwilling to discuss it openly. Ask them why. Some law students, recognizing they will receive little or no compensation for this work if a joint venture can be negotiated, do not raise the compensation issue at all. Their rationale is usually that they expect to have a long term relationship with their client and they are more likely to get future business if their legal and strategic advice results in a good business deal for their client than not.

Question 8. Who did the actual negotiating? Why? What plans were made for handling issues not anticipated in the strategy session? For caucusing?

Teams will vary dramatically in how the actual negotiation was handled. Typically, the lawyers will open the negotiation, testing each other's perception of the legal positions in the case. This approach can lead quickly to impasse unless the parties (lawyers or managers) begin discussing settlement alternatives. In some groups, the lawyers will continue to act as chief spokespeople in proposing and discussing settlement alternatives. In other groups, when joint ventures begin to be discussed, the lawyers turn the negotiations over to the managers, believing that the managers can best hammer out an agreement that meets their business interests and that the lawyers' role should be as counsel, helping their clients evaluate alternatives and making sure that any agreement is complete. (See question 4b.)

Question 9. It is interesting to ask the students why they did not initiate the negotiation with a proposal for a joint venture, since almost no one is likely to have done so.

This question raises the broad issue of whether it is appropriate to begin a negotiation using a cooperative strategy or whether doing so risks exploitation by an opponent following a competitive strategy. In this case, the manager on each side knows the interests of the manager on the other side. A joint venture proposal conveys a message that the proposing party recognizes those interests and moves the negotiation quickly into a joint problem solving mode. The argument for this approach is that it is in both parties' interests to enter into a integrative agreement. In order to begin to move in that direction, someone who recognizes the joint interests must initiate the discussion. Both parties may be more open to such a discussion if they have not opened focusing on legal positions. This opening strategy is a way of speeding up the negotiations.

The counter argument is that in any negotiation one never knows exactly how the other party will perceive the merits of his/her case. Opening with a joint venture agreement assumes that one's own assessment of interests is accurate. If the other party perceives that he/she has negotiating strength, a joint venture opening could be seen as a perception of negotiating weakness on the part of the proposing party.

In addition, few situations in the real world are pure opportunities for integrative bargaining. Within the expanded joint pie, there is still going to be a distribution. Some might argue that in order to maximize their share of the expanded distribution, it is better to let the other party broach the joint venture solution, or at least not to suggest it until you have made it clear that you believe that you have a strong negotiating position.

Students also respond to this question by saying that if they opened with a joint venture proposal, there would be little or no role for the lawyer in this case. This response opens the following line of questioning.

Question 10. When should a manager engage a lawyer or other expert to represent or assist in a negotiation? What role should the manager play? What role should the lawyer play?

There are at least four situations in which a manager should engage a lawyer or other expert as a representative in a dispute:

a. When technical advice is needed, e.g., legal advice;

b. When negotiating skills are needed which the manager does not possess;

c. When the manager is so emotionally engaged in the dispute that he/she does not trust him/herself to negotiate a beneficial settlement;

d. When the manager's time is more valuable than the representatives.

The roles of the manager and lawyer depend on the reason that the expert was engaged. In Rapid vs. Scott, the lawyers were engaged for their legal expertise. In addition, because they as well as the management students have had a course in negotiation, they should be useful in helping their client design a negotiating strategy.

In order for synergy to develop in a lawyer-client relationship, the manager must know and disclose to the lawyer his/her business interests and the lawyer must provide sound legal advice, even if it cuts against the client's position, as is true for Rapid.

Question 11. What did management and law students learn from the experience of working together?
The management students are not likely to have had much experience being represented in a negotiation. Because they engaged their lawyer for legal skills, not necessarily negotiation skills, they are unlikely to wish to turn the entire negotiation over to the lawyer. There will be considerable tension in some lawyer-management teams when the roles of each were not well worked out in the strategy session. In the teams in which the roles were well delineated and enacted as planned, students are likely to focus on the utility of having a knowledgeable negotiating partner with whom to work out strategy and evaluate the utility of potential settlements.

The law students are not likely to have had much experience representing clients, particularly ones with similar negotiating skills and significantly greater financial acumen. Some law students find the limited role of counseling a knowledgeable client a shock. One commented, "I think I'm in the wrong field; it's the managers who get to make all the decisions."

Question 12. What was the major learning point of this exercise?

a. Legal or financial strength does not always create bargaining strength. Thus, a good negotiator should not despair of achieving a satisfactory agreement because his or her legal or financial position appears weak.

b. A good negotiator will recognize that "victory" over another party will not always further his or her interests, and will search for the outcome that best does so.

EXERCISE 2.8:	FG & T TOWER

Teaching Instructions

Divide the students into groups of six. Each group constitutes the executive committee of a law firm, which must meet to decide whether to purchase the building in which the firm is presently renting space.

While this is an exercise in coalition building as a means of influencing group decision-making, we think the exercise is more successful if students are not explicitly told this. Instead, we tell the students that they are to prepare for the forthcoming meeting of the executive committee in any way they wish, including pre-meeting discussions with other members of the committee. The alert student should realize the importance of coalition-building in advance of the scheduled committee meeting. Not only do the private instructions encourage individual negotiations as a means for each committee member to attain his/her goals; those instructions also forbid private discussions once the executive committee meeting has begun.

EXERCISE 2.8:   FG & T TOWER

Confidential Information for
Andy Aldrich*

You are strongly opposed to the purchase of the building and you will do everything you can to prevent it. You support the affirmative action plan advocated by Dana Douglas, which requires hiring five minority attorneys a year, beginning with this year.

Unfortunately, the building issue could not have arisen at a worse time for you. A major ward redistricting case has just come into the Litigation Department, and you must dig into it as soon as possible. The first item you must resolve is whom you will select to work with you on the case. (You have already decided that you will be the lead attorney, since this is a case that is almost certain to go to the Supreme Court, and you've not yet had a case in the Supreme Court.) There is certain to be intense competition for the second chair position, but you have already narrowed your choice to either Erin Edward or Dana Douglas, each of whom would do a first-rate job. You marginally prefer Douglas, however, and you've already discussed the assignment with him/her, albeit in a highly tentative fashion. You've not yet said anything to Edwards, however.

---

*Note: You may be uncomfortable with the role you are asked to play in this exercise. Strictly for the sake of learning, please play that role according to the instructions you are given.

EXERCISE 2.8:   FG & T TOWER

Confidential Information for
Blair Barrister*

You are strongly opposed to the purchase of the building and you will do everything you can to prevent it. You are also opposed to the affirmative action plan that has been proposed by Dana Douglas, since you are concerned about its effect on the quality of the firm. You suspect that the supporters of affirmative action may attempt to use the building vote as an opportunity to institute the affirmative action plan by trading support. You will agree to support the affirmative action plan only if it is absolutely necessary to prevent the purchase of the building.

---

*Note: You may be uncomfortable with the role you are asked to play in this exercise. Strictly for the sake of learning, please play that role according to the instructions you are given.

EXERCISE 2.8:   FG & T TOWER

Confidential Information for
Chris Carlisle*

Ultimately, you are going to vote to purchase the building because of its potential profitability. However, you hope to bluff Forrest into paying a price for your vote. Ideally, you want Forrest to resign the chairmanship of the Hiring & Promotions Committee and support you as his/her replacement. You want to be named the head of the Real Estate Department, and you want to be made a named partner. On other issues, including affirmative action, you will vote for whichever group offers you the most in return.

---

*Note: You may be uncomfortable with the role you are asked to play in this exercise. Strictly for the sake of learning, please play that role according to the instructions you are given.

EXERCISE 2.8:   FG & T TOWER

Confidential Information for
Dana Douglas*

The number one item on your agenda at this time is the institution of an affirmative action plan. To be sure, Andy Aldrich has talked to you about the possibility of your being second chair on the big ward redistricting case that just came into the office, and that's an exciting prospect, but not as important to you as affirmative action at FG&T.

If possible, you are going to use the building vote to accomplish the institution of an affirmative action plan. Ideally, you want a plan that requires hiring five minority attorneys a year beginning with this year. If that plan cannot be obtained, however, you will accept a plan for hiring three minorities each year beginning with next year. You will not pledge your vote to either side of the building decision until that side can guarantee the three votes, other than yours, necessary to institute an affirmative action plan. If both sides ultimately guarantee three votes, then you will vote with the side that guarantees the best plan. If neither side guarantees three votes, then you will vote to purchase since you are convinced that the building will ultimately be profitable, and you have no pressing need for additional current income.

---

*Note: You may be uncomfortable with the role you are asked to play in this exercise. Strictly for the sake of learning, please play that role according to the instructions you are given.

EXERCISE 2.8:   FG & T TOWER

Confidential Information for
Erin Edwards*

The building issue puts you between a rock and a hard place. On one hand, you do not want to oppose Forrest. On the other hand, you do not want the firm to purchase the building because you believe that would be an unwise use of partnership assets. Extra cash should be used to hire able lawyers, not to buy buildings.

You have decided that you will vote against purchasing the building only if two conditions are met. First you want Aldrich, whom you suspect is opposed to purchasing the building, to place you in charge of the big ward redistricting litigation that has just come into the office. You have handled some voting rights cases since you've come into the office but nothing of that magnitude, and you would really enjoy the challenge (and notoriety) that would come from being the lead attorney on a case that is almost certain to end up in the Supreme Court. Indeed, you are so excited at the prospect of being involved in that case that you would settle for second chair, You won't let Aldrich know that, however, unless he turns down your bid to be lead attorney.

Your second condition for voting against purchasing the building is that your vote must be absolutely necessary to form a majority opposing the purchase. You are uncomfortable at the prospect of voting contrary to Forrest's wishes, and will not do so if the opponents of purchasing the building can get a majority against the purchase without your vote.

You are aware that Douglas is anxious to institute an affirmative action hiring plan for FG&T, though he has not spoken to you about it. You have no strong views about such a plan one way or the other.

* Note: You may be uncomfortable with the role you are asked to play in this exercise. Strictly for the sake of learning, please play that role according to the instructions you are given

EXERCISE 2.8:   FG & T TOWER

Confidential Information for
F.L. Forrest*

You want the firm to purchase the building and you will vote both your vote and Glenn Gleason's vote in favor of the proposal. While you don't know where Andy Aldrich and Blair Barrister stand on the proposal, you feel fairly confident that Erin Edwards will vote with you if you make clear how strongly you feel about the proposal.

You also believe that you can obtain Dana Douglas' support by supporting Douglas' efforts to institute an affirmative action plan. You will agree to a plan requiring the hiring of three minorities a year beginning with next year. You will not agree to a plan that commits the firm to more than three minority hires per year. You are not opposed to affirmative action, but do not want to move too fast in that direction, because you are concerned about maintaining the quality of the firm.

The member whose vote you are least certain about is Chris Carlisle. While it would seem that Chris would be crazy to vote against a proposal that is certain to be ultimately profitable, Chris dislikes you enough that he/she just might vote against the proposal to spite you. Therefore, you must be prepared to pay for Chris' vote if you perceive that Chris is planning to vote against you. You know that Chris wishes you to resign your chairmanship of the Hiring & Promotions Committee and you are willing to do that. You are also willing to support Chris as your replacement in that position if it is unavoidable. In the extreme, you will agree to support Chris as head of the Real Estate Department. Under no circumstances, however, will you agree to make Chris a named partner.

* Note: You may be uncomfortable with the role you are asked to play in this exercise. Strictly for the sake of learning, please play that role according to the instructions you are given.

EXERCISE 2.8:   FG & T TOWER

Teaching Notes

This exercise is intended to demonstrate that a group decision is often the product of a series of individual negotiations in which group members seek to advance both group and individual interests. These individual negotiations may lead to the formation of coalitions, with the stronger coalition effectively making the group decision. In order to be successful in this negotiation, each student should trade those interests he/she values less for those which he/she values more. In some instances, this can be done through one-to-one negotiations; in other instances, the formation of a bloc is necessary.

If no negotiations take place prior to the executive committee meeting, or if those negotiations which do occur are unsuccessful, the vote will be 5-2 to purchase the building (with Aldrich and Barrister voting against), with, at most, a 3-person affirmative action plan. If the maximum amount of successful, pre-meeting negotiations take place, the vote should be 4-3 against purchasing the building (Douglas and Edwards joining Aldrich and Barrister), with a 5-person affirmative action plan. In addition, Edwards and Carlisle will have attained some of their individual goals.

Spelling out the latter scenario more precisely, Aldrich should approach Douglas, who will agree to vote against the purchase if Aldrich can guarantee 3 votes (plus Douglas) for the best possible affirmative action plan. Aldrich should next approach Edwards, who will vote against purchase if he/she gets second chair on the ward re-districting case (though Edwards should try to negotiate for lead chair) and if his/her vote is necessary for a majority against purchase. Aldrich should not surrender first chair, should say that second chair may be possible (he/she should not commit on this without clearing with Douglas), and that Edwards' vote may be necessary for a majority against purchase. Aldrich should also be able to obtain Edwards' commitment to vote for a 5-person affirmative action plan, since Edwards has no interest in this issue, and Aldrich can use Edwards' vote on affirmative action in dealing with Douglas. Aldrich should then approach Carlisle, who will give Aldrich nothing.

Aldrich should then tell Barrister that he/she must have Barrister's support on a 5-person affirmative action plan to prevent purchase; under those conditions, Barrister will accede. Aldrich then tells Douglas that if Douglas will give up second chair on the re-districting case, and will vote against the purchase, Aldrich can assure him/her a majority (Aldrich, Barrister, Douglas, Edwards) for a 5-person affirmative action plan. Douglas should accept, since he/she values affirmative action above all else. Aldrich then returns to Edwards, tells Edwards he/she can have second chair, and that his/her vote against purchase is necessary for an anti-purchase majority (Aldrich, Barrister, Douglas, and Edwards). Edwards should then agree to vote against the purchase, and Aldrich is able to block the purchase. (The order of these negotiations, and who initiates them, may vary, but they must all take place if a majority against purchase is to be constructed).

If Aldrich does what he/she is capable of, Forrest cannot put together a pro-purchase majority. Forrest cannot get Edwards' vote because Aldrich controls assignments to the redistricting case, and Forrest cannot get Douglas' vote because the strongest affirmative action plan Forrest can offer is a 3-person plan. Thus, Forrest will obtain only 3 votes in favor of purchase: Carlisle, Forrest and Gleason.

In order to determine how successfully each student has advanced his/her interests in these negotiations, it is necessary to determine what results he/she obtained. If each negotiated well, the individual outcomes should be these:

Aldrich -- No purchase. Retains lead chair in re-districting case. Has not taken second chair from Douglas to give to Edwards without Douglas' consent. Five-person affirmative action plan.

Barrister -- No purchase.

Carlisle -- Has Forrest's support for chair, Hiring and Promotions committee, and head, Real Estate Department. Carlisle should use, as bargaining chips, his/her vote on both the building and the affirmative action plan.

Douglas -- Five-person affirmative action plan.

Edwards -- Second chair on re-districting case. No commitment to vote against purchase until assured vote necessary.

Forrest -- Purchase of building (not possible if Aldrich and Barrister do a good job). Agreement to support Carlisle for as few leadership positions as possible. Get Carlisle's vote for 3-person affirmative action plan.

General -- In addition, the negotiation is institutionally successful for all only if the relationship between the members of the executive committee remains good. If there are significant hard feelings as a result of tactless negotiations, all members of the committee, and the firm as a whole, are losers. This is a point that students often forget in their zeal to put together a "winning" coalition.

EXERCISE 2.9:   MEDICAL MALPRACTICE CLAIM

Teaching Instructions

This exercise is designed to focus on value claiming and value creating negotiating approaches and on the advantages and disadvantages of client presence during negotiations. It is patterned on the simulation in Leonard Riskin's film series (cited in the text) so that the students can engage in the negotiating themselves and then compare their own negotiation to that in the film. The advantages of having the students do the negotiation first are that they will be more intent when watching the film and that they will have a basis for arguing that a different approach (perhaps their own) would have been better. The advantage of showing the film, in addition to having the students do the simulation, is that the teacher can focus discussion on one example, while permitting the students to raise important segments of their own negotiations. This seems to reduce the discussion time needed in a large class, while giving the students a basis to gauge their own effectiveness as negotiators.

The students should be divided into groups of 4, with 2 assigned to be counsel and 2 to be parties. The lawyer and client on each side receive the same confidential instructions. The negotiation is likely to take about two hours.

EXERCISE 2.9:	MEDICAL MALPRACTICE CLAIM

Confidential Instructions for Plaintiff's Counsel
(To be read by Plaintiff also)

Your client believes that defendant represents the worst of the medical profession, those who care about nothing except processing patients quickly to increase their own incomes. At the first visit, the doctor gave no warning that numbness might occur and might interfere with performances. In fact, the doctor never asked about the client's occupation. At the second office visit, scheduled quickly in response to the client's demand, the client waited for an hour, was given x-rays by office staff, and then was seen by the doctor for only 30 seconds. Your client then had twenty sessions (at $1,000 each!) with a different specialist and is now fine. In the meantime, your client not only missed paying engagements but also a favorite pro bono performance, the annual Children's Home concert.

You advised the client that the first lawyer was mistaken -- there is no basis for the battery allegations or for a punitive damage recovery. Your medical expert indicates that the doctor should have advised that numbness was a potential side effect. In your opinion, there is about a 50/50 chance of a plaintiff's verdict on the negligence claim. An optimistic estimate of the amount would be $90,000 to $125,000. The client accepts, albeit with misgivings, your request for authority to settle for a payment of $60,000. The doctor's callousness has left the client furious.

EXERCISE 2.9:	MEDICAL MALPRACTICE CLAIM

Confidential Instructions for Defense Counsel
(To be read by Defendant also)

Your client's reaction to this suit is a combination of fright, because the insurance lapsed, and righteous indignation. The doctor did a postgraduate fellowship at Stanford University that included special instruction in AR-21. Plaintiff should have mentioned an unusual occupation such as piano performing. At the time of the second visit the doctor had been called about an emergency and assumed that the staff had informed the patient that there was only time for a quick conversation then but that the doctor would be glad to talk to the patient further after taking care of the emergency.

Some aspects of the case favor your client. This client will be an appealing witness. Despite a busy practice, the doctor donates time weekly at the Children's Home. You have an expert witness who will testify that the doctor was not negligent. There is no basis for the battery claim or for the request for punitive damages.

Nonetheless, you have advised the client of defense costs plus a likely verdict of about $100,000 with a chance that the verdict could exceed $200,000. You asked for and received authority to pay $90,000 to settle the case.

EXERCISE 2.9:	MEDICAL MALPRACTICE CLAIM

Teaching Notes

After the students have done the exercise, one might begin the class by showing the tape. Several groups of students might be asked to focus on one part of the film: tracking the positions of the negotiators, noting the explanations given for moving to a new position or request, noting evidence of a value creating or value claiming approach, or noting advantages and disadvantages of the parties' presence. As the tape is shown, I find it useful to skip those portions involving commentary, thereby encouraging the students to provide the commentary. At the end of the tape, each group reports and comparisons are made with the simulations done by students.

The position map looks about like this:

	Plaintiff	Defendant
1.		Drops battery claim and punitive damage request
2.	$175,000 - 200,000	
3.		$40,000 & confidentiality (might stop Children's Home work)
4.	$50,000	
5.	$90,000	
6.		$70,000 (probably Children's Home work)
7.	$80,000	
8.		$75,000
9.	$75,000	
10.		$77,500

Students might be asked to make comparable position maps for their own exercises.

The students should have observed some value claiming by defense counsel, who secured the first offer from the opposition, started low, conceded slowly, misrepresented settlement authority (client says that $50,000 is maximum; I'll have to talk her into...), exaggerated the merits of his/her defense ("doubtful liability"), and arguably took advantage of plaintiff's disclosed interest in the Children's Home to insert a false demand, that the amount be low enough to permit the doctor to continue his/her work in the Home. Counsel for both parties may have also engaged in value creating, in admitting that some allegations could not be sustained, in permitting clients to speak about their interests, in the apology, and arguably in the efforts to continue the work at the Children's Home. Did the plaintiff's candor about his/her interest in the Children's Home result in her achieving a lower settlement?

The clients' attendance may have had the following benefits: counsel were well prepared; the clients had a chance to tell each other about their own frustrations with the way each was treated; they began to see a human side of each other; they learned that they had a joint interest in serving the Children's Home; and an apology was given and accepted. At the same time, each had authorized settlement prior to the negotiation, so their presence may not have been necessary in order to produce a settlement. In addition, each was inconvenienced by attending; the plaintiff's disclosure may not have improved her negotiating stance; and the real changes in positions occurred without the clients present, with defense counsel claiming that the client was not willing to concede as much as he.

More detailed teaching notes for this exercise accompany the videotape.

These teaching notes were excerpted from notes prepared by Stephen B. Goldberg and Professor Jeanne M. Brett, Kellogg Graduate School of Management, Northwestern University, for an American Arbitration Association Task Force on Teaching Dispute Resolution in Law and Business Schools. Hence, their form differs from that of other teaching note

CHAPTER 3 – MEDIATION

A.   Questions

Unnumbered question, page 136: Arguments against lawyer participation are made most frequently in the community and divorce context, but could apply in the family-business dispute. Here are views related to divorce mediation:

> ... Professor [Joshua] Rosenberg argues against any type of lawyer involvement in mediation – not just legal argument -- because the advocacy role that attorneys play may promote reluctance "to explore helpful and creative solutions. Possibilities that might help both parties could be permanently lost." Professor Thomas Carbonneau warns that adversarial attorney interaction in divorce mediation "threatens to compromise the viability of the process, " adding that lawyers who do not agree with mediation goals are "likely to become a dysfunctional element in the process, not only jealous of its intrusion into their domain of competence, but also unable to adapt professionally to a situation of controlled and defused, rather than polarized and contentious, conflict." Mediation proponents also suggest that lawyer participation may reduce commitment to, and thus compliance with, the settlement reached (Craig A. McEwen, Nancy H. Rogers & Richard J. Maiman, Bring in the Lawyers: Challenging the Dominant Approaches to Ensuring Fairness in Divorce Mediation, 79 Minn. L. Rev. 1317, 1354-55 (1995) (footnotes omitted).

Unnumbered question, page 139: It may be helpful to put up a copy of Leonard Riskin's grid from his Harvard Negotiation Law Review article, p. 25, before beginning discussion of these questions.

Riskin views the grid as descriptive of practice. Joseph Stulberg has responded by arguing that effective mediators use a style that would fit on Riskin's evaluative side but without the evaluation. Stulberg suggests that the effective mediator prepares on the law and background of the dispute and is "assertive, firm, forceful, imaginative, creative, active, " and "focused " Joseph B. Stulberg, Facilitative Versus Evaluative Mediator Orientations: Piercing the "Grid" Lock, 24 Florida State Law Review 985, 1002 (1997).

Arguably, Weinstein merely challenges the lawyer by saying that he does not see $500, 000 or even $100,000 for most juries, perhaps even fitting Stulberg's non-evaluative but forceful mediator. Aaron seems to argue, though, that the challenge approach (a "dose of reality") does not represent a difference in kind from an evaluation.

The answer to the questions regarding whether evaluation is appropriate largely depends on the goals for mediation. Do the parties' goals define what are appropriate goals for the mediator? If so, the parties seem intent on settlement, and their lawyers seem to welcome the evaluation as helpful in making their clients more realistic.

The commentators typically suggest waiting until later in the mediation for evaluation, but Weinstein's use of a challenging early evaluation in a caucus does not appear to disrupt the process.

Unnumbered question, page 141: Many commentators would suggest this approach. Here are some notes on this:

Sam Kagel and Kathy Kelly:

If the parties are so discouraged that they are reticent to display any movement, it is generally best to start with issues of lesser importance so that some confidence in the process can be built before the most challenging issues are approached (Kagel & Kelly, 1989: 120).

Kimberlee Kovach:

If any progress at all has been made, acknowledge and positively reinforce it. This can go a long way in motivating further movement (Kovach, 1994: 128).

Unnumbered question, page 143: Summarization would seem to be helpful in helping Wofford and Holloway understand that they have much to gain in removing a bump that has arisen on a previously successful road in their personal and business relationships. In the context of this case, Weinstein might summarize by noting the long and positive business and personal relationship shared by this brother and sister, the regret that both feel at the disruption of it, the desire to resolve the issues in a manner that will allow them both to pursue their business careers productively, and the progress that has been made in narrowing the financial differences and other between them. At this point, though, it may be difficult to list the remaining issues without either ignoring the positions stated by the parties or further encouraging them to see the negotiations in a positional way.

Unnumbered question, page 144: Students tend to assume that mediator bias falls along lines of economic status, ethnicity, or judgment about how a case should be "decided." The question is designed to secure their acknowledgment that bias is much more complex.

Unnumbered question, page 146: At this point Weinstein is trying to get Holloway to appreciate the depth of his sister's anger, so arguably the exchange was useful.

Unnumbered question, page 154: Arguably, Weinstein has tried everything else at this point so has little to lose in employing this tactic. Nor is this a situation in which the parties are unrepresented and pressures might cause a reluctant party to cave in. Rather, the parties either are unlikely to settle or are procrastinating. Dwight Golann argues, "The point is to give the participants a sense of urgency, the fear that at some point in the near future 'the mediation train will leave the station.'" (Golann, 1996: 156).

Unnumbered question, pages 156-159: This is an appropriate opportunity to ask the students to reflect on the Fisher and Ury excerpt on single text negotiation. Does this differ? Fisher and Ury focus on a deal-making example. Maggiolo's comment points out the reasons for delaying a proposal in dispute settlement mediation. Would Bush and Folger view the architect in Fisher and Ury's example as removing opportunities for the parties to find their own solutions? Is the mediator's non-involvement in the dispute and knowledge from caucuses like the architect's expertise in permitting the mediator to imagine solutions that the parties are unlikely to suggest?

3.1   The answer depends on the goals for the court-connected program. In terms of settlement rates, there is no reason to match the mediator's substantive expertise with the case, a matching that is likely to increase costs. Also, if the program seeks to discourage evaluation by its mediators, it would have every incentive *not* to match expertise and case. On the other hand, a program seeking to maintain satisfied mediators may say that any added administrative cost of matching expertise to case is worthwhile.

3.2   Weinstein employs a number of techniques to deal with emotionalism, ineffective communication, and differing perceptions of the alternatives to settlement, including:

a. Emotionalism: In joint sessions, the mediator controls the level of anger, permitting its expression while reminding the parties, for example, that accusations and interruptions are counterproductive. In the first caucus, the mediator encourages Wofford to express her feelings. In this caucus away from her brother, there is no risk of an angry reaction that might prematurely terminate the negotiations. Weinstein attempts to make Wofford feel that he understands, though some students will point out that he might be more persuasive on this point if he picks a more specific response than, "I understand how you felt . . . ." The mediator seems to adopt the approach to the parties' emotionalism suggested by Rogers and Salem, "[S]ome mediators provide a controlled forum for a limited venting of feelings early in the process on the theory that the expression and acknowledgment of hurts and frustrations helps to humanize the conflict, surface underlying issues that must be addressed in order to resolve the dispute and facilitate a rational discussion . . . ." In addition, when Holloway seems not to understand why his sister is angry, Weinstein restates her feelings, giving Holloway an opportunity to reflect on his responsibility for them ("You heard her yesterday. She said she was 'crushed' after all her work to be fired out of hand, no warning."). Building on this, Weinstein encourages an apology, recognizing the importance of the technique discussed in the note following the Wofford/Holloway mediation.

b. Ineffective communication: The parties and their lawyers seem prone to focus on what happened in the past and what is likely to occur in litigation. The mediator, after hearing them out on these points, changes the focus to their future business interests. He encourages problem-solving. Further, he provides an excuse for Holloway to abandon his adamant position that no letter of recommendation was appropriate, pointing out that things have changed since that position was last expressed. In addition, he learns in separate caucus about Wofford's hopes for the future, something she was not comfortable discussing in Holloway's presence. Thus, he was able to see a solution that would probably not have been evident in joint negotiations.

c. Differing perceptions of the alternative to agreement: Weinstein provides assessments of the parties' chances of prevailing in litigation. The assessment seems to plant doubt in the minds of the parties about the validity of their positions, enough to make them more flexible during negotiations. By providing the assessments in separate caucuses, the mediator avoids the resentment that might result if the mediator undermined one party's position in the presence of the other. Despite its effectiveness in bringing about settlement, there is some debate about whether the mediator should assess the merits. Opposition to the practice is based both on legal ethics (legal advice to persons whose interests conflict) and on philosophical grounds. The ethical problems, discussed in more detail in Chapter 3E, seem minimal here, because the parties have their own lawyers and will not rely on the mediator's assessment as if it were legal advice. The philosophical objection is based on a view that a key advantage of mediation is its tendency to strengthen the abilities of the parties to resolve their own disputes and the assumption that the parties will acquiesce in the view expressed by the mediator.

d. Other: The mediator also contributes a sense of optimism that motivates the parties to keep working, noting, for example, "some major yielding" on the part of the other party. As an experienced mediator, he also suggests the idea that ultimately proves workable for the parties. A mediator suggestion also avoids a tendency of some disputants to devalue any idea suggested by the other. At the same time, some mediators warn that the parties feel less "ownership" of ideas suggested by a mediator and thus may not have the same enthusiasm for carrying out a mediator-suggested settlement.

3.3   Some mediators view protective or argumentative behavior by lawyers as counterproductive to their efforts to reach settlement. Arguably, the lawyers' role here as a "devil's advocate" to concessions makes the clients feel secure enough to be flexible. If the lawyers had not attended, Weinstein could not have discussed as effectively two things that became significant in reaching agreement -- the likely course of litigation and the possibility of a settlement solution involving financial assistance on a future venture. The role of the clients' presence is discussed more thoroughly in an article by Leonard Riskin, excerpted on pp. 320-324. In this case, attendance by the clients made it possible for them to express emotions and understand each other's emotions. This facilitated the apology and change of heart about the letter of recommendation. It helped the mediator understand the parties' interests and work through the complicated trade-offs required for the solution. At the same time, the clients' presence increased the number of persons involved and thus the complexity of the negotiations. Further, each side risked strategic errors. Some would cite, as an example of a negotiating error, Holloway's agreement to write the letter without demanding a reciprocating concession. On balance, it appears that this settlement would not have been reached without the clients present, so their presence was worth the other risks.

3.4   In domestic mediation, joint sessions provide at least two benefits. First, the mediator can model a workable approach to disputing, something important when the parties must cooperate, for example, in raising children, particularly if they have developed unproductive patterns of negotiating during the disintegration of their marriage. Second, parties undergoing a divorce may find it more difficult to trust the impartiality of the mediator if the mediator hears a separate version from the other party. In the Wofford-Holloway mediation, these benefits of joint sessions are less significant and the countervailing benefits of caucuses (handling emotionalism, testing the parties' assumptions, engaging in candid discussions about their interests) outweigh them.

Students may raise the issue of domestic violence in response to this question. Domestic violence issues are discussed in Chapter 7. Some programs exclude domestic violence cases from mediation. California includes the cases in mediation, but domestic violence victims have a right to insist that the entire mediation be conducted in a series of caucuses, so that they do not have to face their attacker in direct negotiations. Cal. Civ. Code § 4607.2. Apparently, the assumption is that custody mediation does not lose all value merely because it is not held in joint sessions.

3.5   The purpose of the question is to get the students to focus on how "fragile" is the trust that permits the parties to be candid about their interests so that an integrative solution can be fashioned to meet those interests. When the mediator and decision-maker are combined, both lawyers and clients seem likely to speak as advocates, recognizing that the decision-maker will remember such facts as that the plaintiff's own lawyer thought the claim was inflated. It is not hard to see that the apology and the frankness which permitted Weinstein to think of the future agreement as a solution would be casualties of the med-arb approach. On the other hand, the parties would be certain in med-arb to have a solution -- though perhaps not the integrative one evolving in the mediation -- without investing much more time and money to have an independent hearing before a separate arbitrator.

Arguably, the parties act as advocates when discussing settlement before a judge. When the judge acts as mediator, ethical as well as strategic issues arise. Wall, Schiller & Ebert (1984) report that both judges and lawyers believe that judicial involvement increases the chances of settlement. There is substantial disagreement, however, as to when judicial mediation is ethical. More than a quarter of the lawyers surveyed thought it unethical for the judge to use the following techniques: commentary on the credibility of testimony, delay of a trial date to encourage settlement, provision of advice to a lawyer about the strength of the case, or separate discussion with a lawyer or party. Wall, Schiller, & Ebert, 1984: 98-99. At the same time, an ABA-sponsored survey indicates that lawyer opposition to judicial assessments of the merits largely dissipates if the conference is not held by the trial judge. W. Brazil, Settling Civil Suits: Litigators' Views About Appropriate Roles and Effective Techniques for Trial Judges 5-6 (1984).

3.6 Weinstein's legal expertise made credible his assessment of the case on the merits and made it easier for him to discuss effectively with the parties' lawyers the possibility of a new business agreement. Some would argue that a non-lawyer who is not trained to think in terms of the litigated alternative attends more to the interests and emotions of the parties, yet it is hard to see much support for this argument in the Wofford-Holloway mediation. The question of whether mediators should be lawyers or should be drawn from any particular professions is discussed in more detail in Chapter 3D.

3.7 Wofford does indeed seem to focus more on the relationship and to value (even to be willing to reduce her demand in response to) the apology from her brother. Is she vulnerable because she values the relationship more than money? Some students will feel that she was duped to accept an apology in place of a monetary result. Arguably, because she values the relationship and wants to run a business, she is better served by a reconciliation and a settlement that permits her to start a business venture than by even a substantial monetary recovery after months of litigation.

3.8. a. Kaler's anger about the way that she was treated when she called to complain may well be a reason that she is not more flexible about having Breel fix her teeth, as might be her growing distrust of Breel. Perhaps using the "role reversal" suggested by Stulberg on pp. 163-164, a mediator might encourage Breel to focus on this issue and perhaps offer an apology and effort to compensate Kaler for that incident. Kaler's distrust of Breel may still make her resist a proposal that involves Breel re-doing her teeth. The mediator may want to explore the reasons for the distrust in a caucus, using the "hidden issue" approach discussed by Golann on p. 163. Also, the mediator may ask Breel to prioritize her interests as suggested by Stulberg on p. 162, especially her general concern about her reputation if litigation occurs versus her concern about having a single additional dentist learn about the problem. Kaler might be asked to prioritize her desire for immediate relief from the green teeth and her desire to secure a payment to permit her to get help from another dentist.

b. The girlfriend-boyfriend issues seems to be the block, despite the mediator's attempt, through an announcement, to make it otherwise. Here, Golann's advice (p. 163) to search for hidden issues seems important. Once the interests are identified, then Slaikeu's advice to turn positions regarding the girlfriend and boyfriend into specific interests might lead to a resolution. The mediator might be able to have the parties list those interests that have highest priority, perhaps those related to their child as opposed to their own issues with each other. The fact that all other issues have been settled by also be used, as Goldberg and Stulberg suggest (p. 163), to motivate the two people to find ways to resolve this last item.

c. A likely source of impasse is the differing views on the likely outcome of litigation if the matter is not settled. The matter is complicated by that fact that the City's authority comes from city council, and city council members are not at the table. Here, the construction of a decision tree (pp. 329-335), which could be shared with city council member, could be helpful. Alternatively, the parties might be asked for alternatives to full settlement. For example, they might agree to submit the sovereign immunity issue to the court based on a summary judgment motion, and settle on amounts and payment schedules to be paid under both a ruling for and against summary judgment.

3.9 This question is designed to focus on the lawyer's role advising a client about mediation, in contrast to Question 3.13, which focuses on the policy issues arising when the government or court encourages parties to use mediation.

a. Does "likely to lead to settlement" mean a 90 percent chance? Here an early settlement is very important and if mediation increases the chances even slightly, it may serve the client's interests to try it. If the neighborhood residents' reaction is based on fear and misunderstanding, a skilled mediator's provision for the expression of the emotions and improvement of communications may overcome these obstacles to settlement. At the same time, there is a risk that the neighbors have made an informed and rational decision to delay your client's efforts, so that your client will be forced to locate the group home elsewhere. In the latter case, mediation may contribute to the delay and is unlikely to result in settlement. Perhaps the client's interests would be best served by encouraging the client to arrange one mediation session in order to assess more accurately the neighbors' situation. This would not cause much expense or delay and would place the client in a better position to decide whether further sessions would be helpful.

b. If you accompany the client to the mediation session, you can assist in negotiations and there is little danger that she will agree to a settlement that does not serve her interests. At the same time, mediation may be a waste of time if you do not know the extent of her husband's assets. Perhaps a solution that facilitates efforts to find an alternative to a bitter custody battle is to condition the agreement to mediate on the pre-mediation disclosure of tax returns or other records of assets. Some mediators attempt to separate issues of custody from monetary issues in order to avoid the use of custody as a bargaining chip, but the husband may refuse to agree to the separation of issues.

c. It seems unlikely that mediation will result in a monetary settlement, when the other party stands to gain more by delay, and trial is not imminent. At the same time, with the construction company in financial difficulty, your client may prefer a settlement requiring repairs to an uncollectible judgment. This, in turn, may be interesting to the construction company. A mediator may be able to find out about each party's interests through separate caucuses and suggest such a solution.

d. Here mediation is likely to be a waste of time. The city council would like to be able to cite a court order as the reason for admitting those wearing swastikas. There is little reason to believe that the citizen group will agree to stay away. In the latter aspect, the problem differs from the neo-Nazi Skokie case, which was mediated to settlement by the U.S. Community Relations Service. In that case, neo-Nazi marchers had reason to fear violence during their threatened march through a community that included many survivors of the Nazi camps and thus may have had a reason to agree to stage the march elsewhere. See N. Rogers & R. Salem, 1987: 34-36.

3.10 Under some circumstances, two mediators can more effectively gain the trust of both parties. For example, during divorce some parties doubt the neutrality of members of the opposite sex, and co-mediation by a man and a woman may alleviate their concerns. In addition, co-mediation permits a wider range of expertise. This, in turn, may help the mediators understand alternatives to settlement and propose solutions, such as when a lawyer and environmental expert use a one-text procedure in environmental cases. Because co-mediators consult with each other on strategy and often de-brief afterward, co-mediation may serve an important training function. At the same time, co-mediation increases the expense, the scheduling problems, and the complexity of the mediation session. On balance, this suggests that its value varies depending on the type of dispute, level of distrust among parties, expense, logistics, and experience of mediators. Co-mediation by lawyers and non-lawyers sometimes presents ethical issues, discussed in Question 3.26.

3.11 The court could establish a default system. Perhaps the mediator would be instructed to be facilitative unless the parties agreed otherwise. Stulberg is right though that defining the default solution involves a policy judgment about the most appropriate approach. Also, what would be a party's recourse if the mediator evaluated despite that party's preference for the facilitative approach?

3.12   We have found that students learn from discussion of this exercise after completing their study of mediation techniques. If you plan to assign the chapter on Dispute System Design, you may want to delay use of this exercise until that point.

Our own experience has led us to believe that students make more progress toward thinking through the third party's potential role in assisting negotiations across cultural differences if we raise these issues first in an unfamiliar context (questions A-D) and then later (question E) bring the issues closer to home. Also, we think that minority students bear a heavier burden in discussions about racial and ethnic issues set in this country and that this burden may distract these students from focusing on and learning about the third party's role. With this in mind, we would assign A through D each to a particular subgroup of the class for discussion and preparation and ask them to report back to the group as a whole. Then after discussing the reports on A through D, we would ask the entire class question E.

a.   It may be impossible to design a process that meets all of the Chairperson's goals with equal force. For example, the response most likely to reassure faculty of her support might be to do nothing in response to the student memo, but obviously this course of action would not meet the Chairperson's other goals. To overcome this problem, the students may want to ask the Chairperson to give them a sense of priorities among goals.

The Chairperson's goals cannot all be achieved without accommodating some of the students' goals. It may be important to interview representative students about their goals and priorities among them.

The parties' likely goals can be achieved only through some communication process, and any communication process in this context risks misunderstanding and an escalation of hostility. The process most likely to avoid escalation would seem to be a closed, confidential mediation among representative parties, with use of caucusing when joint sessions appear likely to heighten anger. At the same time, the memo indicates that the students may not be willing to participate in a confidential process or one involving the use of representative parties. One alternative might be to convene a mediation among representative parties to discuss and possibly plan the open forum. The mediation might set out the issues, identify the flashpoints to anticipate at the open forum, secure agreement on ground rules to overcome them, and even come up with a short-term solution so that the class can continue until a forum can be held on the broader issues.

b.   Some of the problems presented by an open forum might be press coverage that would aggravate tensions and encourage posturing at the forum, the appearance of persons from outside the Department whose agenda may be only to disrupt rather than to solve the problems, and the high and escalating emotions that may lead to disruption and the possible loss of control by the facilitator. As a result, the facilitator may be unable to turn the forum into a problem-solving or even future-focused session. In addition, one might anticipate frustration on the part of persons who are unable to speak because of time constraints. Also, personal attacks may occur during the forum, creating yet new controversies.

The students may interpret the refusal to hold an open forum as a lack of interest in talking, and they may escalate their actions. The Chairperson might be encouraged to think more broadly than a simple no, despite the risks. She could begin to explore intermediate steps that would provide more information about the risks, for example, by interviewing students and faculty or holding a mediation among representative parties. The resulting conversation may convince her that the open forum is likely to be constructive, on balance. Alternatively, the concept of an open forum could be structured so as to involve less risk, for example, by arranging for speeches reflecting a variety of viewpoints followed by question and answer.

 c. The group may need to help the Chairperson understand the importance of involving students and faculty in this choice. Could most mediators effectively facilitate or should only facilitators trained or experienced in inter-cultural disputes be used? What about co-facilitation by a Catholic and Protestant? Should a Traveler be represented in the facilitation team? Should one facilitator be a faculty member and the other a student? How much substantive expertise in either diversity issues or academia is important? Will a larger team be required in order to interview parties prior to the forum? Would a respected public figure be more likely to maintain control of the forum?

 d. The Chairperson's goals sound somewhat like the goals Baruch Bush urges for mediation (pp. 124-125), so arguably his advice on technique would be instructive. Does there need to be closure (settlement) on some issues, such as the coverage of the class? If so, then more traditional mediation techniques may be appropriate for these. One might expect disagreement here on how active the facilitators should be in suggesting solutions. Unlike a mediation of interpersonal matters, the facilitators may seek to limit expression of emotions because those involved may feel an identity with groups that have a history of violence.

 Regardless of the general mediation approach, the size of the group and intensity of feelings may suggest the need for ground rules. The ground rules may need to specify who may attend (exclusion of all but students and faculty?), how much time each person may speak, and whether repeat comments will be permitted by one speaker before others have been heard for the first time. Should the ground rules specifically prohibit personal attacks and interruptions, as sometimes is done in interpersonal mediation? An important issue is how ground rules will be enforced. If the mediation described in b is held and results in agreement on the ground rules, those involved in that session may be a constructive force at the forum. Alternatively, one could give roving microphones to members of the facilitation team and let them hold the microphone for the recognized speaker and therefore allow enforcement of the rules of discourse.

 Another factor to take into account in planning the forum is the limited time available, the number of potential speakers, and the breadth of issues. It may be possible to shorten the venting portion by interviewing the persons beforehand and putting up a list of concerns on a flipchart, asking the group to review it and ask questions and suggest additions, but with prior agreement to limit the raising of concerns to a particular time period and then to focus on discussing ways to resolve the issues.

 e. Our students were surprised at how similar a process they would suggest for issues that are closer to home for them. We based the exercise on a racial controversy that arose at an American university and then modified it based on comments from a judge in Ulster. When the students start to pull out their own usual response to the situation in this country (for example, "But doesn't it make sense for the professor to emphasize in history the background of the majority of students in a history class?"), either they or others recognize the similarity to what happened in Ulster and their failure to raise a comparable point there. It helps them realize the attitudes they bring to a culture-bound conflict in which they have a group identification.

 Still, the students will note some differences in a conflict set here or in Ulster. The recent history of violence in Ulster presents one significant difference. Another may be the greater tendency of American students to stake out firm positions in the initial memo. One can imagine that the American students will have named themselves ("Students for Equity and Excellence in Teaching," for example) and listed their demands, creating another barrier to moving them to a problem-solving focus.

3.13   In contrast to Question 3.9, which asks the students to play the role of a lawyer seeking to advance the client's interests, this question places the student in the role of a public policy maker. Another way to use the examples in this question is to ask each student to respond as if he or she were one of the commentators in the "Varying Viewpoints" (pp. 171-177).

a. Here the public interest in settlement (less disruption in the lives of existing residents) seems great. Further, a resolution selected by the parties has a better chance of success than one imposed on them by a judge. The resources needed to obtain an adjudicated result might come from funds that would otherwise be used for housing. A mediator might increase the chances of settlement by facilitating communication, making the parties realistic, promoting a productive level of emotional expression, and providing ideas and resources.

At the same time, some commentators would argue that important legal precedent might be lost if parties are encouraged to mediate and thus settle this case (Fiss). In addition, the solution might differ from a litigated one and thus be less "just" in the eyes of those equating court judgments with justice (Terrell). Further, the community might not hear as much about low-income housing problems and might not be as moved to find solutions to those problems (Auerbach and Edwards).

b. Here the public interest in settlement appears lower than in (a). Certainly, there is some interest in reducing the court's time, but it is not clear from the research reported by McEwen that such a reduction is likely here unless settlement prospects exceed those in a typical case. Here, mediation might significantly improve the chances of settlement if it affords the defendant a more realistic view of the alternatives to settlement than that provided by an embarrassed defense counsel. If the costs of mediation would be substantial for the court and would require costly travel by the parties, the effort seems unwarranted. However, if the costs of mediation by a staff mediator are small and the mediation could be conducted by phone, mediation might provide a public benefit, on balance.

c. The public has an interest in both the enforcement of the criminal laws and the public's perception that the laws are being enforced. This interest is not counterbalanced here, as in some neighborhood disputes (Beer), by a need to maintain relationships and community tranquility, though there may be some public interest in encouraging restitution for medical expenses. Professor Albert Alschuler has written about an incident similar to this problem involving Bernard Goetz as the victim. Goetz did not know that the scheduled mediation was not held and that the apprehended attacker was sentenced to jail. Subsequently, Goetz purchased a gun and shot four youths who approached him for money on a New York subway, an incident that gained much national publicity in 1984 and fueled a debate about whether the public could rely on the public justice system to enforce the law. See Alschuler, Mediation With a Mugger: The Shortage of Adjudicative Services and the Need for a Two-Tier Trial System in Civil Cases, 99 Harv. L. Rev. 1808 (1986).

d. In contrast to (c), the public interest in punishment and deterrence is slight in a truancy case. The more substantial public interest is to encourage regular school attendance before the youth gets further behind in schoolwork. If mediation is likely to result quickly in a lasting settlement (Tyler, McEwen & Maiman), the public benefits would seem substantial.

e. Public encouragement of mediation here probably will result in the consumer receiving less than he is entitled to receive under the law. At the same time, Stover is not going to hire a lawyer in litigation either. Without a lawyer, Stover might not secure the judgment authorized by law through litigation (Folberg and Taylor). If encouraged to litigate, however, the chances of consumer agencies or other consumers hearing about the practice increase somewhat (Edwards).

f. In this problem, the public interest in developing precedent is substantial (Fiss). At the same time, Sanford has an interest in settling so that she does not further strain her relationship with her employer (see Beer). If mediation would facilitate a settlement she would prefer to further litigation, is there a public interest in encouraging her to litigate the precedent-setting issue?

3.14 One response is that the burden of persuasion should be placed on the party who advocates a change in the status quo. At the same time, the status quo (whether it is what occurs in the courts or administrative agencies) is under heavy criticism. Thus, one might also argue that an innovation with a favorable reception by the parties should continue until empirical evidence shows that the status quo is better.

3.15 The higher standards do not reflect merely the public's role in encouraging use of mediation. Settlement discussions between counsel or parties are also publicly encouraged in a variety of ways, including, for example, the "meet and confer" requirements of many local court rules governing discovery. The higher standards for mediated settlements may reflect, in part, the greater involvement of the public in choosing mediators and an acknowledgment that the mediator has an effect on the outcome of the mediation, a fact now documented by social science research. See, e.g., Greatbatch and Dingwall (1989); Cobb and Rifkin (1991).

3.16 Bargaining imbalances favoring the bank include: counsel more experienced both in negotiation and litigation and greater financial ability to take risks (as compared to the Thompsons, whose home is in peril). Bargaining imbalances favoring the Thompsons include the ability to create unfavorable publicity for the bank (and the bank's vulnerability on this point), the ability to litigate without incurring legal fees, and their near-insolvency. All these bargaining imbalances could produce results influenced by relative resources of the parties rather than based on the simple application of law to fact. Thus, the bargaining imbalances might produce unjust results. Arguably, these bargaining imbalances also would affect the results in litigation or negotiation without a mediator's assistance. Thus, it is unclear what process is most likely to lead to a "just" result even under this measure.

3.17 As McEwen and Maiman reported regarding small claims cases, payments after settlement, with or without a mediator, tend to be lower than judgments. Does that mean that settlement tends to favor defendants? Perhaps we should assume that the settling plaintiff, after consulting with counsel, has properly assessed the advantages of settling earlier, saving litigation costs, having certainty, and gaining distance from the abuser, and that the result is therefore fair to the parties. At the same time, the litigated result may have been more beneficial to the non-parties, because the publicity of trial might have warned potential targets of this defendant's harassment and deterred harassment by others.

3.18 The potential costs of imposing degree requirements include an increase in the expense of mediation as the size of the pool of mediators is reduced, the unavailability of mediators in some rural areas, and the reduction in diversity of the mediator pool. There is little agreement on whether public confidence is initially higher for programs with highly educated mediators. One might argue that diversity among mediators, mediation skills, and expense of mediation are more important than educational degrees in securing public confidence. It may not always be possible to achieve these aspects of the program if the pool is restricted by advanced degree requirements.

3.19 Mediators can be inexpensively evaluated based on the percentages of settlements in cases they mediate. It is more difficult, and probably more expensive, to evaluate mediators' effectiveness in dealing with power imbalances. Peer evaluation might be required. At the same time, if advancement or recognition depends almost exclusively on settlement rates, and effectiveness in dealing with power imbalances is not assessed and valued, one can expect that mediators will rarely intervene in an attempt to balance the scales. The dialogue that follows this question shows the disagreement about whether the program should encourage mediators to adjust the bargaining balance.

3.20 In Howard v. Drapkin, cited in the question, the majority recognized an immunity for a neutral psychologist-expert, even for the period before she was appointed by the court. The court's reasoning, which was extended in the opinion to mediators not appointed by the court, was that the psychologist's work was integral to the court process even before the court appointed her. The court distinguished psychologists and mediators from lawyers on the basis of the mediators' and psychologists' neutrality. The neutrality presumably would require them to take positions disliked by at least one of the parties and thus subject them to increased risks of suit. Further, the court reasoned that recognition of immunity would expand the pool of mediators and thus encourage dispute resolution processes that would be less expensive and stressful for parties and would relieve court congestion.

Most states have not enacted statutes guaranteeing immunity for mediators. Arguably, without immunity there would be no recourse for behaviors like those alleged in the problem. No agreement resulted and therefore none could be set aside. There usually are no other remedies, since mediators are generally not licensed. In contrast to a judicial ruling, the mediators' actions are not subject to reversal on appeal.

Other means of holding mediators accountable, discussed in the text, include licensure, criminal penalties, and court referral only to certified mediators. None, of course, is without disadvantages.

3.21 The quoted language is from Kansas Statutes Annotated § 23-604(b). The question raises a slightly different issue than that discussed in the accountability dialogue. There, the mediator and professor debated what a mediator should do as a matter of choice. This question raises the next issue -- whether the mediator should be required by law to look out for non-parties and what should be the consequences. If one consequence is liability, one can expect some defensive reactions by mediators; they must not only look out for the children's interests but they must be able to convince a jury later that they did so. This may result in an unwarranted burden on the mediation process. Thus, the professor who believes that mediators should look out for children nonetheless may oppose enactment of a statutory duty to do so.

3.22 It may indeed be difficult for judges to provide a check against unfairness without knowing the content of the negotiations. At the same time, disclosure might significantly reduce the confidentiality of the agreement. In a case involving settlement negotiations, the First Circuit ruled that financial statements submitted to the judge approving the settlement must be released to the public. FTC v. Standard Financial Management, 830 F.2d 404 (1st Cir. 1987).

3.23 The Qualifications Commission emphasized that the need for entry requirements increased as the parties' choice of neutral decreased. The peremptory challenge procedure re-introduces the possibility of a "market place" check on quality. Arguably, it thereby reduces the need for entry requirements. Further, the presence of counsel provides a check on the influence of the mediator and thus the harm that can be done through mediation. This may further reduce the need to set qualifications.

3.24 This asks the student to propose a better statutory scheme, combining entry requirements for mediators, accountability for mediators, and other procedures. The proposed Uniform Mediation Act may provide a helpful basis for discussions on this. The most current draft will be available at www.stanford.edu/group/sccn/mediation.

3.25 Several aspects of the New York opinion address Crouch's concern that the lawyer-mediator might intentionally exploit one party, either to gain advantage with the other party or to increase the chances of settlement. For example, the opinion states that the lawyer-mediator and should not represent either party in the future on a related matter. The mediator should be impartial. Further, the mediator should encourage the parties to check with independent counsel prior to signing a mediated agreement, though the opinion does not require the three-day period for revoking the agreement suggested by Crouch. The opinion requires the explanation suggested by Crouch about the differences between the lawyer-mediator and independent legal counsel.

One might argue that the New York opinion's limitation of the participation of the lawyer-mediator to relatively simple cases may not be justifiable. If the parties are told about the problem and persist in seeking the mediate without independent counsel, the lawyer-mediator may proceed to mediate, simply avoiding any evaluation of the legal issues.

3.26 Amendment of the ethics code might serve to encourage the organization of family mediation practices to serve the broader needs of clients. At the same time, the fee-splitting prohibitions are designed to protect the independence of lawyers, and a lawyer-mediator giving advice or drafting agreements may need that independence as much as the lawyer-advocate. The Oregon approach protects that independence and still permits co-mediation, as long as either the lawyer hires the non-lawyer or the lawyer and non-lawyer bill separately for their services. See Massachusetts Bar Ass'n Ethics Op. No. 85-3(1984); Washington State Bar Ass'n Informal Ethics Op. No. 608.

3.27 It is unclear how the *McKenzie Construction* court would have ruled on a screening procedure, if the mediator's actions had not convinced the court that the screening was ineffective. However, the *Cho* court was not persuaded that screening could work. The *Poly Software* court did not raise screening as a possible way to avoid the problem. Presumably, these courts gave more weight than did the draft rule to maintaining public confidence in the loyalty of lawyers and the neutrality of mediators and preserving confidentiality. They gave less weight to making mediation services broadly available, because the likely result is a refusal by firms to allow their lawyers to mediate. The mediation fairness seems less likely to be affected, except as a party may be surprised by later use of mediation disclosures.

The draft rule's approach for *pro bono* mediation also gives substantial weight to making mediation available at low cost. Otherwise, firms may prohibit *pro bono* mediating by their lawyers. On the other hand, the *pro bono* exception places at risk public confidence in loyalty and preservation of confidentiality.

B. Exercises

EXERCISE 3.1:   THE NEIGHBORHOOD SPAT[1]

---

[1] The exercise was excerpted from N. Rogers and R. Salem, Teacher's Guide to A Student's Guide to Mediation and the Law (Matthew Bender 1987), with permission. A videotape of the role play is available from VCA Teletronics -Rogers/Salem Library, 1200 Thorndale Rd., Elk Grove, Ill. 60007.

Teaching Notes

This simulation provides an opportunity to demonstrate or have students mediate the type of interpersonal dispute that is probably better suited for mediation than litigation. The mediator is challenged to turn a hostile relationship into a more accommodating one in which the parties have a better understanding of each other's needs. This type of case is typical of a class of cases that are frequently mediated at local dispute resolution centers. Prior to using this simulation, you may want students to read Chapter 3 and related readings on the mediation process.

The three role players should be selected in advance of the session at which this simulation is to be used so they have adequate time to study their parts. At the time they are selected, the role players should be given their materials with the instruction to keep this information confidential.

EXERCISE 3.1:   THE NEIGHBORHOOD SPAT

Confidential Information for Fran Moran

You are 19 years old, single and work as a short order cook from 2 p.m. to 10 p.m. Monday through Thursday. When you took this job six months ago, you rented a small house about a mile from work and bought a used motorcycle for transportation.

A couple of weeks after you moved in, your next-door neighbor, T.C. Veranda, a retiree who appears to be about 65 years old, started complaining about the noise from a Saturday night party. You turned down the stereo and thought the matter was resolved. But two months later, while you were having a party, a police officer came to the door at 10:30 p.m. to tell you that your neighbor had complained about the noise. You were so annoyed at Veranda that you started gunning your motorcycle when you returned home from work each night at 10:15.

One day your parents visited and while you and they were walking up the front walk, Veranda yelled at you to change your "disgraceful ways" unless you wanted the police to come again. This really embarrassed and angered you. When Veranda yelled at you again while you were with friends a few weeks later, you were enraged. So after a few beers you decided to retaliate. You took a can of red spray paint and on Veranda's front door wrote, "I Love Sex." Unfortunately, Veranda opened the door just as you were leaving and you were caught in the act. Veranda called the police and has threatened to have charges brought against you, but instead had this scheduled for mediation.

EXERCISE 3.1:   THE NEIGHBORHOOD SPAT

Confidential Information for T.C. Veranda

You are 67 years old and retired. You have been living alone in the same house for the past 15 years, leading a quiet life, turning in each night at 10 p.m. Most Friday mornings you take a crosstown bus to your sister's house and stay with her and her daughter until Sunday morning when you return home.

Six months ago, the house next door was rented to a youth who appears to be about 19 years old named Fran Moran and you have known no peace since then. There are noisy and wild parties until all hours about once a month. And there is the motorcycle--you are certain that Moran is racing the engine when coming home late at night just to wake you up. While the other neighbors do not seem concerned about the situation, you are afraid of Moran and Moran's friends. They ride their motorcycles down the street during parties, and they look tough.

Because Fran was unresponsive to your complaints, you took matters into your own hands. You called the police to quiet the loud parties, but that didn't help much. A couple of times you were so angry that, when you saw Moran coming up the walk with some other people, you shouted out a warning that you would call the police again if they didn't change their disgraceful ways.

Last week another neighbor phoned to tell you Moran was doing something to your front door. When you opened the door you saw Moran running away with a paint can. On the door, in big red letters was: "I Love Sex." You phoned the police and reported what occurred. At the police officer's suggestion, you decided to try mediation. The police officer indicated that it was unlikely the prosecutor would charge Moran. You are not sure you can afford to file a civil suit.

You want Moran to pay to have your door repainted (a piece of burlap is covering the red paint) and you would like to figure out a way to restore peace and feel safe in the neighborhood. Why can't Moran respect your need for sleep and have parties somewhere else or when you are away?

EXERCISE 3.2:   A SHORTAGE OF LOW INCOME HOUSING

Teaching Notes

This role play is designed to provide a basis for a discussion of mediation practice issues related to a complex public policy dispute.* The mediator must make a number of decisions. Who should be present (should the City Coalition be present for all negotiations?)? How should the mediator handle conflicting interests about the release of information to the media? How will the mediator learn quickly about the parties' interests in order to discuss with them how the continuation of mediation will serve those interests? How should the mediator frame the legal and other issues (e.g., how can the parties achieve their common goal of providing decent housing for low income residents of Steeltown?) and order the issues (interim agreement to halt demolition plans?) so that some progress is made during the first session? The fact pattern may also provide the basis for a discussion of confidentiality in Chapter 3D.

The students may be divided into groups of varying sizes, so long as each group has at least 5 persons to play the mediator and the 4 lawyers. Extra persons can be assigned, in any numbers, to play the party representatives.

---

*For another public policy dispute simulation, see Exercise 9.2.

EXERCISE 3.2:   A SHORTAGE OF LOW INCOME HOUSING

Confidential Instructions for Plaintiff Class
Representatives and Their Legal Services Lawyers

The Christopher and Kingsford housing projects now house about 1000 residents. SMHA officials insist that they will build better housing for those displaced by the planned demolitions of Christopher and Kingsford, but their record of compliance with such assurances is dismal. Also, given the national political climate, federal funding for new housing construction may not be available a year or two from now.

Hence, your strategy is to prevent demolition. As long as the housing stands, it provides a roof for people who might otherwise be on the streets. Further, your experts indicate that the housing is structurally sound and could become quite nice with investment in rehabilitation.

HUD and SMHA have violated HUD's statutory demolition approval requirements. However, it is not clear that the courts will recognize a private right of action against HUD or SMHA on behalf of the plaintiff class. It would be a feather in the cap of the legal services organization and a help to plaintiffs elsewhere if you are able to obtain a ruling that public housing residents have a cause of action for violation of the statute. Of course, even if you succeed, the SMHA will ultimately re-submit the application for demolition, this time meeting the requirements of the law, and the demolition will probably be approved. Thus, the victory will not provide the housing relief sought by this plaintiff class.

EXERCISE 3.2:   A SHORTAGE OF LOW INCOME HOUSING

Confidential Instructions for the City Coalition
for Affordable Housing and Its Attorneys

You have many beefs against this city administration, with the failure to provide adequate public housing being only one. The best overall solution to this and other problems is to bring about the defeat of the incumbent officials at the next election. Publicity about SMHA's mismanagement and political favoritism may help next year at election time.

You are sympathetic to the plaintiff class' view that the demolition should be stopped. It is uncertain whether federal funds will be available for the new units SMHA intends to build to replace the 1000 units in the Christopher and Kingsford housing projects. If the plaintiffs could protect existing housing through this litigation, you would subordinate your broader political agenda to help them do so. However, if that seems impossible, your involvement will help you bring these issues to the public's attention.

EXERCISE 3.2:   A SHORTAGE OF LOW INCOME HOUSING

Confidential Instructions for Defendant SMHA
and Its Attorneys

The plaintiffs' allegations about the plans to sell the Kingsford and Christopher housing project land to developers for a sports arena are true. The sale would be profitable to SMHA and increase political support for SMHA within the city administration. Unfortunately, the public will not react positively to these plans, if this information becomes public. They will view it as placing sports above the basic needs of 1000 poor residents for housing, even if you plan to replace the housing. Also, every time a news story appears, the bribery allegations are repeated. Thus, it is very important that what is said during the mediation be confidential.

In addition, the HUD audit of SMHA is not going well. HUD has threatened privately to either take over management of SMHA or cut off all federal housing funds to the City of Steeltown.

EXERCISE 3.2:   A SHORTAGE OF LOW INCOME HOUSING

Confidential Instructions for HUD Officials
and Their Justice Department Attorneys

SMHA has been badly mismanaged, and publicity about it does not help HUD's image. It is also a little embarrassing that the HUD employee (later fired) who worked on the applications for demolition did not follow HUD procedures. HUD would like to have nothing to do with this litigation. You do not know, however, whether the court will rule that tenants have no private right of action for violation of the demolition approval laws.

HUD has been working to straighten out SMHA. HUD officials privately threatened to either take over management of SMHA or cut off all federal housing funds to the City of Steeltown. Both options would bring poor publicity to HUD and the latter would hurt thousands of low income persons in need of housing. At the same time, it would be irresponsible to provide the present SMHA management with the replacement funds for the 1000 units that SMHA seeks to have demolished in the Christopher and Kingsford projects.

If you can think of a good solution to this problem, you are willing to play the role of the 800-pound gorilla with SMHA in these negotiations, using the threat already communicated to it.

EXERCISE 3.3:   THE RED DEVIL DOG LEASE[2]

Teaching Notes

The exercise is designed to provide a basis for practicing mediation skills. The students may be asked to do the mediation outside of class and then may watch a videotape of the same roleplay as a

---

[2]"The Red Devil Dog Lease" in Leonard L. Riskin (1991) Instructor's Manual for Tape III. Mediation: The Red Devil Dog Lease, Dispute Resolution and Lawyers Videotape Series. St. Paul: West. Copyright 1991 Curators of the University of Missouri. The exercise was adapted by Nancy H. Rogers from Dale A. Whitman (1987) "The Missing Tenant: A Negotiation Exercise for Property Law," in Leonard L. Riskin and James E. Westbrook, Instructor's Manual for Dispute Resolution and Lawyers 200. St. Paul: West. Reprinted with permission.

means to de-brief the roleplays. Used for this purpose, it is best to fast forward over the commentary portions of the tape and instead ask the students to compare the approach used by the mediator on the tape with the approach used in their own roleplay.

EXERCISE 3.3:					THE RED DEVIL DOG LEASE

Confidential Information for the Prospective Tenant

You have always dreamed of running your own Cajun restaurant. To get experience, you have taken part-time jobs assisting in the management of friends' restaurants Recently, you decided to be practical and begin your restaurant career with a name that would draw customers. You purchased a Red Devil Dog restaurant franchise, borrowing half of the $40,000 purchase price and reaching into your savings for the rest. When you signed a five-year lease, you gave a $2,000 deposit and had delivered $9,000 worth of new equipment. The rent is high, $1000 per month plus 3 percent of gross, but the location is right next to campus and students have flocked to Red Devil Dogs elsewhere. The landlord was very cooperative, reinforcing the roof to hold the sign and changing the windows to fit the franchise specifications. You planned to quit your job as a nurse next month and begin a new career.

Then the news of the Red Devil Dog bankruptcy broke! You don't know when, if ever, you'll see the $40,000. Your dreams are dashed. When notified, the prospective landlord responded by changing the locks so that you could not remove the boxes of equipment and sending a letter demanding performance or $80,000. Talk about being cold--at the very least the mediation will permit you to tell that jerk what you think of such a response.

The whole thing is a nightmare. If you don't get the equipment out within two weeks, you will not be able to get a refund; in fact, you'll have to sell it as used equipment for half price. Your savings are now down to only a few thousand dollars. If you try to start a Cajun restaurant without a national franchise, it will take a while to establish a clientele. Paying $1000 a month in rent is out of the question. You have no idea what the landlord is entitled to collect under the law, but if you retain a lawyer, your savings will be completely depleted.

You may elaborate on these facts if it helps to play the character. Just remember to stay in your role, even if the other students deviate from theirs.

EXERCISE 3.3:					THE RED DEVIL DOG LEASE

Confidential Information for the Prospective Landlord

After searching for a year, you finally found a tenant for commercial space near the university. The prospective tenant works as a nurse but has won awards for Cajun cooking and has some experience in the restaurant business. Shortly after signing a lease for the Red Devil Dog restaurant, you received an offer, still open, from a national restaurant chain for $600 per month plus 1 ½ percent of gross sales. Still, you were pleased with the better deal under this five-year lease ($1000 per month plus 3 percent of gross sales) and looked forward to working with the tenant, who had even advanced a $2000 payment as a sign of good faith.

When the news broke about the Red Devil Dog bankruptcy, you were hopeful that the restaurant would still open under another name, but the tenant seemed anxious to wiggle out. And that was after you had spent $2500 to reinforce the roof for the sign and modify the windows to look like a Red Devil Dog restaurant. Your lawyer is not optimistic about a substantial recovery.

You decided to act tough. Despite your lawyer's warning that it might subject you to liability to withhold the tenant's property, you changed the locks so that the tenant could not remove the boxes of restaurant equipment. You also sent a demand letter for $8000 or performance. If the tenant will not perform, you want as much money as possible.

You may elaborate on these facts if it helps to play the character. Just remember to stay in your role, even if the other students deviate from theirs.

EXERCISES 3.4, 3.5, and 3.6:   BARRY v. KNIGHT, SANTARA v. KESSEL, BRYAN v. OAKDALE

Teaching Notes

In order to give each student an opportunity both to act as a mediator and to experience mediation from the perspective of a party, the class should be divided into groups of three. Each group will mediate all three of the assigned cases with a different student acting as mediator each time. The exercises are not complex; approximately 45 minutes is ample for Barry and Santara, 60 minutes for Bryan. Class discussion of these exercises should be delayed until all of them are completed.

EXERCISE 3.4:   BARRY v. KNIGHT

Confidential Information for Kellen Barry

You are 45 years old and single. You have lived for about 15 years at 17 Ocean View Drive in a small, pretty Cape-style house, overlooking the Atlantic Ocean. The place is beautifully landscaped, with some lovely tall hemlocks as well as various low evergreen bushes.

The problem is your neighbor, Sandy Knight, an ebullient young business school graduate who moved in the house behind yours a couple of years ago. Although you would like to be good neighbors with Sandy, there have been a number of minor irritations over noise, precise delineation of boundaries, etc. But what has you really disturbed is that one Sunday afternoon two weeks ago when you were out, Sandy trimmed a couple of feet off three of the prime hemlocks behind your house. Sandy claimed that the trees blocked the view, and that he/she had repeatedly asked you to trim them. You recall some vague discussions about this in the course of some of your encounters with Sandy - a number of which centered around unresolved arguments over whose property the trees were on - but you feel that nothing specific was proposed. What's more, Sandy did the job in a callous way, without any regard for the beauty of the trees. Maybe they could have been trimmed to meet your and Sandy's objectives, but now it's too late. You want Sandy to pay $600 to replace the three hemlocks.

You are outraged about this selfish and provocative action of Sandy's and worry about what it portends for the future. There have been some neighborhood rumors that Sandy intends to install a hot tub. That is all you need.

You are open to any reasonable solution that the mediator can come up with, provided it meets your basic concerns.

EXERCISE 3.4:   BARRY v. KNIGHT

Confidential Information for Sandy Knight

You graduated from business school three years ago, and are now employed as a financial analyst. You have found work pressured, and hence were pleased to find a lovely, small house in Swamphead, not far from the ocean, which you moved into two years ago.

The problem is your neighbor, Kellen Barry, a middle-aged social worker who has a fetish for shrubs and trees. When you first moved in, the hemlocks behind Kellen's house didn't obscure the ocean view from your sun deck, but things have gotten gradually worse so that until recently your view was totally obstructed. You mentioned this to Kellen several times, but Kellen never did anything about it. So finally one sunny Sunday two weeks ago you trimmed three hemlocks sufficiently to restore your view. You don't quite understand what all the fuss is about; you only took a couple feet off three trees. Moreover, it is not at all clear the trees aren't on your land. Apparently the precise boundary has never been determined.

You feel sorry that Kellen is upset; after all, neighbors should try to get along together. But you think Kellen's demand that you buy 3 new trees is absurd. If the mediator can come up with some modest reasonable solution to this tempest-in-a-teapot, you are certainly willing to listen, particularly since you plan to install a hot tub in your backyard shortly and would like to work things out with Kellen so that these continuous squabbles cease.

EXERCISE 3.5:   SANTARA v. KESSEL

Confidential Information for Brett Kessel

You are a 23-year-old college drop-out. While at Hampshire College in western Massachusetts, you became interested in cooking. About a year ago, after having had a variety of jobs in the food service field, you encountered Randy Santara, a 29-year-old accountant who was looking around for a way to invest some spare cash. In the course of some discussions between the two of you, you took note of the increasing demand for home catering, perhaps due to the rising incidence of working spouses. Early this year, the two of you decided to go into business together under the name of Ring-and-Serve.

The arrangement between the two of you was quite informal. Essentially Randy was to put up the necessary capital to get the operation started; as it turned out this amounted to just over $4000 as follows:

Cooking Equipment	$1420
Dishes etc.	1430
Advertising	1200
	$4050

Your contribution consisted of going to a crash course in a local gourmet cooking school (which cost you $650) as well as utilizing a large number of recipes carefully accumulated by you over the years. You also spent a substantial amount of time preparing sample menus and price lists.

The agreement was that there would be a modest salary of $125 per week for you, since this was your sole source of income. Thereafter, the profits would be split 50-50 between you and Randy.

By last spring, things were ready to start, with your large apartment serving as the culinary headquarters. The general plan was that you would pretty much run the cooking end of things, while Randy would attend to the business details. The service would consist either of delivering a complete meal to a house to be served by the hostess, or you also offered to supply the necessary help and equipment to handle the entire meal yourself.

Initially things worked out fairly well. You got a good write-up in a local newspaper and that produced quite a spurt of business, almost more than you could handle. Initially there was not quite enough money coming in to cover even your full salary, but in June there was a "profit" distributed of $213 to each of you. Then came the summer lull.

Since the fall, however, there has been nothing but trouble, stemming you believe, largely from Randy's insensitive interference with your running of the business. For example, Randy called up some of your waiters and told them Ring-and-serve could no longer employ them as they were too expensive. They then made other arrangements, and now you are unable to handle any large parties since you haven't been able to find any other employees. Then, in September, Randy called up the printer who was about to print your fall price lists and considerably upped all the prices, as a result of which business has really dropped off. Every time Randy comes over to your apartment, he/she urges you to use less expensive ingredients and "to stop feeding the city on my money." The crowning blow is the lawsuit Randy filed last month, demanding a return of his/her investment and an accounting for all profits.

You are really hurt and bewildered by all these developments. You feel you have knocked yourself out to make a go of this business, and, judging by many comments received, have managed to develop a good reputation. But Randy, for reasons altogether unclear to you, is bent on scuttling the entire venture. As regards the future, you really would like to see the fruits of all your labors by giving the business a chance, but unless some new operating plan can be developed you are determined, too, to end the venture. In that case you want recognition of all your contributions as well. Although there has been no formal audit, the business owns assets that could be sold for perhaps $2000, and there are also about $2600 in net accounts receivable (after paying off about $500 in accrued liabilities). But you have not been paid your full salary since July 1, since all the extra money had to be ploughed back into the business. You received only $200 "on account" in September and October.

(Assume that it is now November.)

EXERCISE 3.5: SANTARA v. KESSEL

Confidential Information for Randy Santara

You are a 29-year-old accountant practicing by yourself. In the course of your accounting work you have become aware of the desirability of using some of your spare money to invest in promising ventures. About a year ago, you met through mutual friends a young would-be chef, Brett Kessel. Following some extended discussions the two of you decided to set up a business under the name of Ring-and-Serve for doing home catering.

The arrangement between you was quite informal. Essentially you were to put up the necessary capital to get the operation started; as it turned out you contributed over $4000 as follows:

Cooking Equipment	$1420
Dishes etc.	1430
Advertising	1200
	$4050

Brett's contribution consisted of going to a crash course in a local gourmet cooking school (which cost $650) as well as making use of a large number of recipes Brett had accumulated over the years. Brett also spent some time preparing sample menus and price lists.

The agreement between you was that Brett would receive a salary of $125 per week; thereafter the profits would be split 50-50.

By last spring things were ready to start. Brett's apartment served as the culinary headquarters. The general plan was that Brett would pretty much run the cooking end of things, while you would attend to the business details. The advertised service would consist either of delivering a complete meal to a house to be served by the hostess, or Ring-and-Serve offered to supply the necessary help and equipment to serve the entire meal.

Initially things worked out fairly well. Ring-and-Serve got a good write-up in a local newspaper and that produced quite a spurt of business, almost more than Brett could handle. Initially there was not quite enough money coming in to cover even Brett's full salary, but in June there was a "profit" distributed of $213 to each of you. Then came the summer lull. Since the fall, however, there has been nothing but trouble, stemming, you believe, largely from Brett's unbusinesslike management. You think Brett pays much too much for help; as a result you were forced to lay off a horde of high-priced butlers. And you've told Brett time after time that the business either has to cut costs or raise prices. When Brett seemed to be entirely deaf to this need, you finally called the printer to raise the prices yourself for the fall menu list. Of course all of this has not pleased Brett, but how else could you avert imminent bankruptcy?

Finally last month things reached their nadir and when you mentioned your difficulties to a lawyer friend he suggested filing a lawsuit for dissolution of the partnership "as a bargaining ploy." You are most concerned about all the money you have sunk into this enterprise, and are really puzzled by Brett's Kamikaze course.

As regards the future, you are torn between trying to realize the potential inherent in this business and seeing your investment being gradually dissipated by unsound management practices. At least now there are still some assets around. Although there has been no formal audit, the business owns assets that could be sold for perhaps $2000, and you believe there are also about $2600 in net accounts receivable (after paying off $500 or so in accrued liabilities). Of course Brett undoubtedly will bring up the fact that he/she has not been paid a full salary since July 1, since all the extra money had to be ploughed back into the business. (Brett received only $200 ' on account" in September and October.) But you feel that is Brett's tough luck. It was really as a result of Brett's loose practices that the business began to go downhill. You rather suspect, though you really have no proof, that Brett may even have been siphoning off some funds for personal use. In any event, if the business were to continue you think you probably should get more than half of the profits. After all you put up most of the capital, and Brett gets salary right off the top to boot.

(Assume that it is now November.)

EXERCISE 3.6:   BRYAN v. CITY OF OAKDALE

Confidential Information for the Plaintiff, D.V. Bryan

Three months ago, you were driving home from work in your new Chevrolet. It was nighttime and you were observing the speed limit. As you turned down Andover Street, a two-way street in Oakdale, you noticed two orange barrels, warning lights, and construction signs blocking the opposite lane. But there were no barrels, signs, or lights in the lane in which you were traveling. You concluded from this that only the opposite lane was closed for construction.

As you proceeded down the street, however, you saw a gaping 4' x 6' hole in the street ahead of you. You noticed this hole when you were only two feet away from it. You slammed on your brakes but could not stop fast enough to avoid it. The front end of your car landed in the hole, causing extensive damage to the shock absorbers and the body of the car.

You pulled your car over to the side of the road to survey the damage. You saw 4 other cars on the side of the road that also had been damaged by the hole. There was an ambulance parked beside one of these cars and a doctor was attending to its driver.

A policeman, who was already on the scene, came over to investigate your accident. You asked him why there were no warnings posted around the hole. He told you that warnings had been placed around the hole three weeks before. However, they had been stolen or misplaced since then. A resident of Andover Street also talked to you at the scene. She told you that there had been approximately a dozen accidents caused by the pothole within the past two weeks. She and others had called various City Hall officials to inform them of the dangerous condition of the street and to request them to place new warnings around the pothole. Yet the City still had not responded to their requests.

The next day, you took your car to a mechanic and obtained an estimate of the cost to repair its damage. You have the estimate with you today. It indicates that it would cost $444.93 to install new shock absorbers and repair the damage to the body of the car.

Two days after the accident, you filed a claim with your insurance company for $444.93. Three days later, a representative from the company called to inform you that the company would not pay the claim since you have a $500.00 deductible on your policy. Instead, the insurance company wrote a letter to the city stating its belief that the city was responsible for your accident. You waited one month for a response from City Hall. When you received none, you called the City Clerk's office to find out what, if any, action the city planned to take. The woman who answered told you that the only way you could possibly recover on your claim against the city would be by suing it in Small Claims Court. Thus, two months ago you filed this tort action against the city requesting $444.93 in damages and $25.00 in court costs.

Since then, you have had your car repaired by a friend who charged you only $325.00, including the shock absorbers.

A week after you filed the claim, Lee Carnevale, the Assistant City Solicitor, offered you $200.00 to settle it. However, you refused this offer. As far as you are concerned, this case involves more than just money. You are angry about the total lack of responsiveness the city has shown to you. It does not dispute the damage to your car or that there were no warnings posted at the time of the accident. Yet, it is trying to avoid paying for the damage caused by its negligence by raising tricky legal arguments that you do not understand. The city argues, for example, that you did not give it proper notice of your accident. However, it is clear that the city knew about it. After you filed your claim, the Oakdale newspaper reported that the City Council planned to discuss your claim at a closed City Council meeting.

It seems to you that this is a clear case of the "Big City vs. the little guy." Four hundred forty-four dollars and ninety-three cents may seem like a trivial amount to the mayor's fancy-talking lawyer, but to someone like you, who makes only $500.00 per week, it is a significant sum to absorb. You refuse to allow the City to shirk its responsibilities to you and to the public in this manner.

Two weeks ago, you received a letter from the Clerk of the Small Claims Court suggesting that you try to resolve this dispute by mediation. You agreed to do so, and are now about to enter the mediation session at the Oakdale Neighborhood Justice Center.

The only thing that concerns you is that you have no basis for determining the validity of Carnevale's legal arguments. You are afraid that a judge may be sympathetic to them. Ask your mediator what s/he thinks the outcome of this case would be if a judge were to decide it on its legal merits.

EXERCISE 3.6:					BRYAN v. CITY OF OAKDALE

Confidential Information for Defendant's
Attorney, Lee Carnevale

You are the Assistant Corporation Counsel for the City of Oakdale. You are not familiar with all the details of plaintiff's allegations, but you do know that plaintiff's car was damaged when plaintiff drove the car into a hole where road construction was taking place. It was nighttime, and there were no lights or signs in front of the hole. They had been placed there, on both sides of the road, but had been stolen from the side on which plaintiff's accident occurred about three weeks before the accident, and had not been replaced. Plaintiff has an estimate indicating the cost of repairing the car would be $444.93.

When the city refused to pay plaintiff's claim, plaintiff filed suit in Small Claims Court against the city, demanding $444.93 in damages and $25.00 in court costs. You offered $200.00 in settlement, but plaintiff refused. Subsequently, the case was referred to mediation by the Clerk of Court, and, on behalf of the city, you agreed to mediate.

You do not dispute the plaintiff's account of the facts of this case. Nevertheless, you are confident that the city would win if this case were to go to trial. You believe the plaintiff would be unable to establish legal liability on the city's part for several reasons. First, plaintiff failed to comply with a statutory requirement of notice. Under Chapter 84, Sections 18 and 19 of the General Laws of

Illiana a person whose property is damaged by reason of a defect in a public way must notify the city of such damage within thirty days. The statute mandates that such notice must be signed by the person whose property is damaged or by someone acting on his behalf and must specify the time, place, and cause of such damage. Plaintiff's insurance company wrote a letter to the city informing it of the accident. However, such notice was defective because it was not signed by plaintiff, plaintiff did not state that the insurance company was acting in his/her behalf, and did not specify the exact time and location of the accident. Under the statute, notice by knowledge simply is not good enough.

Even if plaintiff's notice were to be found sufficient, plaintiff would still have problems establishing the city's liability. Under Alana law, there can be no recovery unless a road defect was the sole cause of the property damage sustained by the plaintiff. Carroll v. City of Lowell, 321 Alana 98 (1974). The plaintiff admits being told that the City took steps to warn the public about the road defect.

It placed barrels, warning lights, and signs around the pothole. Vandals, not the city, removed those warnings. Where, as here, "the wrongdoing of a third person combines with the defect in the way to cause the damage, the municipality is not liable." Carroll, at 99.

Finally, the plaintiff is likely to encounter evidentiary problems in proving the extent of the claimed damages. Plaintiff has an estimate of $444.93, but does not have proof of any actual out of pocket losses. Moreover, the estimate is probably inflated. The plaintiff probably could get the work done for half that amount.

Although you believe plaintiff's case to be quite weak, you would rather not waste the time it would take to prove the city's legal position at trial. You also have a private practice. The city pays you a set salary of $31,000.00 per year. Every day you spend trying cases for the city is one less day you can spend trying cases for your private clients. Thus, you are prepared to renew your prior settlement offer of $200.00 to the plaintiff. You would rather not go much higher than that, however.

EXERCISES 3.4, 3.5, and 3.6:

BARRY v. KNIGHT, SANTARA v. KESSEL, BRYAN v. OAKDALE

Teaching Notes

As stated previously, the primary purpose of these exercises is to acquaint the student with the process of mediation, which will be a novel experience for most of them. Additionally, at least two of the substantive issues raised by the readings should arise in the course of these mediations. What is the mediator's role when faced with an agreement which he/she thinks is unfair to one of the parties? Is it appropriate for the mediator to give legal advice to the parties?

Among the questions which the instructor might pose in discussing these exercises are the following: What did the mediators do to assist the parties in reaching agreement? Did any mediators meet separately with the parties? Make settlement proposals? Seek to defuse hostility? Were these steps helpful in reaching agreement? Were there any negative reactions to what the mediator did?

Did any mediator think that the parties were entering into an agreement that was unfair to one of them? or that was unlikely to be carried out successfully? If so, what did the mediator do? Was that appropriate? What was the parties' reaction to the mediators' interventions?

Was any mediator asked for legal advice? How did the mediator respond? Was the response appropriate?

In general, what did you think of mediation when you were the mediator? What were the similarities between your behavior as a mediator and your behavior as a negotiator? What were the differences? Did you learn anything from your experience as a mediator that will be useful to you as a negotiator?

What did you think of mediation when you were a negotiator? Did you learn anything that will be useful the next time you mediate?

Note: One common student reaction to these exercises is that the mediator is unnecessary, perhaps even a hindrance to settlement, and the parties could have settled just as well without the mediator. The instructor can point out that these exercises differ from the "real world" use of mediation in that, in the "real world," a mediator will not normally be called in until after the parties have been unable to reach agreement on their own. Thus, it is not surprising that in these exercises, in which the students have not negotiate to impasse prior to mediation, some of them should find mediation unnecessary.

If an instructor wants to demonstrate the power of mediation under more realistic circumstance, this can be done by assigning a difficult negotiation exercise in which some groups are bound to reach impasse. Then, after they have done so (and without advance notice), have one group continue negotiating, this time with the assistance of a skilled mediator. For maximum instructional value, the mediation portion of this exercise should take place in class as a demonstration. (If you want to do this, it is important that you tell the students in advance of their negotiation that they should not exchange confidential information sheets when they have finished negotiating, as students sometimes do.)

EXERCISE 3.7:   LITTLE v. JENKS

Teaching Notes

While the previous exercises demonstrate the difference between mediation and negotiation, this exercise demonstrates the difference between mediation and adjudication. The students should be divided into groups of three and assigned roles - one student will be the neutral, one will be Little, one will be Jenks. The neutral will be a mediator in the first scenario and a judge in the second scenario; the other roles will remain constant.

The students should first be directed to attempt to mediate a resolution of the dispute. If the exercise is done in class, 30 minutes should be ample for the mediation. Then, regardless of whether or not they reached a settlement in mediation, they are to argue their cases to the judge, each party seeking judgment in its favor. This, too, should take no more than 30 minutes. Thereafter, the students return to class for a discussion of both mediation and adjudication.

EXERCISE 3.7:   LITTLE v. JENKS

Confidential Information for Chris Little

You are 23 years old. Three months ago, you got a job in Holbrook that required a car. Around the same time, you learned that one of your best friends, Sandy Jenks, was advertising to sell a five year old Camaro. You knew that Sandy enjoys tinkering with cars, and figured that any car owned by Sandy should be in good shape. You asked Sandy to sell the car to you. Sandy said he/she preferred not to sell the car to a friend. You repeatedly stressed how much you needed the car for your job. Finally, Sandy agreed to sell you the car for $1,500. After you paid Sandy, you heard Sandy say to his/her father, "Well, now all my headaches are gone."

Within one week, you figured out what Sandy's comment meant. You began to develop headaches from the fumes which filled the car whenever you drove it. Two weeks after buying the car, you took it to Schein's Garage. Schein explained that the entire exhaust system needed to be replaced. It would cost at least $400 to complete the job. Schein also suggested that whoever sold you the car probably knew about the problem at the time of the sale.

You were surprised and angry. Sandy had told you about various things that were wrong with the car, also that the car had been parked on the street and that road salt and snow had caused some rust problems. But, Sandy never said anything to you about the exhaust system. How could a friend sell you such a lemon?

You called Sandy immediately and said you wanted your money back. Sandy agreed to take the car back and return the money. The next day however, Sandy called to say that he/she had decided not to take the car back, that it was your car now and that you could get it repaired.

You were shocked by Sandy's phone call, since you had always considered Sandy a good friend. You never expected Sandy to cheat you this way, and you have not spoken to Sandy since.

EXERCISE 3.7:   LITTLE v. JENKS

Confidential Information for Sandy Jenks

You are 20 years old and have been unemployed for 6 months. The only income you have-- about $50.00 per week--comes from doing odd jobs in the neighborhood.

Shortly after you were laid off from the grocery store in which you had been working, you decided that you had to sell your car, a five year old Chevy Camaro. You placed an ad in the local paper, and a few days later Chris Little approached you about buying the car. You were reluctant to sell it to Chris. You had always considered Chris to be one of your best friends and, although you enjoy tinkering with cars, and are a pretty good amateur mechanic, this car had been one big headache to you from the moment you bought it. You feared that if anything went wrong with the car later, it might hurt your friendship.

You told Chris about various things that were wrong with the car, including the fact that the car had been parked in the street and had some rust problems due to road salt and snow. Nevertheless, Chris persisted, explaining that he/she had just obtained a new job in Holbrook, 25 miles away, and was in dire need of an affordable car. Finally you sold it to Chris for your advertised price of $1,500 three days after you first advertised the car.

Chris seemed extremely happy with the car on the date of the sale. Two weeks later, however,

Chris called back to say that the car was undriveable because of a faulty exhaust system, which would cost $400 to repair. Chris wanted to return the car to you and get his/her money back. You agreed because you felt bad for Chris and because you were sure the problems with the car could be fairly easily repaired.

The next day, however, you changed your mind. You realized that it was going to be extremely difficult to refund Christ purchase price, since you had already spent the money you had received. Besides, you had warned Chris that the car was not perfect at the time of the sale. It seems unfair to you that you should be held responsible for defects that arose after you sold the car to Chris.

EXERCISE 3.7:	LITTLE v. JENKS

Instruction for Third Parties
Mediation

Introduction

My role as the mediator is to help you find a satisfactory settlement of this case. If you are unable to resolve this case at mediation, I shall advise the clerk to schedule it for a court date. The only ground rules are that each of you gets a chance to talk without being interrupted. We will talk together, as well as separately. Anything that you say to me in private, I will not repeat to the other party without your permission. I may give you some advice, but you do not have to take it. If the case does go to court, nothing that I say can be used by either party, nor can any offers or admissions by either of you be used against you. In other words, all this is off the record. Any questions before we begin?

Process

Suggested questions and strategy:

1. How about telling me about this case? Who wants to go first? (Listen to both sides, then separate them.)

2. To Sandy: Why won't you give Chris the money back?

3. To Chris: Why are you asking for your money back? Do

you really need the money or transportation?

4. To Sandy: Is there anything you could do to help Chris get the car in shape?

5. To Chris: Is there anything Sandy could do to help you get your car in shape?

6. To each: What would be a fair way to settle this case?

7. To Chris: Is there anything you could do for Sandy if Sandy helped you out?

Continue to shuttle until you get a settlement or time is five minutes to running out. If you get a settlement, bring parties back together to commit to it. If you aren't getting anywhere, bring the parties together and ask Question 6.

End

You have agreed

> OR

Since you have not reached a settlement at mediation, I shall advise the clerk to schedule your case for trial.

EXERCISE 3.7:   LITTLE v. JENKS

Instructions for Third Parties
Adjudication

Introduction

My role is that of a judge. I shall listen to arguments from both sides and then make a decision which is final and binding. Chris will get to go first, then Sandy, then Chris will have a chance to respond and finally Sandy. We have plenty of time so I won't cut you off unless your argument is excessively long. Are there any questions? If not, take a few minutes to prepare your arguments.

Process

Follow the process specified above. Refrain from asking questions.

End

I have found Chris bought a car from Sandy three months ago for $1500. The car has problems with the exhaust system, which will cost at least $400 to repair.

I have decided ....

EXERCISE 3.7:   LITTLE v. JENKS

Teaching Notes

It is useful to begin the discussion of this exercise by having the students describe some of the results reached in each of the processes. Generally, the results of adjudication will be zero-sum, while those in mediation will be compromises, typically with Sandy agreeing to repair the car at little or no charge to Chris, who may agree to pay for any necessary parts. Subsequent questioning is designed to stimulate discussion of the differences in the two processes, and the extent to which those differences affected the parties' satisfaction with each, both when they were acting as a neutral and when they were acting as a party.

Some of the questions that the instructor might ask those who played party roles are: How did the processes differ from your perspective? Did they differ in your ability to control the process? The information that was presented to the neutral? Your ability to control the outcome? How you felt about the outcome? In general, which process did you prefer? Why?

Questions that might be asked those who played the neutral roles include: How did the processes differ? In which did you find your role more clearly defined? In which were you more powerful? Which did you find more challenging? In general, which process did you prefer? Why?

Neutrals might also be asked whether they learned any facts when acting as a mediator that were not presented to them when they were acting as a judge. If so, did they nonetheless consider what they learned as a mediator in reaching a decision as a judge? If there were students who did so, or who were tempted do so, you can discuss the problems inherent in judicial settlement efforts, as well as in med-arb.

Questions that can be asked of all students include: Based on this experience, what do you see as the strengths and weaknesses of mediation compared to adjudication? Again based on this limited experience, are there particular circumstances in which one or the other might be preferable?

EXERCISE 3.8   THE GRINDER

There are no confidential instructions for this exercise.

EXERCISE 3.9:   PROSANDO, INC. v. HIGH-TECH INTERNATIONAL*

Teaching Notes

This exercise, like Rapid Printing v. Scott Computers (Exercise 2.7), was designed to provide students with the experience in negotiating (and mediating) in the roles of lawyer and businessperson respectively. Thus, the instructor should consult the Teaching Instructions for Rapid v. Scott.

The CPR Institute for Dispute Resolution has produced a 35-minute videotape of this exercise, Mediation in Action: Resolving a Complex Business Dispute, with an accompanying Study Guide, which are available at an educational price of $62.50 plus $5.00 handling charge from CPR Institute for Dispute Resolution, 366 Madison Avenue, New York, NY 10017. We recommend showing and discussing the videotape as part of the post-exercise discussion.

This exercise is somewhat complex, and the instructor should allow a minimum of two hours to complete it.

---

*This exercise was written by Professor Stephen B. Goldberg, Northwestern University Law School, and Catherine Cronin-Harris, Vice-President, CPR Institute for Dispute Resolution. Copyright 1994 by

CPR Institute for Dispute Resolution, 366 Madison Avenue, New York, NY 10017.

EXERCISE 3.9: PROSANDO, INC. v. HIGH-TECH INTERNATIONAL

Confidential Instructions for Prosando's Lawyer

Your strongest argument is that High-Tech had no express contractual right to terminate the contract. The contract had no at-will termination clause and no clause to terminate for dissatisfaction. If High-Tech were dissatisfied with Prosando's progress in establishing a distribution network, High-Tech had the Clause D right to terminate the sole distributorship aspects of the contract, but not all distribution rights. Moreover, High-Tech should have given Prosando notice of its dissatisfaction and an opportunity to cure that dissatisfaction, before termination, in view of the fact that the contract, by its express terms, was for five years.

You also think that High-Tech's reliance on clause F termination rights for failure to negotiate and agree to annual purchase orders each year is erroneous. You'll argue that the purchase requirements clause intentionally had blank dates because the parties had orally agreed that they needed a full year of operation before they could determine annual purchase requirements. At the time of the June, 1992, termination, they had only conducted one full year of operation, since the Century line was only granted in June, 1991. Secondly, High-Tech's failure to initiate negotiations for future orders, or to object to Prosando's failure to place orders, constituted a waiver of any claim that Prosando had breached Clause E or F as of June, 1992.

Still, you are concerned that a court could find that Prosando committed a substantial and material breach of contract in never ordering 100 computers (Clause E) or establishing a distribution system in any country except Chile as of the date of contract termination. The court could imply a termination right into the contract for such a substantial and material breach.

Litigation could get very messy regarding who breached the contract first. Your position is that Prosando's slow startup and failure to place orders were direct consequences of High Tech's initial and anticipatory breaches in insisting upon contract renegotiation, canceling Futura A, and withholding Century. The determination on initial material breach is quite uncertain.

You are also concerned that Prosando's damage assertions of $10 million, drafted by inhouse counsel without a litigator's perspective on proof and legal theories, are excessive. The contract expressly excludes "lost profits or prospective profits arising out of or related to termination." These lost profits are also quite speculative. The claimed $6 million lost profits is based on 150 lost sales per year for the remaining 2 ½ years of the contract, with profits at $16,000 per sale. However, actual sales never exceeded 50 a year.

Your theory is that, despite Clause G, lost profits are due Prosando under the fraud assertions. Fraud is not a contractual claim and all damages arising from fraud are recoverable. You are not certain, however, that the court will accept this theory.

Your strongest claim is for $3 million in actual reliance damages (leasing of premises, engaging personnel, promoting and advertising the product, travel, etc.). You will argue that Prosando is entitled to such damages because High-Tech interfered with Prosando's ability to obtain the benefits of the contract, through its immediate insistence on renegotiating the contract, cancellation of Futura A, refusal to negotiate on new model availability, and then improperly terminating the contract.

If your client asks, you will advise against a settlement that would provide for Prosando to distribute High-Tech product in the future. High-Tech was a difficult business partner from the beginning, and you are aware of no reason why Prosando should want to do business with them again (certainly not without a contract much more tightly drafted than the original contract).

EXERCISE 3.9:   PROSANDO, INC. v. HIGH-TECH INTERNATIONAL

Confidential Instructions for President of Prosando

You were shocked at the June, 1992 notice of termination issued by High-Tech. You believe that it was High-Tech's initial actions, particularly its insistence on renegotiating the agreement, that impeded Prosando's development of a reliable reputation for sales of High-Tech equipment, and slowed Prosando's development of a distribution and support network. Although you don't know if High-Tech exercised its right to sell directly in South America, the existence of that right had a strongly negative effect on Prosando's ability to secure distributors. Potential distributors were leery about joining the Prosando network because they feared that their selling efforts could lead to direct sales by High-Tech, on which they would receive no sales commissions.

In addition, High-Tech's discontinuance of the Futura A series and refusal to negotiate Prosando's distribution rights for the new Century series (which was essentially a substitution for the Futura A system) were infuriating. In your view, this behavior was fraudulent because High-Tech sold product to Prosando that it knew was about to be discontinued, and then refused, at least initially, to supply the new product. To be sure, Futura B was always available, but it was more expensive, with features that Prosando's customers didn't need and wouldn't pay for.

You know that Prosando had some problems that impacted on the relationship. Prosando had trouble establishing its distribution network due to its lack of expertise in sales and servicing of computers, an expertise it had exaggerated when courting, High-Tech. Prosando had never dealt with computers before, had no distribution contacts in place, and had to hire all new computer sales and service staff. However, just as Prosando had everything in place, High-Tech repudiated the contract. At the time of termination, Prosando had established four distributorships in Chile and, unknown to High-Tech, had firm commitments to establish eight more distributors in Argentina and three in Brazil, although it had made no headway in any other countries. (This information should not be revealed to High-Tech unless you believe that doing so will lead to a desirable settlement. If settlement discussions fail, you don't want High-Tech pirating those distributors.)

If this case proceeds to trial you are going to press for recovery of all actual damages, lost profits, and loss of reputation damages. High-Tech's behavior has truly been outrageous and has had a real impact on both Prosando's finances and its reputation as a reliable distributor.

At the same time, you would like to continue to distribute High-Tech's computers, albeit under a much more carefully drafted contract. You believe that there are enormous potential profits to be made in the South American computer market, and you want the opportunity to utilize the system of distribution and service that Prosando built over two long years to reap those potential profits. High-Tech is clearly the most desirable company for Prosando to do business with, since High-Tech's newer equipment has generated great interest in South America.

Prosando is not alone in seeing High-Tech as a desirable business partners. You have heard that two other South American dealers, CALFO and Ventura, are competing for the right to distribute High-Tech computers. CALFO, which is based in Uruguay, is also strong in Venezuela and Colombia. Ventura, which is based in Brazil, is also strong in Paraguay.

You believe that your original sales goal of 150 computers per year, which would generate $2.4 million in annual profits to Prosando (and which provides the basis for your claim of $6 million in lost profits in the lawsuit) is entirely realistic, based on profits of $16,000 per sale. That goal was based on having 12 distributors, and Prosando now has commitments for 15 distributorships. To be sure, actual sales never exceeded 50 computers per year, but that was due both to High-Tech's initial actions in interfering with implementation of the contract, and to Prosando's initial inexperience in selling and servicing computers.

EXERCISE 3.9:   PROSANDO, INC. v. HIGH-TECH INTERNATIONAL

Confidential Instructions for High-Tech's Lawyer

You assert that Prosando breached the contract in not setting up a distribution network to High-Tech's satisfaction by June 1991 (or even by June 1992), in not negotiating annual purchase orders, and in not purchasing 100 computers by June, 1990. (You concede that the six month renegotiation extended the date of the first purchase requirement of 100 units for six months.) High-Tech is not responsible for any damages since it terminated the contract with sufficient good cause based on Prosando's material breach of contras.

However, you have advised your client that High-Tech faces some uncertainty regarding a court's interpretation of the poorly drafted contract termination provisions. Clause C of the contract requires establishment of the distribution network to the "satisfaction" of High-Tech, but that provision carries no express termination provision. Clause D requires establishment of the distribution network within 1 ½ years, but failure results only in termination of Prosando's status as exclusive South American distributor.

You will press the court to apply the express contract termination provisions of Clause F (termination is allowed upon 90 days' notice for failure to negotiate and reach agreement on yearly minimum purchase orders). You face an uphill battle, however, on proving that the contract was terminated correctly. First, High-Tech did not afford 90 days' notice. Second, the date in clause F is blank, supporting Prosando's assertions that the date was intentionally left blank to arow for a joint determination on minimum requirements- after a full year of operation. Third, High-Tech never complained of Prosando's failure to negotiate minimum purchase orders, did not itself initiate negotiations for new orders, and did not give Prosando notice of its dissatisfaction or an opportunity to cure that dissatisfaction before its sudden termination of the contract.

If you cannot establish proper termination under clause F, your alternative theory is that the right to terminate arises from Prosando's total and material breach of the core purposes of the contract. You will argue that termination rights arise from the "satisfaction of High-Tech language of Clause C, and that Prosando's failure to establish the distribution network was a material breach. Even if the court accepts that argument, it may not be satisfied that High-Tech's 30 days notice was sufficient. The court might still award damages to Prosando to substitute for a sufficient period to allow for wind-up of business affairs, and some recoupment of investment expenditures.

You are also concerned that an implied termination theory is weakened by High-Tech's insistence on renegotiation, cancellation of Futura A, and withholding of Century, all of which could be construed as impairing Prosando's ability to develop its distribution network and its sales efforts.

If High-Tech was warranted in terminating the contract under Clause F, some damage payments may be due because of failure to give 90 days' notice. Conversely, if a court held that High-Tech couldn't terminate under either Clause F or under an implied termination rights theory, High-Tech might be responsible for the $3 million in actual damages claimed by Prosando, reduced by whatever amounts Prosando did or could have lessened those damages by canceling leases, terminating employment contracts, etc.

In your view Prosando's claims are unsound. The contract limited sales to the Futura A and B models, and implicitly excluded new computer lines such as Century. The contract also bars recovery for lost profits on termination, so Prosando has no valid claim to such profits. The initial renegotiation was voluntary, since Prosando was told either renegotiate or there would be no deal. Had High-Tech breached at that point no damages would have accrued. Nor was there any fraud regarding cancellation of Futura A. That machine was selling reasonably well in January 1990, when the contract with Prosando was signed. It was not until six months later that sales dropped so sharply that sound business judgment required cancellation.

If your client asks, you will advise against a settlement that involves High-Tech reengaging Prosando as a distributor. Prosando was a difficult business partner from the beginning, and you can see no reason why High-Tech would want to do business with Prosando again (certainly not without a contract much more tightly drafted than the original contract).

EXERCISE 3.9: <u>PROSANDO, INC. v. HIGH-TECH INTERNATIONAL</u>

<u>Confidential Instructions for High-Tech's Executive</u>

As High-Tech's Senior Vice-President in charge of operations, you want to resolve this matter as rapidly as possible.

This entire operation was botched right from the start. Prosando represented itself as skilled in electronics office equipment sales and service, and claimed to have a distribution network ready to come on line. While your recent investigation of the South American distributorship situation has turned up evidence that Prosando may have subsequently engaged skilled personnel, and expanded its potential distribution network beyond Chile, none of this was true when the contract was signed in 1990, or when it was terminated in 1992.

Admittedly, the contract was not a model of clarity. The presence of translators made it difficult, and the legal department was never consulted to perform its standard review in significant contract matters. You attribute the initial problems to a maverick former High-Tech manager, Bill Heid, whose execution of the contract without review by the legal department was typical of his inappropriately aggressive sales tactics. When the legal department saw exclusive distributorship granted in every South American country, they hit the roof. They forced a renegotiation of the exclusivity provision, and refused parts shipment until renegotiation was complete. High-Tech admits no fault or contract breach in not offering the Century series to Prosando. Under the contract it had no obligation to offer new series, only updates to Futura A and B. Prosando's slow start in implementing its distribution network led High-Tech to decide to distribute the Century models on its own. In any event, distribution rights for the Century were eventually granted to Prosando.

High-Tech also denies fraud or misrepresentation in canceling the Futura A model in early1991. Sales of that model trailed off sharply in 1990, and its cancellation was the only justifiable business decision available. Prosando always had rights to distribute Futura B in any event.

When Prosando's failure to establish a satisfactory distribution network, and its failure to place minimum orders are combined, it is clear that Prosando breached the, essential terms of the contract. Hence, High-Tech was warranted in terminating the contract, and should pay no damages.

You would reluctantly concede, however, from a business perspective, that the 30-day period given to terminate the contract was so short that it did not allow Prosando sufficient time to wrap-up or wind-down its commitments. Thus, some payment to Prosando may be appropriate to absorb some of the $3 million they say they've lost.

You are authorized to offer up to $1.5 million to fully resolve the matter, but you are reluctant to offer anywhere near that amount because you think High-Tech acted correctly. You will, however, to show your reasonableness, offer $250,000 fairly early on in the negotiations to make up for the abrupt notice of termination. Thereafter, you will be guided by your business judgment in determining how much you will spend (within your $1.5 million authority) to achieve a resolution.

You have a particularly strong interest in getting this matter resolved, since High-Tech still sees South America as a vast potential market for its products. (Your marketing people estimate the market in Argentina, Brazil and Chile alone as in excess of 150 units per year. At an estimated per unit profit of $20,000, this would mean annual profits of $3 million.) You are now in charge of penetrating the South American market. In attempting to do so, you have determined that High-Tech cannot hope to achieve meaningful South American sales acting as its own distributor. Too many on-site managers, technicians and trainers are needed to support direct sales effectively in South America, and High-Tech has no interest in recruiting and managing a South American sales and support staff. Thus, High-Tech's right to distribute product on its own, which it insisted on in the January - June, 1990, renegotiation, has turned out to be meaningless. (This is embarrassing, and you certainly don't want Prosando to discover it.)

Your investigations in South America have turned up no distributor with continent-wide capability. Two promising regional distributors have surfaced, however. CALFO is strong in Uruguay, Venezuela and Colombia, while Ventura is strong in Brazil and Paraguay. As soon as the Prosando matter is resolved, you hope to begin negotiations with CALFO and Ventura, as well as to intensify your search for other regional distributors. High-Tech is determined to succeed in South America.

EXERCISE 3.9:   PROSANDO v. HIGH-TECH

Teaching Notes

The dynamic of the exercise is fairly straightforward. Each party has a somewhat uncertain legal position, and each would benefit substantially if they could re-establish their business relationship, albeit somewhat modified, and with a better-drafted contract.

The maximum likely recovery to Prosando is $3 million (though recovery of this amount is by no means certain). On the other hand, if Prosando can re-establish its deal with High-Tech, it can earn annual profits of approximately $2.4 million. This assumption requires that Prosando have 12 distributorships, and that is exactly the number it will have if High-Tech gives it distributorships in Chile and Argentina. High-Tech should be willing to do this, since it is anxious to penetrate the South American market, with great potential profits for it also, but has found no other potential distributor with sales capacity in Argentina and Chile.

The amount of damages (if any) that will be paid to Prosando by High-Tech will turn entirely on the distributive negotiation skills of the students, since High-Tech has a $1.5 million settlement authority, and Prosando can settle for any amount it wishes.

Whatever the terms of an agreement may be, capable negotiators should certainly clear up the ambiguities of the prior agreement. High-Tech, for example, should obtain a better-drafted clause on annual purchase requirements, and Prosando should clarify its rights to new computer product developed by High-Tech. The termination provisions of the agreement should also be more certain.

One interesting potential trade to be made involves High-Tech's right to distribute in Prosando's territory. The existence of that right proved to be of little value to High-Tech, but it curtailed Prosando's ability to obtain distributors. Skilled High-Tech negotiators (or a resourceful mediator) might be able to trade a surrender of High-Tech distribution rights for something of value to High-Tech, e.g. a reduction in High-Tech's damages payment to Prosando.

In the videotape, when Prosando rejected High-Tech's $1.00 million settlement offer, insisting on $1.25 million, and the mediator knew that High-Tech would go to $1.25 million, the mediator did not go back to High-Tech for authority to offer $1.25 million. Instead, the mediator proposed to Prosando that it accept $1.00 million in exchange for High-Tech's surrender of distribution rights in Prosando territory. (The mediator knew that High-Tech viewed those rights as of little value.) Prosando accepted this proposal and a deal was struck at $1.00 million

One might criticize the mediator for enabling High-Tech to obtain a more favorable deal than it would have if the mediator had simply transmitted Prosando's $1.25 million demand to High-Tech. Still, Prosando was under no obligation to accept the mediator's suggestion, and it could have told the mediator it wanted both $1.25 million and a termination of High-Tech's distribution rights (which it probably could have obtained). From either perspective, the videotape demonstrates that parties to a mediation cannot rely on the mediator to get the best possible agreement for them, but must accomplish that goal for themselves.

CHAPTER 4 – ARBITRATION

4.1   While arbitration would appear preferable to litigation, for reasons spelled out in the Dialogue, mediation is another alternative that should be considered. These parties have a long-term relationship, and mediation may be less harmful to that relationship than an adjudicative procedure, regardless of whether the latter takes place in court or arbitration. Mediation might also be less expensive than arbitration, and spending even the $20,000 estimated for arbitration seems expensive for a $75,000 dispute. (See Goldberg, Green, and Sander, 1989).

4.2   There are a variety of devices other than a waiver of all damages by which to reduce the risk to defendants of a high damage award. For example, plaintiff might reduce its damage claim, it might agree to a liquidated damages sum in the event of a liability finding, or it might agree that regardless of the amount of damages awarded, defendant would not be liable above a specified sum. See pp. 274-275.

4.3   Among the terms that would surely be proposed by the Consumer's League would be that the procedure be speedy, inexpensive, and sufficiently informal that legal representation would not be necessary, though permissible. In addition, the Consumer's League will want some control over arbitrator selection, in order to protect against biased arbitrators. It will want to have an equal voice in the selection and dismissal of arbitrators for the panel, and perhaps for individual cases. It may want the arbitrator to be paid equally by the consumer and the manufacturer, though in light of the financial burden this would place on consumers, it may prefer to have the manufacturer pay all, counting on its ability to select and dismiss arbitrators as adequate protection against bias. Undoubtedly, Consumers League will want all arbitration outcomes reported to it, both so it can maintain scrutiny of the arbitrators, and so it can publicize those results. Consumers would thus have the information on which to decide whether to arbitrate future claims. The Consumers League would also be able to see when there was a product that was the basis of much arbitration, and to encourage class action suits to deal with claims relating to that product. Finally, Consumers League may wish to have the arbitration binding only on Appliances, Inc., not on the consumer. (Compare the discussion of Question 4.6, *infra*.)

If Appliances, Inc., is highly motivated to establish an arbitration procedure, it is likely to accept most of the Consumer's League proposals. The most troubling of those proposals is probably that providing for Consumers League's ability to publicize arbitration outcomes in the hope of stirring up class action suits, since publicity and class actions are just what Appliances is seeking to avoid. The acceptability of the provision for arbitration to be binding only on Appliances, not on the consumer, is likely to turn on Appliance's calculations regarding the frequency with which arbitration, though not binding on the consumer, will in fact be the end of the line, either because the consumer is satisfied with the outcome, or because the consumer has no appetite for further procedures. In fact, some manufacturers do offer arbitration that is binding only on them, not the customer.

If Appliances accepts all the Consumer's League demands except for allowing Consumers League to publicize arbitration results, Consumers League will be faced with a difficult decision. Should it support a program that is fair to the consumer who elects to use it, but that may deter broad-scale class action efforts to deal with major problems with the product?

4.4   One can sympathize with the courts' desire not to micromanage the arbitration process, but some explanation of the arbitrator's decision - whether it be called an opinion or memorandum - seems essential if the court is to provide any meaningful oversight. Moreover forcing the arbitrator to document her reasoning process provides additional protection against arbitrary decisions, and that is presumably what led the framers of the Due Process Protocol to adopt such a requirement (p. 256). See also the discussion of Question 4.6, infra. Whether such an explanation would have led to a different result in the Halligan case is open to question. In a case like this, where the issue is manifest disregard of the weight of the evidence, the appellate court's judgment seems grounded on a straight disagreement with the district court. But an opinion might be particularly helpful in "manifest disregard of the law" cases.

4.5   None of the arbitrator's six most recent cases may have involved the employer in this dispute, but the arbitrator may have decided many other cases involving this employer. Accordingly, you would want to know how many cases the arbitrator has decided involving this employer, and you would want copies of the arbitrator's decisions in all such cases. In that way, you could better protect your client against the risk the arbitrator persistently rules in favor of the employer.

4.6   Judge Edwards certainly makes a strong argument that the source of payment for a particular case creates less of a risk of bias in favor of the employer than does the arbitrator's knowledge that the employer is, or may be, a repeat player, while the employee is a one-shot player. This creates a risk that the arbitrator, albeit not corrupt as Judge Edwards uses the term, may nonetheless be disposed, even if only subconsciously, to make close calls in favor of the employer. This would be a particular danger if the arbitrator had many cases involving the same employer.

The best means of protection for employees against this risk of bias would be a requirement of written arbitral decisions in all statutorily based cases, and the development of a nation-wide organization of attorneys representing employees in such cases. If attorneys representing employees in all statutorily-based cases were to make all arbitrators' decisions available to their colleagues, the plaintiff's bar would then become the functional equivalent of a repeat player, and the arbitrator would be under no temptation to favor the employer as the sole repeat player. (This is the system of information sharing used by labor unions to insure that they are on an information parity with employers in selecting an arbitrator.) Alternatively, publication of all arbitral decisions on statutory claims might be required as a means of insuring full information on arbitrators.

4.7   As in many other cases, a skilled mediator may be capable of moving the parties from focusing exclusively on their rights to focusing also on their underlying interests, so enabling them to achieve a mutually satisfactory resolution of their dispute. (See the discussion of grievance mediation on pp. 275 – 277.) To be sure, mediation involves the risk that the employee will settle for less than he might ultimately have received in court (or arbitration), but that risk is inherent in all settlements, and is not a basis for refusing to use mediation. It does, however, suggest that an employee in this situation should have the benefit of advice from competent counsel before he agrees to enter into a settlement of his statutory claim.

4.8   The vice of requiring an employee to pay for the arbitration of statutory disputes, according to Cole, is that Congress' intent in creating statutory rights to be enforced before a free federal judge would be frustrated if the beneficiary of those rights had to pay to have them enforced in arbitration. It is a big leap from that to striking down the paid mediation of all employment claims, regardless of whether they involve statutory rights. Cole would support the employee's refusal only if her claim was predicated on a federal statute.

4.9 Not necessarily. The employee who is forced into arbitration under Gilmer is no worse off in arbitration than she would have been in court. In either situation, the employee is free to select the representative of her choice, subject to whatever economic constraints there may be. If a union-represented employee were forced into arbitration, she would arguably be worse off than if she were allowed to go to court because she would have no choice in arbitration but to be represented by a union, for which the duty of fair representation includes the duty to consider the interests of other employees. In court, however, the employee, again subject to economic constraints, is free to select an attorney who will have no interests to further but those of the employee. The Supreme Court in Wright refused to overrule the Alexander case, stressing also the fact that in a collective bargaining situation there has normally been no explicit waiver of a judicial remedy by the employee. Thus even if the collective bargaining grievance clause were broadly worded, allowing both contractual and statutory claims, the absence of a clear waiver of judicial access by the plaintiff employee would still bar a court from compelling him to resort solely to arbitration.

4.10 The enforcement of state law in this situation could be attacked on either of two bases. Initially, the Supreme Court has held, most recently in Doctor's Associates, that a state is barred by Section 2 of the FAA from invalidating arbitration agreements under state laws that are not of general applicability, but that apply only to agreements to arbitrate. To be sure, state law, if applied to this situation, would not invalidate the entire agreement to arbitrate, as was true in Doctor's Associates, but would invalidate only a portion of the remedy provision. Still, the state law does bar the arbitration agreement from being fully enforceable, on the basis of a doctrine applicable only to arbitration agreements, and might be overturned on the ground that it conflicts with Section 2 of the FAA, and is preempted for that reason. Additionally, the state law is preempted because it conflicts with that portion of Title VII that provides that a prevailing party may receive both compensatory and punitive damages.

CHAPTER 5 - COMBINING AND APPLYING THE BASIC PROCESSES

A. QUESTIONS

5.1 The point of this question is to suggest that there are some circumstances in which, despite the general reluctance to submit interest disputes to arbitration, such arbitration may benefit both parties. Thus, in this case, though each party could abandon the negotiations, and look elsewhere to satisfy its needs, each has invested considerable time and expense in the negotiations, and the potential buyer is convinced that looking elsewhere is unlikely to prove satisfactory. Furthermore, the negotiations have narrowed the outstanding issues to price, so that the arbitrator's discretion will be quite limited.

Whether final offer arbitration should be proposed is unclear. Conventional arbitration is suggested by the fact that if the buyer agrees to arbitrate at all, it would not appear to have any particular objection to a compromise decision by the arbitrator. On the other hand, the prospect of final offer arbitration may be sufficient to spur both parties to alter their positions sufficiently that agreement can be reached without resort to arbitration.

It is unlikely that med-arb would be useful here, since there is no indication that mediation efforts preceding arbitration would be productive.

5.2 You should be quite wary of agreeing to med-arb in this dispute. As pointed out in the text, one risk of med-arb is that a party who discloses damaging information to the neutral when she is acting in her mediator role may suffer if the dispute does not settle in mediation, because the damaging information may be used against that party by the neutral in her arbitrator role. That risk is apparent here. The client is not a sophisticated business person but an associate professor at a small midwestern college (presumably unsophisticated). As such, he may inadvertently, or out of a mistaken view it will support his position, tell the mediator of his job offer. However, if no settlement is reached, the mediator turned arbitrator may use this information against your client, reasoning that since he already has had substantial career advancement, he needs first authorship less than does the other professor (Goldberg, 1990).

5.3 The strength of this proposal compared to classic med-arb is that the same person does not serve as both mediator and arbitrator. The weakness is that the proposed joint fact-finding hearing is apt to be quite impractical. The arbitrator will want to get out those facts and arguments that bear on which party is right and which is wrong under the governing contract or law. The mediator will want to pursue those facts and arguments that will be useful in bringing the parties to a settlement. The two lines of inquiry will be quite different, and conducting a hearing in which both are pursued more or less simultaneously may be wholly impractical.

One slight variant on the proposed procedure, that might alleviate this problem, would be to have the mediator proceed first with his questions and settlement efforts, while the arbitrator sat by, learning what he could, but not speaking. Nor would the arbitrator follow the mediator into private sessions with the parties. If the mediator were unsuccessful in achieving a settlement, the arbitrator would then take over. He would have some knowledge of the dispute by virtue of having sat in on the joint sessions of the mediation, yet would be unlikely to know anything that he shouldn't know, since he would not have sat in on the private sessions. It is possible that simply on the basis of what was said in joint sessions the arbitrator would have enough information to render an award immediately following the mediation. If not, he would supplement the information he gained from mediation by asking those questions and eliciting that information that he viewed necessary for an arbitral decision. While this approach would not be quite as efficient as the joint fact finding process, there would not be much of an efficiency loss and there would be a very substantial gain in terms of the practicability of the process.

Arb-med appears to meet a number of the objections to med-arb. Here the arbitrator's decision precedes the mediation phase and hence is not tainted by the information elicited in the mediation phase. And the parties should be less reluctant to reveal confidential information in the mediation since it cannot be used against them in the arbitration. But will it be possible so neatly to separate the two processes? Will the focus on rights-based adjudication generate such a "win-lose" atmosphere that the parties are unable successfully to make the transition to mediation, in which the goal is to find a mutually acceptable outcome? If the arbitrator allows any hints of his leanings, as sometimes happens, will he be regarded thereafter as neutral by the apparent loser? Suppose in the mediation phase, the parties ask the neutral for an evaluation of their case? Should he do so - based on the case as he now knows it or on the opinion he wrote down previously? And won't the extended arbitration hearing and decision-writing seem wasteful if the case is subsequently settled?

5.4 Among the first considerations that might occur to the company's attorney is that if grievance mediation is adopted, and is successful, his firm's arbitration work is likely to diminish substantially. Nor is it likely to be made up by increased mediation work, since the company may well decide that it does not need attorneys to mediate, but can do so with labor relations personnel. It is clear, however, that such considerations of self-interest ought not influence the attorney's recommendation.

On the merits, the central question is whether the Company's success at arbitration should lead it to oppose a mediation step prior to arbitration. The answer to that question turns on the costs of arbitration to the Company. First, there are the transaction costs -- attorney's fees and lost time of managerial personnel. Secondly, there are the relationship costs. Is the Union sufficiently unhappy with the transaction costs and frequent losses in arbitration that a refusal to mediate will seriously compromise the union-management relationship? Have the transaction costs of arbitration deterred the union from pressing some claims in arbitration, with the result that employees are bitter at never having had the opportunity to be heard by a neutral? If so, has that bitterness had a negative effect on their productivity?

After analyzing the responses to these questions, and weighing them against the potential gains of mediation, counsel should be in a position to respond to the company's request for advice.

5.5 (a) NWPIRG may argue that it was improper for a public regulatory agency to take into consideration the opinion of a private party (the neutral advisor) handed down in a private proceeding at which neither it nor any member of the public were present. This question raises issues of exploitation by the parties of the imprimatur of a mini-trial neutral advisor to gain an advantage in matters affected with a public interest. Regulated industries, in particular, may be attracted to the mini-trial because it may appear to lend credibility to a settlement that may later be challenged by a public agency. On the other hand, a regulated industry may simply want to arrive at a reasonable settlement, but be afraid to do so because of a concern that it will be unfairly criticized for "caving in." Going through a mini-trial, where the merits of the case are aired, may alleviate this concern. A regulatory agency, however, should give no greater or lesser weight to a private settlement reached through a mini-trial than without one, regardless of the credibility of the neutral advisor. NWPIRG might also point out that the presidents of Pipeco and Northwest are friendly, and argue that they may have colluded to create evidence favorable to the petition for a rate increase.

(b) This question raises the issue of the confidentiality of mini-trial proceedings. To some extent, the same issues are present in any ADR process. Parties to a mini-trial usually want confidentiality. They do not want to worry about mini-trial discussions coming back to haunt them at a later trial. Thus, the parties usually agree that the entire mini-trial process is a settlement discussion and thus inadmissible under FRE 408 and state counterparts. But any agreement does not bind nonparties and FRE 408 only goes to admissibility, not to discoverability. Also, the rule results in exclusion only if the evidence is offered to prove liability or amount. The attorney-client privilege probably would not apply and it is not clear whether a mediator's privilege would apply to the neutral in a mini-trial.

In this case, where a regulated industry seeks a rate increase and has itself offered the neutral advisor's opinion as justification for including the disputed costs in the rate base, public policy would seem to be on the side of full disclosure of the neutral advisor's thinking and of her notes. Those notes may very well show that the full story was not presented at the mini-trial. Compare McLaughlin v. Superior Court, 149 Cal. App. 3d 473, 189 Cal. Rptr. 489 (1st Dist., 1983), in which the court held that due process in a child custody dispute required that the party disadvantaged by a mediator's custody recommendation to the court have an opportunity to cross-examine the mediator, despite the existence of a mediation privilege.

5.6   The principal objectives of the insurance company in a dispute resolution procedure under these circumstances would appear to be minimizing costs and obtaining a neutral opinion (to persuade the inexperienced plaintiff's attorney that his demand is exaggerated). Both early neutral evaluation (ENE) and mediation rate high in the Fitting the Forum to the Fuss (FFF) tables on cost minimization, and ENE rates high on providing a neutral opinion (though an evaluative mediation would rate equally high). The impediments to settlement are different views of the facts (plaintiff's disability) and the law (the damages to which plaintiff is entitled). Once again, ENE and mediation, particularly evaluative mediation, are about on a par. Thus, either evaluative mediation or ENE would be a sound recommendation.

5.7   In view of your client's objectives - low costs, high speed, privacy, and, most important, restoring the potentially profitable relationship with Acme - mediation would seem the clear choice under Table 1, FFF. The emotions that this conflict has engendered seem the primary barrier to settlement, and that, too, suggests mediation. (See Table 2, FFF.)

5.8   While it is difficult to apply the FFF tables in this situation, it should not be difficult to come up with a process recommendation. Since your client needs to tell her "story" in a safe and somewhat formal setting, but not a lengthy trial, and since there are disputes about both liability and damages, either arbitration/private judging or a summary jury trial would seem appropriate. Any of these would also serve defendants interest in privacy, and provide them with either guidance (summary jury trial) or a binding decision (arbitration/private judging) on the liability and damages issues.

It is possible that an MDC case screener, with the public interest in mind, might be reluctant to recommend resolution in a non-public forum of a dispute in which the safety of medical equipment is at issue. The case screener might think that there is a public interest in knowing the facts about the failure of the anesthetic equipment, and that only a trial, despite its costs, will accomplish that goal.

5.9   This is essentially a neighborhood dispute. While your client's parents undoubtedly want a sufficient recovery to take care of all their medical expenses, and something extra for the scarring, they should also have a strong interest in restoring their relationship with defendants, without which their son, and perhaps other neighborhood children, will be deprived of a place to swim. There also needs to be an agreement on pool supervision. All this calls out for mediation. The mediator should also be able to help the parties agree on a damages amount. See Tables 1,2,FFF.

5.10   This is an extremely difficult problem. The costs of settlement are apt to be quite high, both in present dollars and in the risks of future litigation. Trial costs, while substantial, will be much less than the costs of settlement. Going to trial is also a high risk, high gain strategy. A series of victories in the individual suits will make the costs of settling the remaining suits minimal and largely eliminate the risk of future litigation; a series of losses will have the opposite effect, and be enormously costly.

If one looks at the FFF tables for guidance, it is apparent that while the client would like a dispute resolution procedure that would minimize costs, and while it may wish to maintain/improve its relationship with the citizens of the city, its primary interests are in minimizing recovery and in obtaining a binding precedent that would protect it against the risk of future suits. This suggests that court might be the best option. Ideally, the client will be able to first litigate a case in which the sympathy factor is less strong, and, if it wins there, use that victory to drive down the price of settlement in the remaining cases.

5.11   It is arguable that since judicial review will lead to delay, and since none of the processes that might be recommended by the case screener can lead to an imposed outcome, judicial review ought not be allowed. On the other hand, since participation in any of these processes will require the expenditure of time and resources by the parties, it is also arguable that there should be some opportunity to challenge a clearly erroneous decision. Stempel suggests that an appropriate balance might be a standard of review somewhere between the extraordinary events that would lead to a successful mandamus and that of an ordinary appeal. "The reviewing judge would examine challenges to ADR directives looking (but not painstakingly searching) for a clear abuse of discretion or the imposition of serious inconvenience or expense that is not likely to move the dispute toward resolution."(1996:375).

5.12   1. "More discovery needed." At times, an objection that more discovery is needed will be genuine, in which event the case screener might suggest to opposing counsel that the necessary information be furnished promptly, so that the settlement process can go forward. (Gray gives an example of such a situation.) Frequently, however, the need for discovery will be either a pretext for delay or a product of the attorney's belief that if she engages in sufficient discovery she will uncover the "smoking gun" that will immediately resolve the dispute in her client's favor. In fact, the results of discovery are rarely that dramatic. Furthermore, most disputes can be settled after comparatively little discovery. One study of 800 mediations in four Ohio courts showed that the mediation settlement rate did not differ significantly between cases mediated before and after the completion of discovery. The same study showed that mediation prior to the completion of discovery led to cost savings for clients. Accordingly, case screeners should be somewhat skeptical of the objection that a case is not ready for ADR because more discovery is needed.

On the other hand, there is little point in forcing an attorney to mediate if she has a genuine belief that she needs more information in order to assess settlement possibilities. Thus, the best approach may be for the case screener to attempt an independent assessment of the need for additional discovery, and, where it is necessary, or, perhaps, where there is a good faith belief in its necessity, to allow limited and supervised discovery as a precursor to ADR. In other cases, however, the case screener should not delay ADR to enable additional discovery to occur.

2.   "The case is a clear winner." Alas, experience shows that most cases are not as "clear winners" as the advocates assert. Indeed often the other side believes the same certain outcome in its favor! But both sides cannot be correct. Hence some type of case evaluation or evaluative mediation may be called for. Moreover, even if the case really is a "clear winner," there may still be reasons - such as saving transaction costs or preserving the relationship between the parties - for looking to an early settlement that will of course reflect the high probability of winning. See Chapter 5E infra on Decision Analysis.

3.   My client won't let me, even though I'm in favor." The first question in this situation

is whether the lawyer has fully informed the client concerning the downsides of going ahead with the litigation (e.g., cost, delay, risk of adverse outcome). The judge may want to set an early pretrial conference at which the clients are required to be present and issues like those just alluded to are canvassed. If a client, after being fully informed of the costs and benefits of ADR still doesn't want it, yet the court believes that some kind of ADR may be helpful, perhaps this is a case for mandatory nonbinding ADR (such as mediation) if the court has that authority. Research reveals (p. 393) that the likelihood of settlement is as great for mandatory ADR as for voluntary ADR.

4. "There are dispositive motions pending." This argument is similar to No. 1 (more discovery needed) and No. 2 (case is clear winner). Occasionally a dispositive motion goes to the heart of the case (cf. the related claim: "There are other actions like this pending, and we need to take a strong stand against this kind of holdup") or the case presents novel arguments that have not been judicially evaluated before. But in most situations, the claims underlying the dispositive motions can and should be factored into a decision tree, so that the cost and uncertainty of that route can be properly accounted for.

5. "It's a matter of principle." This ambiguous phrase may mean different things. If the principle referred to is a legal principle, then the question is whether that principle is a novel one (cf. Brown v. Board of Education) or one that has been previously established. If the latter, then, as pointed out previously, that factor needs to be plugged into the settlement equation, rather than justifying nonresort to ADR. If the principle referred to is a strongly held personal belief, then the case may be more difficult, but still not impossible, to settle. A skilled mediator may, for example, be able to identify a solution that bypasses the strongly held view, as happened in Skokie, Illinois, when a clash between NeoNazi marchers and Holocaust survivors was averted by getting the marchers to take a different route.

5.13 While it is intuitively obvious that certain types of neutrals are best-suited to resolve certain disputes, there is no research that confirms this hypothesis. To the contrary, one study found that among trained and highly skilled mediators, different mediation styles did not lead to significant differences in settlement rates (Brett, Shapiro and Drieghe, 1985). Additionally, efforts to match mediators to disputes are likely to be time-consuming and expensive. On the other hand, if those efforts are engaged in by the attorneys for the disputing parties, rather than by court personnel, the attorneys' belief that they have found the "right" mediator to help them resolve the dispute may be a self-fulfilling prophecy.

5.14 Although some of the criteria set forth in the Administrative Dispute Resolution Act pertain specifically to government ADR (i.e., particularly paragraphs 2 and 6), most of the factors advanced in the Act have general applicability. Thus the first factor corresponds closely to one often referred to outside the administrative agency context. Of course in the private sector it is almost always open to the parties to settle the case, even if it is one that the judge or intake official might regard as appropriate for the formulation of a general rule. The administrative context is more akin to the criminal one, in that one of the parties is the government and hence can control the terms of any settlement.

The second and third factors also have application outside the government context since they point again to the need for the formulation of a general principle, rather than piecemeal disposition of a number of related but independent cases. Compare for example the situation presented where a number of consumers buy defective tires from a company that is engaging in fraudulent practices. Here, too, there is a need for a collective resolution, which is unlikely to be accomplished in a series of independent mediation proceedings. But that goal may be unattainable unless a government agency, such as the Attorney General Consumer Protection Bureau, brings a pattern and practice action against the offending seller.

The fourth factor seems highly relevant but overbroad, unless it were amended to add "and those parties could not be made part of the proceeding." One advantage of mediation is its amenability to bringing in all the relevant parties. Hence it is not clear why the absence of necessary parties should lead to an adjudicative rather than a mediated proceeding.

The fifth factor, as such, does not appear to have a counterpart outside the government. But it is closely related to the topic of access to ADR proceedings that is discussed in Chapter 7. Thus an intake official at the Multidoor Courthouse might not send to mediation a case raising major health issues with respect to some widely used product. But, as what pointed out above, that would not normally prevent the parties from reaching a private settlement, at least if they do so prior to any court filing.

The sixth factor also has its counterpart in court cases, in that many cases of institutional litigation (e.g., over restructuring a prison to conform to constitutional mandate) require subsequent court monitoring, and hence may be less appropriate for ADR. Still, in such cases the courts often appoint a special master mediator who will try to work out the implementation issues, always retaining the possibility of recourse to the court should that be necessary.

5.15   The difference, of course, is that a confidential statement may include sensitive information that is not known to the other side (either about the facts of the dispute or about views concerning acceptable settlements) while a nonconfidential statement does not. From the perspective of the mediator, confidential statements are clearly more useful, provided they are honest and forthright. The trouble for you, the plaintiff's lawyer in this case, is that you do not know what the other side will do. Clearly you do not want to reveal sensitive information if the other side does not, since that may harm your client's position. Ideally it might be best if you can discuss the matter with the other side and agree either both to file confidential premediation statements, or in the absence of such agreement, both file nonconfidential statements. Even if you do agree to file confidential statements, there are difficult questions concerning just how candid you will be (e.g., in disclosing your "true" bottom line). But the more you tell the mediator about your real concerns, the more likely she will be able to achieve a settlement that is beneficial for you.

5.16   Keeping in mind that the goal of a mediation is to achieve a mutually acceptable settlement with the other side, the question posed gives your client a major opportunity to create a climate for settlement. Thus your client might express considerable sympathy for the plaintiff and his condition even while gently reiterating his (the defendant's) lack of responsibility therefor. Such an approach is premised on the proposition that if the plaintiff feels some support or sympathy from the defendant, he (the plaintiff) is much more likely to come to a settlement than if the plaintiff regards the defendant as hostile and adversarial. The delicate tightrope your client has to walk is how to exude such sympathy without admitting legal responsibility for the plaintiff's condition. One can well imagine a lawyer and client preparing for a mediation rehearsing such a scene several times since the question and its response could well be a critical element in the success of the mediation. See Jonathan Cohen, Advising Clients to Apologize, U.S.C. L. Rev., May 1999.

5.17   Theoretically the lawyer's role is no different whether the parties were required to go into mediation or choose to do so. But the danger is that in the former case lawyers and clients will simply go through the motions rather than using the opportunity to resolve the dispute without going to trial. Of course much depends on the reaction of the other side. If they are treating the mediation pro forma without entering the discussion in good faith, then, unless you can get the mediator to change their approach, it will probably not be to your advantage to act any differently. Research shows (p. 393) that even where parties were compelled to go into mediation, settlements are just as likely as where they went involuntarily. Hence it is in your interest to turn the mediation into a productive session rather than a "going through the motions" experience.

5.18   The advice seems clearly misguided. The whole point of bringing in a mediator is that the use of a neutral third party often brings in new ideas and new techniques. For example the reason why the parties may have reached an impasse may be reactive devaluation (see p. 96). The mediator, by acting as a go-between, can avoid the effect of that phenomenon. Or there may be need for a realistic third party evaluation of each side's likelihood of success in court. Or the use of separate sessions with each side may reveal important information concerning the real interests of the parties that has not surfaced in their face-to-face negotiations.

5.19   Urging your client to go to mediation even though you do not discuss with her the full reason does not seem to raise any ethical questions. See M. Moffitt, Casting Light on the Black Box of Mediation: Should Mediators Make Their Conduct More Transparent, 13 Ohio St. J. Dis. Res. 1 (1997). Indeed it could be argued that it is part of your job as a lawyer to help your client get a realistic estimate of his success in court. If you have qualms about hiding your reason, conceivably some neutral formulation might be employed such as "it might be particularly useful to have a third party neutral who could try to help the parties get a realistic third party estimate of their likelihood of success".

There may also be issues of the different financial interests of the agent and principal. If the lawyer is being paid on an hourly basis he may have a financial interest in dragging out the case as long as possible. Hence trying to encourage settlement is arguably all the more commendable since it is against the lawyer's financial interest. But the lawyer may be on a fixed contingent fee, in which case a quick settlement might be more beneficial than going to trial. If the lawyer were to strongly urge settlement on the client solely for that reason it would raise ethical issues. But in the present situation where the primary interest of the lawyer is to get a more realistic estimate of the likelihood of success for the client that objection would not appear to be present.

5.20.   Courts have acknowledged that the standard for malpractice liability is likely to affect a lawyer's willingness to make effective use of settlement processes before formal discovery. In one case, a state supreme court changed the malpractice liability standard, expressing a hope that the change would encourage lawyers to recommend settlement. Like the *Collins* case, cited in the text, the plaintiffs in *Muhammad v. Strassburger, McKenna, Messer, Shilobod & Gutnick*, 526 Pa. 541, 587 A.2d 1346, cert. den. 502 U.S. 876 (1991), had accepted their attorney's recommendation, settled a medical malpractice case, and then sued the attorney for malpractice for recommending the settlement. The Pennsylvania Supreme Court ruled that, absent fraud, a party who agreed to a settlement could not later recover in a malpractice action against the attorney who recommended the settlement. The court indicated that a key consideration in its ruling was the desire to encourage settlement.

> Lawyers would be reluctant to settle a case for fear some enterprising attorney representing a disgruntled client will find a way to sue them for something that 'could have been done, but was not.' We refuse to endorse a rule that will discourage settlements and increase substantially the number of legal malpractice cases. A long-standing principle of our courts has been to encourage settlements; we will not now act so as to discourage them (587 A.2d at 1349).

Courts in other states have rejected any change to liability standards, and the Pennsylvania Supreme Court has limited its holding in *Muhammad* to the facts of that case. *McMahon v. Shea*, 688 A.2d 1179, 1182 (Pa. 1996). Some courts rejecting *Muhammad* mention the fear that attorneys who commit malpractice will try to insulate themselves from liability by recommending settlement. They emphasize the importance of settlement but argue that its importance weighs in favor of maintaining a high level of legal advice regarding settlements. For example, the Supreme Court of Connecticut reasoned.

> Although we encourage settlements, we recognize that litigants rely heavily on the professional advice of counsel when they decide whether to accept or reject offers of settlement, and we insist that the lawyers of our state advise clients with respect to settlements with the same skill, knowledge, and diligence with which they pursue all other legal tasks. *Grayson v. Wofsey, Rosen, Kweskin & Kuriansky*, 231 Conn. 168, 646 A.2d 195, 199-200 (1994).

An alternative to the *Muhammad* approach is to recognize malpractice liability for lawyers who through negligence fail to achieve and recommend earlier settlement. A plaintiff corporation urged the court to recognize this theory of recovery in a recent federal court diversity action. The court construed Illinois law as requiring the plaintiff corporation to show that it would have been "successful" in the underlying litigation but for the lawyers' negligence. The court was unwilling to extend "successful" to cover an earlier favorable settlement, mentioning the highly speculative nature of extending liability in this way. *Kirkland & Ellis v. CMI*, 1996 WL 674072 (N.D. Ill. 1996).

Another option might be to build a malpractice standard on the approach suggested by the Model Rules of Professional Conduct for ethics standards -- that the lawyer and client can define the terms of engagement (cf. Rules 1.1, 1.2). As long as the client is clear that the recommendation is based on a limited investigation, and has decided that the cost of securing more information is not worth it given the stakes, the lawyer's failure to investigate should not subject the lawyer to liability.

5.21. The ethical duties referenced in Chapter 5C might include the duty to discuss the advantages and disadvantages of using dispute resolution processes early in the development of the dispute. This duty does not seem to pose the danger, discussed with respect to changing malpractice standards in the Teacher's Manual response to 5.20, that lawyers will give poor legal advice. Indeed, the lawyer's advice might be to wait to make a serious attempt to settle until more information becomes available through discovery. The primary disadvantage of such a duty would seem to be that it would impose additional regulation on the attorney-client relationship and, if satisfied by handing a form to the client, might not achieve the desired goal.

The court might achieve better than a form response by requiring lawyers to appear and discuss the options. At the same time, it might be more efficient for the courts just to schedule the case for mediation, early in the case, because mediation seems to be the process chosen most often. The research discussed in the text would indicate that the settlement rates for cases scheduled for mediation early in the litigation resemble those of cases scheduled later. It is uncertain, however, whether the court's approach would affect lawyers' behavior in other cases. The potential of this device as yeast for change would seem to depend on whether attorneys who had experience with early mediation would decide that early scheduling of mediation was better and would begin scheduling mediation early themselves. If lack of education is not the reason lawyers delay, this court action might not have an impact beyond the immediate case. At any rate, there seems little reason to worry that the quality of the lawyer's advice would suffer, because the lawyers could advise the clients that it was too early to make a serious attempt to settle the case in mediation.

5.22. The problem with blanket approaches such as this one is that there are situations when it may be sensible to settle after formal discovery when it did not appear so before. For example, a case that seemed to be worth more than the $100,000 offered by the defendant midway through discovery may not be worth more than $1,000 after the plaintiff makes damaging admissions during a deposition.

5.23 As shown on the far right of the decision tree, if plaintiff prevails on both liability and punitive damages, he will receive $2,000,000, less attorney's fees, for a total recovery of $1,333,000. If plaintiff prevails on liability, but loses on punitive damages, he will receive $1,000,000, less attorney's fees, for a total recovery of $667,000.

Client's Decision Tree
[SEE Insert 5.2.1]

Since plaintiff, if he prevails on liability, has only a 50% likelihood of prevailing on punitive damages, the recoveries attached to winning and losing on punitives must each be multiplied by 50% (or 0.5) and the resulting figures ($666, 667 and $333, 500) added. Doing so leads to an expected value of slightly over $1,000,000 if plaintiff prevails on liability, and the $1,000,000 figure is entered at the chance node following the win on liability. Multiplying that $1,000,000 by the 60% probability of a win on liability (this figure is derived from the fact that plaintiffs have prevailed in three out of five similar suits) leads to an expected value for the litigation of $600,000, the figure entered at the chance node on litigation. Since the value of the settlement offer of $800,000, after deducting attorney's fees of $160,000, is $640,000, which is greater than the expected value of litigation, counsel should advise the client to accept the settlement offer, particularly if the client needs money promptly for treatment or rehabilitation.

An interesting twist to this question is provided if one constructs a separate decision tree for the lawyer, as is done below.

Lawyer's Decision Tree
[SEE Insert 5.2.2]

In this tree, the recoveries to the lawyer are substituted for the client's recoveries, and the expected value of the case to the lawyer is substituted for the expected value to the client. Doing so, and comparing the two trees, demonstrates that while the expected value of litigating is less for the client than the value of settling, the opposite is true for the lawyer, for whom the litigation value of the case is $300,000, while the settlement value is only $160,000. Nonetheless, it is the lawyer's ethical obligation to recommend settlement, since settlement is in the client's best interest.

5.24 Multiplying the high and low ends of the possible recoveries by the likelihood of each, and adding in the anticipated trial costs of $25,000 leads to an expected litigation value (or cost) to Barry's of $88,000 - $107,850. Since the settlement demand of $150,000 is well in excess of even the high end of the expected litigation cost, the obvious answer to the question is that the settlement demand should be rejected.

On the other hand, there is a substantial reputational cost to Barry's in proceeding to trial. Regardless of whether or not Barry's prevails in the litigation, public knowledge of the incident may harm Barry's reputation and its business. While this cost is not calculated in the analysis, and while it may be difficult to do so (but see Lax and Sebenius, 1986), it cannot be ignored in making the litigation-settle decision. The point of the question is that a sophisticated decision analysis takes into account all the risks of litigation, not only the immediate financial risks of an adverse decision.

5.25 The purpose of this question is to demonstrate a somewhat more complex decision tree.

[SEE Insert 5.2.3]

That tree shows that the expected value (cost) of the case to Barry's is $112,000. This figure is derived by starting at the right of the tree, where the total cost to Barry's under each possible scenario is set out. For example, if plaintiff shows a prima facie case, defeats the "legitimate business reason" defense, and obtains the maximum front pay of $500,000, her recovery would be $600,000. To this must be added Barry's litigation costs of $30,000, leading to a total maximum cost to Barry's of $630,000, the figure attached to the top branch of the decision tree. The figures attached to the other branches of the decision tree are similarly calculated, with differing amounts of projected front pay leading to the different figures. The next step is to multiply the probability of each result by the amount of that result. Thus, .05 times $630,000 is $31,500. Performing the same operation with each of the figures on the far right of the tree leads to a total of $235,000 ($31,500 +$76,000+$69,000+$58,500= $235,000). That amount is entered in the box after the third chance node, as it represents the value (cost) of the case to Barry's after plaintiff has prevailed on the pretext issue.

Since plaintiff's likelihood of prevailing on the pretext issue is .50, the $235,000 figure is multiplied by .50 and the result ($132,500) entered in the box after the second chance node. This figure represents the expected value (cost) to Barry's of the litigation after plaintiff has established a prima facie case.

Finally, since plaintiff's likelihood of establishing a prima facie case is .80, the figure of $132,500 is multiplied by .80. The resulting figure of $112,000 represents the expected value (cost) of the case if Barry's decides to litigate. Since plaintiff's settlement demand is $150,000, it should, absent other considerations (see Question 2), be rejected.

5.26 The purpose of this question is to demonstrate, in a very simple fashion, the use of a sensitivity analysis. If, as the decision tree shows, plaintiff's likelihood of prevailing on the pretext issue goes up to 67%, the expected value (cost) of the case goes up to $139,880, which is still less than the plaintiff's settlement demand, albeit not by much.

[SEE Insert 5.2.4]

Thus, the decision to settle is not sensitive to a change from 50% to 67% in the plaintiff's likelihood of prevailing on the pretext issue. (Actually, 73% is the tipping point. At any value greater than that, the expected value (cost) of the case exceeds the settlement demand.)

5.27 One possibility is for each lawyer to seek a second opinion, another possibility would be for the lawyers to jointly engage a neutral expert for his/her view on the plaintiff's likelihood of prevailing on the pretext issue.

5.28 Initially, you should, in conjunction with the CPP/National joint venture team, diagnose the disputes that have arisen in the past. What kinds of disputes have occurred, why, and with whom? What methods have been used to resolve these disputes, why, and with what success? What have been the costs and benefits of existing dispute resolution methods?

The results of this diagnosis show that the disputes that have plagued the introduction of the new catalogue design and layout system have been a product of the users' inability to utilize the system efficiently. This has led to complaints about computer malfunctions, inadequate training, poor follow-up training, inadequate design assistance, and the costs associated with attempting to remedy those asserted defects. Customers have been engaged in disputes with National personnel in training and customer support, and with CPP graphic arts personnel and the head of the catalog division. They attempted to negotiate resolutions of their problems with each, but with no success. The costs of this lack of success have been enormous -- lost sales by customers, lost contracts for CPP/National, and a shaky future for the new catalogue design and layout system.

The reasons for the frequent disputes between customers and CPP/National, and the parties' inability to resolve those disputes satisfactorily, are manifold. Among them would appear to be that the customers were at different levels of computer sophistication when they attempted to use the new design and layout system, the new system was introduced at a period when speedy production was essential, and there was no agreed-upon means for dealing with problems that might arise in implementing the new system.

Designing a system to deal with these problems begins with devising means for reducing the number of disputes that will enter the system (a topic given perhaps insufficient weight in <u>Getting Disputes Resolved).</u> Prominent among such dispute prevention efforts would be a greater emphasis on tailoring the amount of training to the needs of the customer, so that customers would be capable of using the new system when it was installed, regardless of their previous level of computer use. Suggestions for achieving this goal are a generally higher level of training; operator testing, leading to a certificate of readiness; and motivating sales personnel to encourage training by tying their commissions in part to the customer's successful use of the system. Another obvious dispute prevention idea is to inaugurate the new system at a less critical time. This
should avoid some difficulties and reduce the costs of others.

In designing procedures for dealing with those problems and disputes that do arise in the operation of the new system, an initial question is whether customers should have several points of access to the dispute resolution system or only one access point. Should a customer be able to call, at his volition, the CPP/National sales representative with whom he dealt, the graphic arts technician, the computer installer, the computer trainer, etc.? Or should there be a single contact person/entry point? The advantage of multiple points of entry is that the customer can deal with someone he is comfortable with, so he will be motivated to use the system; the disadvantage is that the person may not be competent to deal with the problem.

Regardless of whether the customer can contact whom he wishes for assistance, or has a single point of entry, such as an 800 hotline number, CPP/National should establish a trouble-shooting group with expertise in all areas of the new system in which problems might arise. Problems that cannot be dealt with satisfactorily by the initial contact person should be promptly referred to the trouble-shooting group. In addition to their technical knowledge, the members of this group should have negotiation training, and compensation tied in part to their successful resolution of disputes. The financial cost of assistance should be clearly spelled out in the contracts between CPP/National and their customers.

Disputes not resolved between the customer and the trouble-shooting group might be sent to a neutral technical expert for advice, then back to the customer and the group for further negotiation. Beyond this, the procedures that might be available for dispute resolution would be negotiation between designated managers, arbitration, and a cooling-off period prior to either arbitration or court. There should also be a provision for the optional use of a mini-trial or summary jury trial in appropriate disputes. Provision should be made for training and motivating use of appropriate procedures at each step.

Two final comments. First, these ideas are neither all-inclusive nor applicable in all situations. Their value depends on how well they fit in the dynamic of a particular relationship. Second, at each step the designer must be conscious of the cost of implementing his design, compared to the hoped-for benefits. Dispute systems design is not like fine art in which the goal is to provide an aesthetically pleasing experience, but more like engineering in which function precedes form, and one aspect of function is costs compared to benefits.

5.29   An appropriate starting place for a dispute resolution procedure that will resolve student problems "quickly, fairly and openly" would be with a -requirement that all student complaints be presented initially to the teacher involved. Disputes which they could not resolve would be presented to a hearing board or committee on which teachers and students are equally represented. Since parents are deeply interested in many of the problems that arise in school, there might also be provision for parent representation (perhaps 2 from each group). There should also be a non-voting chairman, whose function would be that of meeting facilitator and mediator. Step 2 would be an appeal to the Washington High School principal and perhaps a Step 3 appeal to the district superintendent.

Delay could be minimized by tight time limits for appeal from each step to the next. For example, the student might first be required to present his complaint to the teacher involved, then, if no settlement is reached within 10 days, to the hearing board. The hearing board would be required to hear complaints within 10 days of the time of filing, and any appeal to subsequent steps would have to be filed within 10 days. A failure to appeal within the time limits would be treated as stopping the complaint; the failure of the principal or district superintendent to respond within 10 days would be treated as sustaining the complaint.

The next question is whether there should be outside review of a decision of the district superintendent (assuming she is the last step in the internal dispute resolution mechanism). Arguing against the availability of outside review (even of an advisory nature) is that it will create some pressure to accept the outside reviewer's advice. Thus, there will be some loss of power for the district superintendent. On the other hand, outside review and student participation are likely to be the most powerful factors in making this a successful procedure that will be used and trusted by students. Furthermore, if the outside reviewers are carefully chosen, the risk of far-out advisory opinions is minimized. Hence, on balance, a provision for advisory arbitration as the terminal step in the process would appear desirable.

Just to touch on a few remaining issues briefly, the procedure should be open to all student complaints, with the possible exception of complaints about a particular grade. Dissatisfaction with grades is a constant source of low-level student concern, and allowing such complaints into the procedure could overwhelm the system. Furthermore, the subjectivity of grading makes such complaints next to impossible to resolve. Finally, review of their grading decisions is apt to upset the teachers.

A complaining student should be allowed to have representation by anyone in the school community. No outsiders (lawyers or not), as they will tend to polarize the dispute and make settlements more difficult to achieve. This is not unfair to the student, as he retains the right to counsel in any judicial challenge to the outcome of the procedure.

There should be training in dispute resolution skills for all members of the hearing board, and for their future replacements. We cannot assume that they will possess these skills, and they are of the highest importance to the success of this venture. Steps should also be taken to publicize the program extensively, and to assure students that no reprisals will ever be taken against students who press their complaints through this program.

The foregoing approach is not, by any means, exclusive. one alternative would be to develop different procedures for different types of disputes. Another alternative would be to design an ombudsman procedure (see pp. 287-289).

The teacher who wishes to do so may turn this question into a role-playing exercise. Divide the class into groups of 5-10 students, with each student playing an assigned role, e.g. teacher, student, parent. Each student would receive a memorandum outlining the interests of the person whose role he is playing. (Examples of such memoranda follow.) Each group of students is given the assignment set out in the last paragraph of the question, and allowed approximately one hour to complete its assignment. The various groups then return to class for discussion of their proposed procedures.

ROLE DESCRIPTION: PRINCIPAL

You are in your mid-thirties. You are completing your doctorate at the local university. You did undergraduate work in sociology with honors and hold a Master's in Secondary School Education. Your first job was as a social science teacher; you were an academic vice-principal for six years. You came to George Washington High as principal two years ago, after a statewide search. You are resented by some older faculty and administration members but have developed a strong base of support among younger teachers. The students, you feel, are somewhat cynical about you. They liked what you said when you arrived and reacted favorably to your rather relaxed manner with them, but they seem to have lost faith in you as a result of the school newspaper censorship issue.

ROLE DESCRIPTION: HEAD GUIDANCE COUNSELOR

You see the grievance mechanism as a serious threat to your professional integrity. It interferes with treatment programs, such as group counseling, and undermines the counselor's authority to determine what is best for students.

You have a Master's in school psychology and are president of the local chapter of the School Psychologists Association. You have just returned from a week's in-service training workshop on adolescent drug and alcohol abuse.

ROLE DESCRIPTION: VICE-PRINCIPAL FOR ACADEMICS

You are older than the principal, have been at George Washington a long time, and are seeking a higher administration post elsewhere. You are caught between a faculty that is basically unreceptive to the grievance mechanism and an administrator who wants it to succeed. You pride yourself on your open mind. You are deeply disturbed by the deteriorating morale throughout the school, the conflicts between and within groups, and the drop in academic standards. You have a son who is a senior at George Washington who argues vociferously for more student participation in school policy-making.

ROLE DESCRIPTION: DEAN OF STUDENTS

You are a former physical education teacher and pride yourself on your good rapport with students. You believe that a grievance mechanism will open up communications between rival factions. You led a small group of faculty dissidents in the censorship fracas. You believe there is no place for litigation in resolving student disputes with the school system.

ROLE DESCRIPTION: TEACHERS' UNION REPRESENTATIVE

You see the new mechanism as a threat to the teacher's authority and the right to establish rules for class behavior and decorum. You also see it as potentially a threat to the teacher's prerogative to design the curriculum and are afraid that it might even lead to public censure of a teacher's actions. A majority of the union members agree. On the other hand, you are receiving increasing pressure from teachers who are concerned about the rapid deterioration of the learning environment and the threat of litigation, and who believe that teachers may find in a grievance mechanism the tool they need to restore confidence in the classroom situation among their students.

ROLE DESCRIPTION: STUDENT COUNCIL PRESIDENT

An incoming senior, you have just taken office. You are an honor student who is aiming for a prestigious college, law school, and a political career in the tradition of your family. You are defensive about the Council's losing its credibility as the forum for airing student concerns and are afraid that a grievance mechanism would further erode the Council's status. However, you know that the principal wants a grievance mechanism and you do not want to be left out of the mainstream if one succeeds. You want to ensure a role for the Student Council in the procedure.

ROLE DESCRIPTION: PRESIDENT OF JUNIOR CLASS

You are an incoming junior who has recently become an A student. However, you used to be a disciplinary problem in junior high. You are active in extracurricular activities and over the summer organized a Teenage Hotline in the community. You are tentatively in favor of a new grievance mechanism because it might provide students with a real voice in school affairs and disputes for the first time. But you doubt very much that the administration and teachers will permit a mechanism that limits their decision-making power. You have your own ideas on how the mechanism should function, but take a "show me" attitude toward all school authorities.

ROLE DESCRIPTION: P.T.A. PRESIDENT

You are deeply troubled by the diminishing quality of education at George Washington High School, the increasing alienation of the children from school and the learning process, and a breakdown in communication between school and home, as evidenced by the recent rise in litigation. You are delighted that the school superintendent wants a grievance mechanism, because you see it as a means of forcing the school to initiate communication with the home and community. Suspicious of the biases of staff and administration, you favor neutral outside review of grievances at some stage.

ROLE DESCRIPTION: VICE-PRINCIPAL FOR ADMINISTRATION

You got your B.A. from a local teachers college 25 years ago, your Master's in Business Administration over a period of time. You are viewed primarily as a good fiscal manager by the central administration. You are outraged by the destruction and theft of property and believe it is the product of permissive attitudes toward the young. You are a strong believer in discipline and in adhering to rules and regulations. You are cynical about student participation in school affairs; you feel that students are just children, who should be in school simply to learn.

ROLE DESCRIPTION: SOPHOMORE CLASS PRESIDENT

You are considered a leader of the school's radical intellectuals. The suspended student was a good friend of yours. You resent the fact that it took a lawsuit to get the administration to consider the possibility of a student grievance procedure, but you are intrigued by the possibilities of increasing students' power and liberalizing restrictive school policies.

5.30 What makes this problem difficult is that we know the general outlines of the kind of dispute that may arise in the future, but we know none of its details. If one parent decides to move, resolution of the physical custody issue may depend on where and when the parent moves, the reasons for the move, the desires at that time of parents, children, and any new spouses, and a myriad of factors that make up "the best interests of the children" and the psychological state of the parents.

The best the parents may be able to do at this time is to devise a procedure for talking about all of these factors, for negotiating them, and for third-party facilitation if their negotiations fail.

More precisely, some of the issues that need to be addressed in such a clause are:

1. Triggering event (e.g., party contemplating move must give at least x days notice to other party);

2. Processes to be employed (negotiation, mediation, arbitration);

3. Time limits for going from one process to next;

4. How neutrals to be selected;

5. Who will pay for them;

6. Possible participation of

    a. experts

    b. children

7. Standards to be applied (e.g., best interests of children)

8. Preservation of status quo pending resolution under this clause

B.   EXERCISES

EXERCISE 5.1:   SOUTHERN ELECTRIC COMPANY AND
PUBLIC UTILITY WORKERS UNION, AFL-CIO

Teaching Instructions

There are five roles in this exercise – mediator, grievant, Union representative, Company maintenance superintendent, and Company industrial relations manager. In assigning students to play these roles, you may wish to assign the mediator's role to a student who has taken a labor law course, or who has some knowledge of labor relations, preferably in a union-represented workplace.

The exercise is set up as a grievance mediation, in which the mediator has no decisional authority. It may also be used, with appropriate directions from the instructor, as an exercise in med-arb, in which the neutral functions initially as a mediator, then, if agreement cannot be reached, as an arbitrator with authority to issue a final and binding decision (text, pp. 278-280).

If the exercise is conducted as a med-arb, an interesting question will be whether the parties will be capable of reaching agreement, or whether the neutral will be required to decide the matter. And, if they do reach agreement, is the agreement really a disguised decision by the neutral, adopted as an agreement because the neutral indicated to the parties what his/her decision would be absent agreement? In either event, the exercise should demonstrate to the students the tension that exists between the mediation and arbitration elements of med-arb.

If the exercise is conducted as a grievance mediation, the questions are similar, though not the same, once again, the first question is whether the parties can reach agreement, and if so, how they do so. The neutral cannot decide the dispute, but can influence the terms of the discourse, as well as the terms of an agreement, by focussing on the rights of the parties or on their underlying interests. It is tempting for the neutral, particularly if he/she knows something about labor law or labor relations to focus the discussion on the likely arbitration outcome (rights), but the neutral who believes in the virtues of interest-based dispute resolution for parties with an ongoing relationship will avoid this temptation. (A recent case bearing on the likely arbitration outcome is McKennon v. Nashville Banner Publishing Co., 115 S. Ct. 8790 (1995), in which the Supreme Court held, in a suit arising under the Age Discrimination Act, that after-acquired adverse evidence could not be used to defeat the claim, but may be used to limit damages or make reinstatement or front pay inappropriate.)

The most frequent resolution of this dispute, and one that meets the interests of all, is that the grievant is returned to work in a non-driving job. However, the students should resolve several additional issues. Can the grievant return to a driving position some day? Under what circumstances? Will his pay rate be based on the driving or non-driving job? How about back pay? What will be the Union's future involvement in the accident investigation process?

A 35-minute videotape of this exercise, done as a grievance mediation, with a professional mediator and experienced union and management representatives, is available from Mediation Research & Education Project, Inc., Northwestern University Law School, 357 E. Chicago Avenue, Chicago, IL 60611, 312-503-0090, for $30.00.

EXERCISE 5.1:   SOUTHERN ELECTRIC COMPANY AND
PUBLIC UTILITY WORKERS UNION, AFL-CIO

Confidential Information Grievant

You bid out of the maintenance mechanic job seven years ago because you weren't happy working in the shop all day. You like a change of scene during the working day, you like to drive, and you think that you are a good driver. You sometimes drive fast, but not dangerously (in your opinion), and you've never been in an accident that you thought was your fault.

This last accident was clearly not your fault and was not preventable. You think that the police report and the Company report support you on that, and that there's no way the Company can successfully charge you with having had three preventable accidents in the last three years. What you're concerned about, though, is the possibility that the Company may have obtained a copy of your driving record from the State Department of Motor Vehicles. You don't know if they could use that against you, but it certainly doesn't look good -- four speeding convictions in the last five years, as well as three accidents in your personal vehicle, one of which caused injuries to the other driver. (The most recent accident took place one year ago, and was the one involving injuries. The most recent speeding conviction was 15 months ago.) None of the Company people mentioned your record during the earlier steps of the grievance procedure, so you haven't said anything about it to your Union representative, and you won't unless the Company raises it at mediation. The fewer people who know about it, the better!

Your biggest concern is getting back to work. You've got 10 years invested in a company known for its job security and good pension plan, and you don't want to lose it. You'd also like to get as much back pay as you can. You've lost approximately $20,000 wages in the last nine months, and that hurts. Still, if it becomes a question of money or a job, there's no question that you'd go back to work with no back pay to get a job. The only thing that you wouldn't do is go back to work as a maintenance mechanic with no possibility of ever returning to the maintenance driver position. This is partly a matter of the lower pay rate in the maintenance mechanic job ($1.25 per hour less than for a maintenance driver), but is more because you enjoy driving and getting out of the shop from time to time.

EXERCISE 5.1:   SOUTHERN ELECTRIC COMPANY AND
PUBLIC UTILITY WORKERS UNION, AFL-CIO

Confidential Information Union Representative

If Doaks really was a danger to himself and his fellow employees, not to mention the public, you would have little enthusiasm for protecting him. There have been past instances of employees being seriously injured due to the careless driving of other employees, and the Union fully agrees with legitimate Company efforts to eliminate careless driving. Still, that does not appear to have been what happened here. Based on the evidence the Company has put forward so far, Doaks' driving record is not at all bad, and the last accident was clearly not preventable. What you're after here is reinstatement with full back pay, and in view of the weakness of the Company's case, you think you can get it.

The Union did not challenge the two previous findings that Doaks has been engaged in preventable accidents because it did not know about them. There is no system at this Company to notify the Union of preventable accident findings. Unless the employee involved tells the Union, it will not know.

Thus, another goal you should pursue here is getting Union involvement in the investigation of so-called "preventable" accidents. That way, Union representatives might be able to prevent discipline in cases like this, instead of being forced to challenge discipline after it has been imposed. You've raised this in the past without success, but the Safety Department did such a poor job here that the Company may be more amenable to changes in the accident investigation procedure.

EXERCISE 5.1:   SOUTHERN ELECTRIC COMPANY AND
PUBLIC UTILITY WORKERS UNION, AFL-CIO

Confidential Information for Company Industrial Relations Manager

You and the maintenance superintendent have had a difficult time agreeing on what the Company's position should be in this grievance. You understand his unhappiness at the prospect of having Doaks driving a Company truck after having received Doaks' driving record from the State Department of Motor Vehicles -- four speeding convictions in the past five years, as well as three accidents in his personal vehicle, one of which caused injury to the other driver. (The most recent accident took place one year ago, and was the one involving injuries. The most recent speeding conviction was 15 months ago.) Still, you did not receive that information until after the discharge, and think it is unlikely that an arbitrator would let the Company use it to justify the discharge. You also think it is unlikely that the Company can persuade an arbitrator that the third accident was preventable. Thus, you see this case as a loser at arbitration, with the likely result of reinstatement and full back pay of approximately $20,000.

A loss could also lead to an arbitrator's decision criticizing the Company's defensive driving course or its accident investigation procedure. Either of these could have harmful effects
in other disciplinary proceedings.

You have suggested to the maintenance superintendent that you should try to minimize the Company's risks by offering immediate reinstatement with no back pay, but he is dead set against having someone with Doaks' record driving one of his trucks, so he will not agree to reinstatement. He also does not believe you when you tell him the Company will probably lose at arbitration. He has suggested that you try to settle the case with a substantial severance pay offer, and you're willing to try that -- at least up to $25,000, slightly more than the accrued back pay liability.

Your first tactic at mediation, however, will be to come on strong with Doaks' driving record, and see if you can bluff the Union, on the basis of that record, into dropping the grievance in exchange for a modest amount of severance pay. If that doesn't work, you'll gradually move up to your $25,000 maximum offer.

It is possible that the Union will try to use this case to revive its demand for Union involvement in the accident investigation procedure. You are opposed to such involvement, because you fear that it would lead to Union obstruction of legitimate Company efforts to insure safe driving habits. Still, your position is not set in concrete, and you would be willing to discuss the Union's concerns and suggestions.

EXERCISE 5.1: SOUTHERN ELECTRIC COMPANY AND
PUBLIC UTILITY WORKERS UNION, AFL-CIO

Confidential Information Company Maintenance Superintendent

Shortly after the grievant's discharge, you requested the State Department of Motor Vehicles to provide you with a copy of his driving record. You received it about 60 days ago, after the grievance meetings had been completed, and you have not yet discussed it with the Union. It shows that in the past five years the grievant has had four speeding convictions, as well as three accidents in his personal vehicle, one of which caused bodily harm to the driver of the other car. (The most recent accident took place one year ago, and was the one involving injuries. The most recent speeding conviction was 15 months ago.) Regardless of whether his third Company accident was preventable, there is no way, with this record, that you will have him driving for you again. You are certain that any arbitrator would agree with you on this, and cannot understand why your Industrial Relations Manager doesn't see the outcome at arbitration the same way you do.

It's too bad that Doaks got himself into this mess, because he's a good maintenance mechanic, and your expanding department can always use more mechanics, but you are absolutely firm against putting him back behind the wheel of a truck. If I.R. is worried about losing at
arbitration, you would have no objection to the Company paying as much severance pay as necessary to get Doaks to resign, but you will not agree to any settlement that puts him back in a truck.

EXERCISE 5.1: SOUTHERN ELECTRIC COMPANY AND
PUBLIC UTILITY WORKERS UNION, AFL-CIO

Confidential Information Mediator

You have served as a labor arbitrator for 30 years, and are a member of the National Academy of Arbitrators. Approximately two years ago, you noticed a drop in the number of your arbitration appointments, and discovered that other long-time arbitrators were experiencing the same drop. Accordingly, you decided to try your hand at grievance mediation, which seems to be gaining in popularity. Since then, you have mediated approximately 20 grievances.

On the whole, you enjoy mediating, though you are occasionally frustrated at the amount of time that is required to resolve a fairly simple dispute. Your preference is to gather the relevant facts from the parties, analyze those facts based on your years of arbitration experience, and then to encourage the potential loser at arbitration to modify its demands to obtain a settlement.

Still, you have learned that you must proceed cautiously in this respect. At times, the re are factors that have little to do with a potential arbitration decision that are crucial for settlement purposes, and you must understand those factors if you are to obtain a settlement. At other times, your knowledge of likely arbitration outcomes is extremely valuable in moving the parties towards settlement. Thus, a key question for you in your role as a grievance mediator is to know when to use your "pure" mediation skills and when to use your arbitration knowledge.

EXERCISE 5.2   WORLD OIL COMPANY V. NORTHEAST SHIPBUILDING, INC.

Teaching Instructions

In addition to the two exercises set out in parts (a) and (b), the instructor might add or substitute two supplemental exercises. The first supplemental exercise, which would precede what is now part (a), would be this:

Supplemental. Exercise 1: The Internal Decision Regarding a Mini-Trial

Counsel for each party should meet separately to consider whether they wish to explore the possibility of a mini-trial with opposing counsel. Each participant should think about the interests that someone in his/her position would realistically have, and consider the mini-trial in light of these interests.

The point of Supplemental Exercise 1 is to demonstrate that persons in different positions tend to have different views about the desirability of any dispute resolution procedure, that those views are a function of both personal and institutional interests, and that if those interests are not satisfied the proposed procedure may not be agreed upon, even though it may appear to be desirable for the disputing parties. This exercise is most instructive if students are assigned to play the roles of inside counsel, outside counsel, and client, since each will have a different perspective on the desirability of a mini-trial.

Supplemental Exercise 2: Negotiating a Settlement of the Dispute

The other supplemental exercise, which would be done instead of part (b), would be to have students playing the roles set out above attempt to negotiate a settlement of the case. Doing so will take far less time than preparing for and conducting a mini-trial, and may be preferred by those instructors who wish to have additional time to devote to other areas of the course. If the negotiation exercise is assigned, students should not find it difficult, as there is a substantial zone of agreement based on the facts given to each party.

The existence of that zone of agreement is not immediately apparent, as Northeast is willing to contribute only $300 million, while World insists on $875 million. However, Northeast's cost of building a 100,000 ton supertanker for delivery in 18 months is $150 million; for delivery in 24 months it is $100 million. World wants to buy up to four such vessels in the next 18-24 months, and its best bids have been $325 million for 18-month delivery, $225 million for 24-month delivery. Thus, buying two ships for 18-month delivery and two ships for 24-month delivery would cost World $1.1 billion. Northeast can build the same ships and deliver them in the same time at an out-of-pocket cost to it of $500 million. Thus, if World is willing to buy four ships from Northeast, two to be delivered in 18 months, two in 24 months, at a price of $200 million, it will have a savings of $900 million, and Northeast will have an out-of-pocket loss of $300 million. Each of those figures is within the settlement authority of counsel for the two companies, so that a settlement can be reached. (World may be reluctant to buy additional ships from Northeast in view of the problems with the steering gear on the J.B. John, but they have been doing business for many years, with no indication of prior problems, and Northeast is willing to provide an unconditional warranty on the steering gear.)

EXERCISE 5.2: WORLD OIL COMPANY V. NORTHEAST SHIPBUILDING, INC.

Confidential Information for Northeast Shipbuilding. Inc.

You think it is unlikely that Northeast would escape from a trial without both a substantial jury verdict and damaging publicity. This is true less because of the facts that have come out so far than because of other facts of which World is not yet aware, but which are bound to come out in the full-scale discovery that would precede a trial.

After the failure of the J.B. John's steering gear in the English Channel, Northeast immediately sent engineers to examine the steering gear on the three sister ships of the J.B. John (none of which are owned by World Oil). This examination disclosed that on two of the three ships the metal studs which secured the flange showed microscopic cracks indicative of metal fatigue. Northeast immediately replaced the studs on all three ships, and agreed to reimburse the ship operators for the lost revenues associated with each ship being out of service for three days. While each of these agreements contained a confidentiality clause, pursuant to which the ship operator agreed not to disclose either the discovery of the cracks or Northeast's payments to them, these agreements would be no protection against discovery by World aimed at Northeast. Thus you are anxious to settle this matter promptly, and are willing to participate in a mini-trial as a means to that end.

In discussing the terms of a possible settlement with CEO Fay Austin, she indicated her willingness to go to $300 million if that was necessary. Actually, though, Ms. Austin's preference is to settle this case by providing World with ships rather than cash. This may not be easy to do as the world oil market is not good, and it is unlikely that World is planning to add to its fleet in the immediate future. World might also be reluctant to accept ships built by Northeast in settlement of a claim based on faulty ship construction by Northeast.

Still, a settlement of that type has such clear advantages for Northeast that Ms. Austin is determined to propose it. Initially, the depressed world oil market has led to a similar downturn in the demand for tankers, with the result that Northeast will soon be forced to begin laying off some of its experienced employees. Doing so is harmful to the business because the best employees tend to find work elsewhere, and will not return to Northeast when business picks up and Northeast needs additional crews. This leads to both delays and increased training costs. If Northeast can settle this dispute by providing ships, not cash, to World, it can avoid such layoffs, a clear advantage to it.

Northeast prefers not to build additional ships in the 200,000 ton range (the size of the J.B. John), but to focus on ships of 100,000 tons or less. The cost to Northeast of building a 100,000 ton tanker ranges from $100-150 million, depending on the speed with which the ship is constructed. (The price difference is primarily due to the increased costs of labor and material for a rush job.) Typically, a ship of this size can be built at a cost to Northeast of $100 million (including all overhead, but no profit) in 24 months, $150 million in 18 months. Northeast normally charges the purchaser two times its construction costs; if construction costs are $100 million, sales price will be $200 million; if construction costs are $150 million, sales price will be $300 million.

Ms. Austin has authorized you to explore the possibility of settling World's claim by providing ships, rather than cash, up to a maximum out-of-pocket cost to Northeast of $300 million. To be sure, Northeast will have to forego its normal profit on any ships that it provides to World at cost, but in the absence of any other demand for ships, that is purely a theoretical loss, not a real one.

Furthermore, to deal with World's likely reluctance to accept additional ships built by Northeast, Ms. Austin is prepared, if World insists, to give an unconditional warranty on the steering gear for five years, provided that Northeast can keep an engineer on each boat to insure that World is performing the proper maintenance on the steering gear. The two companies have been doing business for many years, with no prior problems, so World should generally be satisfied with Northeast's work, and such a warranty should set World at ease with regard to potential steering gear problems.

EXERCISE 5.2: WORLD OIL COMPANY v. NORTHEAST SHIPBUILDING

Confidential Information for World Oil Company

The $1.2 billion judgment was a major blow, even for a company as large as World (FY 1990 gross income = $10 billion). As a result of that judgment World has a cash flow problem that is particularly serious at this time in view of the weak world market for oil, and World's aging tanker fleet, much of which will have to be replaced in the near future. Happily, the demand for oil shows signs of increasing, particularly in some of the countries where World has a strong presence. Thus, World sees significant profit opportunities ahead, particularly if it can obtain the funds necessary to replace at least three, preferably four, of its obsolete vessels within the next 18-24 months with modern supertankers in the 100,000 ton range (about half the size of the J.B. John). The lowest bid World has received on such ships is $325 million if delivered within 18 months, $225 million if delivered within 24 months. (The price difference is primarily due to the increased costs of labor and material for a rush job.)

The import of all this for you is that World wants to walk away from this litigation with at least $875 million, the amount necessary to purchase three supertankers, two to be delivered in 18 months, the other in 24 months. Normally World would seek bank funding for such a purchase, but its current financial situation is such that two financial institutions have already told it that they would not, at this time, provide financing for ship purchases.

Your goal at trial, then, would be to persuade a jury that Northeast was at least 75% responsible for the grounding of the J.B. John, thus liable to World for $900 million. You will seek to persuade Northeast at a mini-trial that its potential damages are so great that a $900 million settlement would be a bargain.

There is, however, one difficulty with this promising scenario. Your research has turned up certain events connected with the grounding of the J.B. John of which Northeast is unaware, but which would surely come out in full-scale discovery. You have learned, though Northeast has not -- at least yet -- why over three hours passed between the time Captain Griffin called for tug assistance in the English Channel and the time a tow line was attached from the tug Superior to the J.B. John. Most of that time, during which the J.B. John was drifting ever closer to the French coast, was consumed in negotiations between Captain Griffin and the captain of the Superior. Apparently, Captain Griffin refused to accept the standard Lloyd's Open Form Salvage Contract, instead insisting on a towing contract that would have been more advantageous to World. We think Captain Griffin's judgment was doubtful; a jury looking at it after the fact might find it appalling. Thus, we are not anxious for this case to go to a jury.

In sum, you are anxious to settle this case before trial, and see a mini-trial as potentially useful in achieving that goal. In negotiating the terms of the mini-trial there are two procedural issues that concern you. First, you would rather not bring in someone like a former judge to serve as a neutral advisor in the mini-trial. The reason for this position is your concern that having a neutral advisor will transform the whole procedure from a structured negotiation into a real trial. The lawyers will spend so much time trying to score points with the neutral advisor that they will lose sight of their real task, which is to persuade the business people.

Secondly, CEO Blaine Kelly wants to be the World Oil representative at the mini-trial. The sinking of the J.B. John was a major financial loss for World Oil, and Mr. Kelly is determined to make certain that Northeast bears its fair share of that loss.

EXERCISE 5.2:   WORLD OIL COMPANY v. NORTHEAST SHIPBUILDING

Teaching Notes

In debriefing Part a, students should be asked first whether they were able to come to an agreement to do a minitrial and what their agreement consists of. There is likely to be a fair amount of variation in how students deal with various procedural components, such as discovery, presentation format, identity of business participants, role of neutral advisor, and so forth. The point to keep in mind here is that there is no one correct mini-trial format. The flexibility of the mini-trial is one of its strengths. What counts is how well the parties to the dispute deal with the issues that they believe are important in this particular case. In this respect, students may be asked how well the mini-trial agreement reflects their overall negotiation strategy. Did they accomplish their objectives in this meeting? Did they accomplish those objectives while maintaining the relationship with the other side that they want to have?

One point that should be addressed in the discussion of Part a is the identity of World's business representative at the mini-trial. CEO Blaine Kelly wants to play that role, but an astute Northeast team should consider whether, as a result of the media criticism of Kelly in this case, he is too emotionally involved to be able to negotiate a settlement.

Part a also contains an ethical issue that should be addressed. Each side has a potential smoking gun of which the other side is unaware. How did students deal with this issue in discussing discovery and the facts of the dispute? How many found out about the other side's bad facts, or are likely to find out about them given whatever arrangements they made for pre-mini-trial discovery? Is there an ethical obligation to draft discovery rules that will enable the other side to discover damaging material in your files prior to the mini-trial?

Part b is designed to provide students the opportunity to experience what it is like to participate in a minitrial. In debriefing, students may be asked to compare the advocate's role in a mini-trial with the advocate's role in negotiation, mediation, and adjudication. Students might be asked: What were you trying to do in your presentation? What were your goals? Who was your audience? What would you do differently in a straight mediation? At a trial? Do you feel that the mini-trial provided sufficient opportunity to get your side of the case across? Does the mini-trial format meet the minimal criteria of acceptable dispute resolution? What changes would you recommend in the minitrial?

If a neutral advisor is used, students who play this role can be asked to comment on the process from the role of the neutral. How did the neutral advisors see their role? Were the neutral advisors comfortable in the role assigned to them? How does the role of neutral advisor differ from that of mediator, arbitrator, and judge?

EXERCISE 5.3:   THE DAILY BUGLE

Confidential Information for the Daily Bugle Editor

Terry Ives is usually a good reporter, but this time he made two errors. First, he did not check county property records but relied instead on a tenant's statement that Dr. Roark owned the building. Second, when Dr. Roark called to explain the error and asked for a retraction, Ives responded merely, "I stand on the First Amendment." When Dr. Roark reached you, he was angry. You had not spoken to Ives yet and therefore just refused the retraction.

The statement about the Fire Marshall's office is accurate but you must protect the identity of this valuable source. You have other concerns. It would be embarrassing to retract or to have the reporter's carelessness revealed. Also, if you settle for a large amount, it will attract other defamation suits. Already you are sued about twice a month. At the same time, the newspaper's income is down and the insurance policy requires the Daily Bugle to cover the first $100,000 of the litigation costs. (This includes attorney's fees, amounts paid in settlement of litigation, and amounts paid pursuant to a judgment.)

Dr. Roark is a well-respected physician who serves on the boards of several charitable foundations. As far as you know, he has never sought publicity. Terry Ives has mentioned Dr. Roark once before in an article dealing with his youngest son's involvement with drugs.

EXERCISE 5.3:   THE DAILY BUGLE

Confidential Information for Dr. Roark's Lawyer

Dr. Roark sought you out because of your reputation as a litigator. His greatest concern is his reputation. He wants the Daily Bugle to correct the story. Both the newspaper reporter, Terry Ives, and the editor were very cold and uninterested when he called to explain the error. Hence, he also thinks the newspaper should be taught a lesson by paying damages.

Incidentally, there may be a basis for punitive damages because Ives has once before written a story about Dr. Roark when his youngest son was arrested for drug possession, possibly providing evidence of a grudge. You do not know yet what investigation was done by Ives or who were his sources.

You know very little about alternative dispute resolution processes.

EXERCISE 5.3:   THE DAILY BUGLE

Teaching Notes

There are three roles for this exercise - lawyer for Dr. Roark, lawyer for the Daily Bugle, and Charles Warner, editor of the Daily Bugle. But there are no confidential instructions for the Daily Bugle's lawyer; he or she has only the general instructions contained in the text. In Part I of the exercise, the lawyer for the newspaper interviews the editor to learn more about the facts concerning the alleged libel and to advise the client about the ingredients of a successful libel action (tortious defamatory statement, resulting in tangible injury; absence of truth, which would be a complete defense). The parties then canvass the desires of the editor in so far as they may pertain to various forms of alternative dispute resolution. This part can be done out of class.

Part II consists of the subsequent meeting between the two lawyers, going over the facts and culminating in a discussion of a possible choice of an appropriate form of ADR. Options explored, in addition to litigation, might include negotiation, mediation, arbitration, minitrial and summary jury trial. Litigation and arbitration both involve binding decisions that are difficult to predict; this is particularly true of a jury. Hence that path entails large expense and large risk. Mediation, though theoretically very suited to such a case, may be difficult to achieve here in light of the defendant's unwillingness to issue a retraction, and his anxiousness to stand firm against what he regards as predatory plaintiffs. But perhaps something short of a full retraction can be worked out.

A summary jury trial may be a good way to get an idea of how a jury would react to this case, but it is unclear whether the case is presently "ripe" for such a presentation, without additional discovery. Finally a minitrial should be explored since it might not only facilitate settlement as a result of the information exchange but also provide a helpful prediction of the likely outcome by the minitrial presider. Of course both the summary jury trial and the minitrial prediction pose a risk. For if they come out clearly in favor of one party, that party may harden its position and thus make settlement more difficult. All these issues can be discussed after the various teams have completed their negotiation; it may also be useful to have one team do the negotiation in front of the class as a basis for focusing the class discussion.

Additional materials on the libel and ADR aspects of this problem can be found in the extensive Instructor's Manual that accompanies the videotape.

CHAPTER 6 – COURTS AND ADR

A. Questions

6.1 This problem concerns a collateral order, not a judgment as in *U.S. Bancorp Mortgage and Hanovers Trust Company*. Arguably, a district court order regarding sanctions against an attorney have little value as precedent. Still, in *Keller v. Mobil Corporation,* the Second Circuit ruled that the district court could appropriately refuse to grant the parties' joint motion to vacate the sanctions award which was premised on the grounds that their settlement was conditioned on it. The court explained, "The public interest in having rules of procedure obeyed is at least as important as the public interest in encouraging the settlement of disputes." 55 F.3d at 98. Ultimately, the appellate court vacated the sanction order on the merits, ruling that the attorney's conduct was not vexatious.

The district court has discretion to grant vacatur, so arguably the mediator does not act improperly in assisting in the settlement conditioned on vacatur. In this case, the district judge apparently erred, and the settlement might have saved the appellate court the trouble of considering the meritorious appeal. On the other hand, why should the courts invest resources in paying mediators who will seek settlement at the cost of losing judicial rulings?

6.2 Admissibility would present substantial problems. An omitted portion of the SPIDR report (p. 385) states:

> It appears unwise to permit transmission of rejected court-annexed arbitration awards to the court or jury. First, the court-annexed arbitration presentations are likely to be summary in nature and the record less comprehensive than in litigation. The court or jury may give the awards undue weight. Second, one purpose of this arbitration is to provide information for settlement negotiations. The procedure will have more credibility as a settlement device if the arbitration award is not transmitted to the court or jury.

6.3 The undesirability of the kind of severe sanction imposed in the cited case is evident. As stated in another omitted portion of the SPIDR report (p. 262):

> If the amount [of the penalty] is uncertain, such as in shifted attorney's fees for a failure to improve upon the award, few individual parties can afford to take the risk [of filing de novo in court]. Further, for fixed amount disincentives, settlement rates do not seem to be substantially higher when the disincentives are higher. Thus it would be wise to place a cap on the amount of the disincentive. The amount of the cap should not be so great as to result in a disadvantage based on the relative wealth of the litigants and should not be disproportionate to the value of the case.

Quite evidently the sanction imposed in the case described in 6.3 does not meet this standard.

Aside from initial policy objections to such a sanction, how might it be attacked in a specific case? First, one needs to examine the applicable local rule to see whether it authorizes the kind of sizable sanction imposed here. Then, one needs to question whether the court had the authority to issue such a local rule. In Tiedel v. Northwestern Michigan College, 865 F.2d 88 (6th Cir. 1988), a penalty of $47,000 in costs and attorney's fees was overturned because it did not come within the rule-making power possessed by federal courts. There may also be constitutional objections even if the rule and statutory authority are clear.

6.4   The word "mediation" is clearly inapt for the procedure outlined. The program is very close to court-annexed arbitration in that it is a hearing process resulting in an award that becomes final unless there is an appeal. As with many COA programs, the Michigan program also provides for disincentives to appeal.

The principal difference between this program and standard court-annexed arbitration is that typically "Michigan mediation" entails less formal hearings without witnesses. Rather, the attorneys tend to make a summary presentation. The informality of the proceeding is further underscored by the fact that the three neutrals may attempt to mediate the case in the course of the presentations, if they deem that to be appropriate.

6.5   The principal design issues are:

1. Should all tort cases or only certain types (e.g., motor vehicle, malpractice etc.) be included in the program?

2. If all types of torts are included, should there be any exceptions (e.g., environmental torts, civil rights type torts etc.)? What procedure should be provided for opting out?

3. Should there be a maximum jurisdictional amount for the cases to be eligible for the program?

4. When should cases go into COA?

5. What types of sanctions, if any, should be imposed?

There are no definitive answers to any of these questions. But here are some possible responses:

1. and 2.   Although there are some programs extending to specific types of torts (e.g., motor vehicle torts), most court-annexed programs do not distinguish among cases by the type of tort. Hence, at the outset all types of cases might be included, subject to one or two specific exclusions (such as civil rights torts). Alternatively, the statute could provide for no stated exclusions, with the burden being put on any particular party who sought to opt out.

3. Most programs have an upper dollar limit ranging from $25,000 to $150,000. But it is not clear why cases above that amount are not suited for the program; perhaps they, too, could be handled by requests to opt out if there were other disqualifying factors besides the amount in controversy, such as great complexity, as in some environmental tort cases.

4. Since the COA program often is a means to settlement it seems sensible to have the arbitration fairly soon after the pleadings are complete (e.g., 60-90 days thereafter). If the case warrants more extensive discovery, the parties can always move to extend the time, provided the statute allows for such discretionary postponements.

5. The sentences quoted in the answers to questions 6.2 and 6.3 provide suitable guidelines for sanctions.

6.6   a. Although summary jury trials do not usually involve close credibility questions, there is no reason why they might not. Obviously, if a case turned on extended testimony by several witnesses whose credibility was in question, a summary jury trial -- as the name suggests -- would not be appropriate. But if there are one or two key witnesses whose credibility is sought to be determined by the jury, the SJT might well be a suitable device.

b. Such a case was in fact successfully handled through a SJT by Judge Richard Enslen of the Western District of Michigan. One of the lawyers first suggested picking a "best" case, as well as a "worst" one, and one in-between, and then submitting those three to three juries in order to obtain some guidelines for the resolution of the other cases. But after some discussions it was decided to pick just one case and submit that to two different juries. One verdict came in for $2.8 million; the other was for the defendant. Following extensive settlement discussions, the case was settled within a few hours. See 2 Alternative Dispute Resolution Report 46, 145 (1988) for a report of this case. The National Institute for Dispute Resolution in Washington has also prepared a videotape of this case. See 3 *id.* 110 (1989). Thus, even in a very complex series of cases, an SJT may help provide the parameters for settlement.

c. This would seem to be an ideal case for a summary jury trial. There are likely to be intermixed questions of law and fact as to which a jury reaction will be helpful. If the case would be likely to take two or more weeks to try, the possible time saving will be well worth the added effort. Indeed in an earlier videotape made by Judge Enslen for the Federal Judicial Center, such a case is one of three shown successfully disposed of by SJT.

6.7   Although there are some occasional intersections between Allen's comments and the SPIDR report, they are in essence a Rashomon-like example of people viewing the same thing – mandatory ADR – from their own very different perspectives. The SPIDR report seeks to present a carefully balanced policy analysis of mandatory ADR, stressing both its strengths and weaknesses. Allen views the world from the vantage point of a traditional litigator who is a true believer in the full-scale adversary model, and skeptical about any departures therefrom. Of course, it is important to note that Allen does not oppose voluntary ADR, so the issue narrows to why he opposes mandatory ADR. His reasons seem to come down to four: 1) That it deprives individuals of "real" trials (i.e., by judge or jury); 2) that the parties would settle anyway in most instances; 3) that the courts can handle the caseloads; and 4) that the parties do not save as the result of ADR.

Much of this book is devoted to questioning the first reason. Some cases, to be sure, should be handled by full-scale trial. Others, we believe, are more effectively and efficiently dealt with by other methods of dispute resolution. See particularly chapters 1 and 5C. The SPIDR report does not go into these reasons because it is rather narrowly addressed to the question of the case for and against mandatory ADR. The SPIDR report does discuss whether court caseloads are producing delays or party costs are reduced, but indicates that party costs should be a factor to consider (Recommendation 1). An increase in party costs as the result of mediation then might be a contraindication to requiring participation.

One's response to the suggested proposal of mandatory mediation for all contested child custody cases as well as mandatory arbitration for all money claim cases under $50,000 would depend greatly on other circumstances. Such programs have of course been widely adopted. California imposes mandatory mediation in contested child custody cases and Maine in all contested cases involving children; mandatory arbitration for money claim cases under certain jurisdictional amounts is now utilized in many states. As pointed out in the text (particularly the SPIDR report) such programs have to be carefully designed and adequately financed. As indicated in the response to Question 6.5, the design issues involve a number of subsidiary questions, such as timing, staffing, and opt-out procedures. But if those concerns are appropriately addressed, the two programs in question may be very useful. Note, incidentally, that Allen's statement that there is no evidence of reduction of costs is somewhat oversimplified. See the Note on Empirical Data, pp. 384-385.

6.8   There are at least three serious concerns about mandatorily referring cases to outside providers: 1) The general concerns about quality control (see pp. 388-389) become particularly acute here, as was noted by the SPIDR Commission on Qualifications; 2) There is a real danger of cronyism, particularly where cases are referred to retired judges who were formerly members of the referring court. In an omitted portion, the SPIDR Report (p. 385 of text) recommends against referral to individual providers in routine cases. This concern was noted in Florida which originally permitted such referral; as a result of a recent amendment, parties now have a choice of outside providers; 3) There is also a concern about costs. If the costs of the referral are paid by the court, this concern is eliminated except insofar as it involves the general question of efficient use of public funds. But if, as is often the case, the cases are mandatorily referred to a private provider with the parties sharing the cost, then there is a real concern (see SPIDR Report, p. 389). It would seem that in such circumstances there should be a maximum charge set by the court, unless the parties both opt to use another higher priced provider.

6.9   This is a more or less rhetorical question. As stated, facial challenges to mandatory programs have generally been rejected. Where such programs have been invalidated, it has been on peripheral grounds such as the way the program is administered. For further details, see the two references cited in the question.

6.10   The arguments for permitting mandatory summary jury trial are basically similar to those canvassed in the SPIDR report (p. 385). But there is this added point: since the procedure depends so much on the willingness of the parties to make it work, one factor a judge should take into account is that if at least one of the parties resists the procedure, it is probably less likely to be successful. Nevertheless, a sophisticated judge would want to take a closer look at the situation. Sometimes a lawyer's objection is simply to anything new and different; in that case the judge might give that consideration little weight. But if the reasons are related to the nature of the specific case (as in Strandell), then the judge might well reach a different conclusion. Similarly, the reason suggested by the cited North Carolina study, which turned on a local lack of sophistication in case management, may well be appropriate in that setting.

6.11   The first question is whether this case comes under the statute at all, since it concerns the termination of a long-term relationship. But perhaps this is too narrow a reading. By analogy it would mean that divorce cases also would not be subject to the statute, even though those cases have been widely regarded as appropriate for mediation.

If the case does come under the statute, the next question is whether the court should disturb the mediator's finding of noncompliance with the statutory "duty to mediate in good faith." The parties disagree on this issue. Hence a key witness will be the mediator. But at least one court, interpreting its local privilege statute, concluded that such evidence could not be compelled. See Minnesota Bureau of Mediation Services v. Spellacy (Minn. Ct. App. 1988), cited in Rogers and McEwen, § 7:06.

In the absence of testimony by the mediator, how can the court resolve the threshold procedural question (i.e., whether there has been good faith compliance)? Courts generally have tended to find sufficient compliance with such vaguely worded statutes even in cases where one party's conduct was described as hostile, acrimonious and truculent. See, e.g., Graham v. Baker, 447 N.W. 2d 397 (Iowa 1989); Schulz v. Nienhus, 448 N.W. 2d 655 (Wisc. 1989) and Rogers and McEwen, op. cit. One reason for this tendency is the difficulty of crafting a suitable sanction. A specific order to mediate in good faith is unlikely to change the situation. The court can certainly award the injured party its costs in the abortive mediation, but that is really only a minimal remedy.

This problem illustrates the difficulty of policing a "good faith" requirement. In the present case one can see why Martin was angry and wanted to get on with his demand that the security deposit be refunded. If there had been no claim of damage by the landlord, perhaps Martin's argument would be stronger, for then there would be very little to mediate. Here, however, one might well imagine that an effective mediation could have resolved all the issues in the case. Still, if one of the parties does not want to make mediation work, then it is very difficult to compel him or her to do so. Thus the court should probably overrule the procedural objection and get on with a hearing of the merits (i.e., the damage, if any, that warrants retention of all or part of the security deposit).

For the reasons indicated above, statutes that import good faith requirements are problematic. The SPIDR Report came out against such requirements. However, the notion of requiring an attempt at mediation in all cases involving long-term relationships between the parties seems worth exploring. Those are the cases in which mediation may be most effective because of the power of mediation to explore fully the relationship between the parties. Hence, provided it is made clear what is expected by way of participation in mediation (e.g., showing up at one session, coming up with an offer and listening to the other side's offer) and the sanctions, if any, for violation of the duty (e.g., payment of the other party's costs of participating in the aborted mediation session), such a requirement may make a good deal of sense.

6.12   This problem is the arbitration counterpart to problem 6.11 (i.e., it raises the question of what remedy, if any, is appropriate for failure to participate "meaningfully" in mandatory court-annexed arbitration). The answer to this question can be broken down into two parts:

1.   Did Friar participate "meaningfully" in the arbitration? Certainly Friar did not do what normally would be expected of a party in a court-annexed arbitration. He did not even bring his lawyer or himself to cross-examine any of the plaintiff's witnesses. Therefore, the arbitrator really had no choice but to enter a decision in favor of the plaintiff, assuming there was adequate evidence to support such a decision.

But this is not a case, such as some that have arisen, where one party perversely refused to participate in the arbitration. There is some plausibility to Friar's argument that in a small case like this there are duplicative costs to preparing in effect for two trials, even though experienced participants in court-annexed arbitration indicate that much of the preparation for the arbitration is "recoverable" in the trial, if there is one. Hence Friar perhaps made the wrong choice and should have put his eggs in the arbitration, rather than the court, basket. In any event, whether for good reason or not, his failure to take any real part in the arbitration proceeding made that proceeding a waste of time for the plaintiff. That brings us to the next question.

2.   If there was no meaningful participation, what is the appropriate sanction? Unlike some of the prior cases, here there is a specific rule putting the parties on notice that where a party refuses to participate "meaningfully" in the arbitration a range of sanctions including dismissal can be invoked. (Incidentally, the rule quoted in the problem is patterned after that adopted in the United States District Court for the Eastern District of Pennsylvania, following an earlier decision barring a litigant from exercising his right to de novo trial in a much more extreme situation where the defendant did not show up at all and perhaps had no claim in any event, <u>New England Merchants National Bank v. Hughes</u>, 556 F.Supp. 712 (E.D. Pa. 1983)). Under a broad rule such as that quoted in the problem, what are the possible sanctions that might be imposed? There are essentially four: a) to tax the defaulting party for the costs needlessly incurred by the other party in the arbitration; b) to admit the arbitration award in the subsequent trial if that is not expressly barred by other rules or provisions - so that the injured party (Damon) gets some benefit from participating in the arbitration; c) to dismiss the defaulting party's right

to a subsequent trial, as was done in Hughes; and d) to prevent the defaulting party from using any argument in court that was not presented in the arbitration.

The courts have gone all over the lot in past cases, depending partly on the extent of the defaulting party's participation and the prior notice he had of the possible consequences. See Harvard Law Review, 1990. In this case, for the reasons previously given, dismissal would seem to be too extreme a sanction. Indeed some cases have pointed out that such a sanction might raise constitutional questions based on an impairment of a party's right of access to court. In a case like the present, the courts have tended to use the first approach of imposing cost sanctions. Provided these also include attorney's fees, which are often the major cost item, that may well be the fairest result. Admitting the arbitration in the court proceeding, even if specifically allowed, might be too favorable to Damon in that the court or jury may assume that he should prevail, even though Friar's arguments have not really been heard. And while the fourth choice might be theoretically the ideal one, it may be difficult to apply in practice. How would one apply that theory to Friar's otherwise right to cross-examine Damon's witnesses in the court proceeding? Barring him altogether from doing so may be too severe a sanction for action that, though misguided, was not totally unreasonable under the circumstances.

It might be noted in passing that although the present problem does not raise the issue, in some of the past cases the defaulting party appears to have made a tactical choice not to participate in the arbitration for fear of giving away his or her case. Nonparticipation based on that ground seems less justified; for, if a court-annexed arbitration scheme is to work at all, it cannot allow individuals simply to default because they want to preserve their case for the court proceeding. Of course, it would be difficult to police any party who put on some of his case but held back other parts for the court hearing. For such situations a rule like the fourth sanction adverted to above might be ideally suited.

6.13   It is difficult to see how the proposal improves upon mandatory nonbinding arbitration with similar sanctions. Moreover, on its face the proposal, unlike court-ordered arbitration, applies to all civil actions, which may be questionable. And of course it raises all the familiar questions about the legality of imposing sanctions, except that here the sanctions are imposed not for refusing to accept an arbitration award but rather for refusing to go to arbitration in the first place – a very different situation. Also the fact that sanctions are discretionary with the court may make them fairly biteless.

This proposal can be usefully compared with one put forward by Rosenberg, Rient and Rowe in their article *Expenses: The Roadblock to Justice*, 20 JUDGES J. 16-19 (No. 3, Summer 1981). That proposal consists of a mandatory sizing up of the claim by a neutral panel, followed by required settlement offers, with sanctions for unreasonable refusal to accept such offers, as judged by the subsequent court decision. That package seems to make much more sense than this one, which seeks to induce litigants into arbitration but then doesn't give the customary finality to the arbitration award.

6.14   Yes. For the reasons pointed out in the SPIDR report, as well as the excerpt cited in the question, recommendations by the mediator can add an undesirable element of coercion to what should be a voluntary process. They may also lead to diminished candor by parties who know that particular disclosures may ultimately be held against them through the mediator's recommendation to the court. Finally, such recommendations raise constitutional questions, as pointed out in the McLaughlin case cited in footnote 17 of the SPIDR report. See pp. 389-390.

6.15   This proposal, which has been used in the past in the District of Columbia and is presently in effect in some jurisdictions in Oregon, makes a good deal of sense. If one party strongly believes that mediation may be productive in the case, that seems enough reason to make the other party show up for at least one mediation session, barring the absence of special circumstances. Perhaps the proposal should be modified to add at the end thereof some phrase such as the following: "unless the court for good cause shown, concludes that mediation would be inappropriate in the case." That clause would be intended to cover cases such as a challenge to a constitutional provision where the court would have concluded in the first instance not to send the case to mediation. Arguably the fact that one party nevertheless wishes to submit the case to mediation may not be sufficient in such a case to warrant ordering the other party to participate in a mediation session. Moreover, the court should also have the discretion, after hearing the objecting party's reasons, not to order the case to mediation. Compare for example the Strandell case and the answer to question 6.10.

A variant of the proposal in 6.15 is one that does not mandate a particular ADR process but rather requires both parties to discuss what ADR, if any, would be suitable in the case, and then obligates each party to submit a memorandum to the court explaining the process(es) chosen, and if none is chosen, the reasons therefor.

6.16   The primary reason put forward by Mr. Marshall for opposing mandatory mediation seems a bit unrealistic. Of course, if parties and attorneys were fully informed about the pros and cons of different styles of handling conflicts, then perhaps there would be less argument for mandatory mediation, although even then there may be other factors at work. See particularly some of the issues canvassed in chapter 11A.

Mr. Marshall's notion that "the costliest process of the law cannot be applied to every single case, without some consideration of the importance of the issues" seems sound. The question is how one can best implement that principle. He thinks the answer is "public education in the pros and cons of different styles of handling conflicts," concededly a desirable long-term objective. But what should be done in the interim? And, as pointed out in chapter 11A of the text, even if there were pervasive knowledge of the pros and cons of various forms of ADR, there are nevertheless economic and psychological factors that lead parties and their attorneys to avoid using them. Mr. Marshall does not really address those obstacles that have led some jurisdictions to implement mandatory programs.

Note, incidentally, Marshall's interesting observation that diverting cases to various forms of ADR should not be done on a case-by-case basis but rather on the basis of a general rule. Many experts take the contrary view, believing that while individual decisions necessarily import some element of judgment and discretion, that is the only fair way of taking account of the infinite variety of individual cases. Still, for reasons of economy and efficiency, many ADR programs are of a categorical nature (i.e., they refer a whole category of cases to ADR). However, these programs include an opt-out procedure for individual cases that may nevertheless be unsuitable for the mandated ADR process.

6.17   One might argue that all standards for formal accountability of mediators could be eliminated in the staff model. This could be an important cost differential. In North Carolina and Florida, regulatory commissions already monitor the work of court-certified mediators. The Florida commission reviews grievances and issues advisory reports on standards, much like the regulatory groups for licensed professions like lawyers. Attention would still need to be given to assuring that the mediators are qualified under all models. Also, procedural protections, such as the right to bring legal counsel would seem to be equally needed under all models.

6.18   Chernick canvasses well most of the arguments against private judging. The basic question is the one posed by Raven in the instant question – what is the effect of systems of private justice on the public justice system? The advocates of private justice claim that it will improve the public system because it will drain off many difficult cases that the public system will not have to deal with. But against that consideration one has to weigh the risk of draining off of some of the best judges, as well as a resulting loss of push by some of society's key players to improving the public system because many of their disputes are now being handled by the private system. If one could be assured that there would be no adverse impact on the public system, then much might be said for such parallel systems of justice, in that surely one effect of the private system would be to provide some competition for the public system, much along the lines of the relationship between Federal Express and the U.S. mail system.

6.19   The second question seems the more important one – whether the courts should regularly shift the expense of litigation and the decision-making authority for parties who have selected the public process. By analogy, Federal Rule of Civil Procedure 53(b) provides that "reference to a master shall be the exception and not the rule" and requires a showing of the exceptional circumstances. Perhaps implicit in the more limited nature of Rule 53 is the fear that courts will give up their functions as adjudicators, that even greater costs will be shifted to the parties, and that cronyism is more likely in routine referrals.

At the same time, shifting decision-making for discovery seems less troublesome than for the adjudication on the merits.

6.20   The California reference statute can be amended as the policy debate over its effect on the courts develops. In contrast, a ruling like *Gateway Technologies* leaves the matter entirely to the parties. It remains to be seen whether the prospect of appellate review will result in less or more work for the courts.

CHAPTER 7 – CONFIDENTIALITY

A.   Introduction

The introductory material might be reviewed in the context of a fact pattern, such as Exercise 3.2, "A Shortage of Low Income Housing." What are SMHA's various interests in confidentiality? What should emerge from the class discussion is a list of confidentiality concerns regarding:

1. Public disclosure of what was said during the mediation session;
2. Perhaps testimony at Congressional or other hearings, voluntarily or pursuant to subpoena;
3. Admission of testimony about the mediation discussions at trial, if the matter is not settled; and
4. Possibly, disclosure during the discovery process if the matter is not settled.

What types of laws provide some protection regarding each of these concerns? Here the list might become a table:

	FRE 408	Agreement	Protective O.	Privilege
public disclosure		x*	x**	
Congr. subpoena			x**	x
admissibility at trial	x***		x**	x
discovery			x****	x

With these notes:

*The agreement might provide an incentive not to disclose, because of potential civil liability, but, of course, the tenants might still do it.

**A protective order by agreement could be sought since the matter is pending before a court. However, another court may set aside a protective order if lacking in justification or if the need for the information outweighs the need for privacy.

***FRE 408 and comparable provisions in most (but not all) states exclude the compromise discussions (not just offers and responses to offers) if offered to show liability or amount. But part of the discussions might be admitted to show bias or some other purpose.

****If the tenants' lawyer later seeks to depose the mediator, SMHA's lawyer might ask the court to issue a protective order because the burden on the mediation process is great and the tenant has little need for the information, since most would not be admissible at trial. This argument, based on Federal Rule of Civil Procedure 26(b), has occasionally been persuasive, but not always. Compare Bottaro v. Hatton Associates, 96 F.R.D. 158 (E.D.N.Y. 1982) (compromise discussions not subject to discovery when requesting party cannot show how could be used) with Bennett v. La Pere, 112 F.R.D. 136 (D.R.I. 1986) (rejecting Bottaro).

The table now shows the inadequate protection provided by any existing devices except the privilege.

B.   Questions

7.1   The court notes a Congressional recognition that labor peace serves the nation's interests and that federal mediation promotes labor peace. It then notes that the federal agency has consistently maintained that testimony by mediators will interfere with the perceived neutrality of the FMCS. (One quote mentions a broader interest, but the court's own discussion does not emphasize that.) A contradiction to the privilege is the need for tie-breaking testimony about whether an agreement was reached.

The court seems to give little weight to the need to promote frank discussion or to attract potential users who are wary of publicity. The arguments for recognition of a privilege in the context of a community mediation program – protection of the naive party and encouragement of volunteer mediators – were not relevant to the facts of Joseph Macaluso. Further, the opinion provides little guidance as to how the court would rule regarding testimony by the parties, assuming that they objected in a timely way, since the parties had already testified.

7.2   The court may make a determination based on the testimony of the parties, but, without the tie-breaking testimony of a mediator, the plaintiffs who have the burden to establish the oral agreement may fail with more frequency.

7.3   There is no comparable federal statute providing that mediation by non-FMCS mediators is an essential element of labor peace. Arguably, though, industrial peace also depends on the work of private mediators. However, the public interest in preserving the perception of neutrality as to an individual mediator may be lower because other mediators will be available. The judge in this case granted the protective order in a ruling issued from the bench, declining to recognize a privilege explicitly but doing so in practical effect. The court reasoned that the parties' expectations of confidentiality should be preserved to encourage mediation of cases like this, and that the need for the discovery was outweighed by these interests.

Is that rationale applicable to the mediation of all disputes or only to the mediation of labor disputes? Arguably the latter. What is the public interest in settlement of disputes involving the delivery of widgets? Is it relieving congestion in the courts? Improving the quality of life for those dealing with widgets? Educating the public about better ways to resolve disputes? Others listed in Part B?

7.4   The weighing process differs when the mediator makes a public disclosure after an implicit or explicit agreement to keep discussions confidential. A party's expectations have been breached and there is no countervailing need for evidence. Absent such a public interest in disclosure (see Question 3.31), courts should have little difficulty in deciding that the breach warrants damages.

7.5   The purpose of this question is to focus on a brief portion of the Mack Truck argument concerning this issue. As the judge points out, the essential elements of an oral agreement would have to be established as well as whether an agreement was reached. Thus, the parties would never know at the time of the mediation whether everything said might be admitted into evidence on the issue of whether an agreement was reached. If the privilege does not have such an exception, however, the parties may have to assume that an agreement is unlikely to be enforced unless reduced to writing and signed. Is this too heavy a price to pay to preserve the expectation of confidentiality?

7.6   Arguably, all three of these provisions run the risk suggested by the court in Mack Truck, that what starts as a question about one aspect of the mediation may be broadened when the witness is asked to explain. Also, a party would not know at the beginning of the mediation whether a claim of bad faith or mediator malfeasance made after the mediation would result in disclosure of all that was said. It may indeed be a choice between assuring the parties of mediation confidentiality and enforcement of these provisions. Provisions such as those listed in a through c are the exception rather than the rule.

Therefore, students may argue that there are other means to achieve quality control and that assurance of confidentiality should be given priority. Nonetheless, lawmakers occasionally have made exceptions to the privilege in order to cover grievances against mediators, enforcement of compelled participation in good faith, and enforcement of oral agreements reached in mediation. Fla. Stat. § 44.102 (exception for grievances against mediators); Mont. Code Ann. §§ 29-71-2401(4)(c), 39-71-2410 (exception to show failure to comply with mandatory requirements); N.D.Cent. Code §§ 31-04-11 (exception if validity of mediated agreement is in issue).

7.7   It is unclear whether the parties or the mediator or both hold the privilege. If it is to preserve the mediator's reputation for neutrality, it should be held by the mediator. But, if the primary purpose is to protect the parties' expectation of confidentiality, the parties should be deemed the holders and the mediator should testify if they both waive the privilege. The latter arguments ("the standard in the industry... is so clear that confidentiality is assumed....") were made with the most force in the Mack Truck argument, while the mediator's reputation for neutrality was emphasized in Joseph Macaluso.

In Castellano, the mediator was subpoenaed for a discovery deposition as part of a criminal action against Castellano for attempted first degree murder. Absent a privilege, the defendant would be able to find out whether the mediator would corroborate his claim that the victim had threatened him during the mediation session, thus helping to establish his contention that he acted in self-defense.

Thus, the need for the testimony is much greater in Castellano than in Joseph Macaluso. An innocent man may otherwise be convicted. Of course, the defendant could testify about the threat, but with less credibility and perhaps with some compromise to a strategic decision not to take the stand. At the same time, the mediation program's interest in perceived neutrality may not be as strong in Castellano as in Joseph Macaluso. The community program does not improve industrial peace. It may serve a variety of other interests, however.

7.8   The Florida statute would have blocked the deposition of the mediator in Castellano. (1) The privilege probably cannot be narrowed by changing the holder of the privilege. The parties seem to be the holders. Making the mediator the holder, as in Joseph Macaluso, might result in a waiver here, but that would depend on the disposition of the mediator. (2) An exception might be added for disclosure or admissibility in criminal proceedings; several mediation privilege statutes do this to avert a situation in which a criminal defendant might be erroneously convicted or acquitted. (3) Alternatively, the statute may create a "qualified" privilege which would apply in criminal cases but would yield upon a court determination that the need for the evidence or disclosure outweighs the purposes served.

7.9   There is an argument that the defendant's constitutional rights would require the Florida statute to yield in a situation like Castellano (Question 3.28). In Davis v. Alaska, the Supreme Court ruled that a juvenile record confidentiality statute could not be applied to deprive the defendant of evidence to show that the prime prosecution witness had a reason to finger the defendant. The bias evidence excluded by the trial court was the prosecution witness' prior juvenile adjudication for a similar theft, indicating that he might be trying to deflect blame, and also evidence that he was on probation and needed to curry favor with law enforcement personnel. Arguably, the statute should be drafted to accommodate the concerns that form the basis for the Supreme Court ruling.

7.10   This question focuses on the issue of how explicit the mediator should be about the limits of confidentiality. Even when a privilege exists, there are often areas of uncertainty. Have the statutory requirements been met? Whose law will apply when the case is tried? What is the application of statutes requiring the reporting of evidence of child abuse by certain professionals? Suppose the mediator thinks that she should report child abuse even if not one of the designated professionals. If the mediator begins with a long explanation on this point, it may sound something like a Miranda warning, with a similar chilling effect. On the other hand, there is likely to be reliance on the simple statement concerning confidentiality. Some mediators say, "I will not voluntarily disclose what I hear today." That may be no better, especially as it relates to the child abuse requirement. What about saying nothing on the subject of confidentiality?

7.11 Arguably the majority would have given force to the confidentiality provision, despite the attorney's duty otherwise to report an ethical violation. In both cases, there was an obligation to report. If anything, the possible danger of sexual abuse to another child should weigh more heavily in favor of disclosure than the need to protect a party against an attorney with a conflict of interest or to protect future clients from an unethical attorney. But Waller might be distinguished because the mediator did not stand to gain in appearing to submit to the confidentiality agreement and then reporting the ethical violation, in contrast to the parents who achieved a private nonappealable award arguably because the priest valued the confidentiality guarantee. Also, the parents should have known the facts that they wanted to disclose before agreeing to the confidentiality, whereas the mediator in the D.C. case was surprised by the plaintiff's attorney's statement. It does seem better to anticipate situations in which disclosures should be made so that no one relies to their detriment on the assurance of confidentiality.

The plaintiff in Paranzino had no duty to disclose, the situation faced by the mediator in Waller. Arguably no public purpose was served by disclosure. Still, the sanctions ordered in Paranzino seem extreme, even for a willful violation. In an earlier case, Bernard v. Galen Group, 901 F.Supp. 778 (S.D.N.Y. 1995), the court ordered monetary sanctions for willful disclosure.

7.12 Here, there was no reason supported by public policy for the disclosure.

7.13 This case presents another clash of policies -- in this case the policies favoring public access to agreements regarding public officials versus encouraging settlement through enforcement of confidentiality provisions in agreements. In the actual case, Pierce v. St. Vrain Valley School District, 1997 WL94120 (Colo. App. 1997), the court entered summary judgment for the school board and the Court of Appeals affirmed reasoning that an agreement which contravened the public records law was invalid.

7.14 When the case came to the court of appeals, Judge Merritt stayed the proceedings pending argument, distinguishing the prison case from Cincinnati Gas & Electric because of the public interest. The full panel vacated Judge Merritt's staying, applying the rational of Cincinnati Gas & Electric that the nature of the process, not the nature of the case, is the key to determining whether the public has access.

7.15 The quoted provisions are taken from the 1992 Report of the ADR Task Force of the Commission on the Future of the Massachusetts Courts. The Task Force attempted to draw some bright-line distinctions, on the one hand, between court-connected proceedings and private proceedings and, on the other, between adjudicative proceedings and settlement procedures. Obviously both those categorizations will necessitate some difficult line drawing. Thus settlement procedures that take place in court (such as SJT) would be presumptively treated as private, even if they involved issues affected with the public interest. That, of course, is consistent with the result in Cincinnati Gas & Elec. But that case takes the notion of encouraging settlements by keeping the process confidential about as far as it can be taken.

Moreover, the proposal raises some related definitional questions. For example what is a court-connected mediation program? If a case is referred by the court to a community program or to a program run by private providers, should that be treated as "court-connected" or "private"? Arguably any case that is referred by a court ought to be considered court-connected.

Note also that the envisioned scheme does not explicitly take account of cases of particular public importance such as those referred to on p. 443 of the text. Presumably explicit exceptions could be provided for those cases by statute.

7.16   Two steps would seem to be desirable to achieve the client's desired result. First, a confidentiality provision should be inserted into the settlement agreement that obligates the parties not to disclose the terms of the settlement. But this in itself might not be sufficient. If there is no need for later recourse to the court to secure compliance, then the parties might seek to dismiss the court case or at least avoid any court decree incorporating the settlement agreement. That was a fact explicitly relied upon in the Rittenhouse case, p. 433.

CHAPTER 8 – FAMILY DISPUTES

8.1   This question invites the student to differentiate between the roles played by attorneys in most settlement discussions and their roles in mediation. One significant distinction between negotiations conducted with only attorneys present and the typical domestic mediation is the participation of clients. In a thoughtful recent article, Jean Sternlight argues that attorneys should learn from the social science literature about when it is helpful to have clients participate but should also be prepared to play a traditional adversarial role when necessary to protect the client. *Lawyers' Representation of Clients in Mediation: Using Economics and Psychology to Structure Advocacy in a Nonadversarial Setting*, 14 Ohio St. J. Disp. Resol. 269 (1999).

8.2   One would expect that attorneys in Maine could intervene to terminate the mediation, ask that the mediation be conducted through shuttle mediation, or protect the client against entering an agreement that did not suit the client's interests. As in question 8.1, however, some doubt the competence of attorneys, especially with respect to protection of domestic violence victims. Moreover, some parties attend without attorneys. If unrepresented parties are excluded from mediation, they may avoid the possible intimidation in that setting. Without representation, however, they may be unable to litigate their case effectively at a hearing and may feel forced to negotiate directly with the other spouse or the other spouse's attorney. Thus, it is not clear that the alternative to mediation is a setting lacking in coercion.

8.3   A request for advice. This question is intended to encourage the student to recognize that the professional background of the person who provides third-party assistance is likely to substantially impact on the approach that person takes to the problem. Decisions regarding whether to retain separate legal representation may also be impacted by the third-party's professional background. There is evidence that people seeking help do not necessarily go to the most appropriate professional, but rather go to anyone in whom they have confidence. The advice concerning what type of third-party to see should be a function of the nature of the parties' problems and how they wish to deal with those problems. For example, if the parties are certain that they want a divorce, but there is a strained relationship between them and there are also complex financial issues involved, then they might each want to seek out independent lawyers. On the other hand, if the problems were complex but they were eager to approach divorce as a joint problem solving exercise, then use of a lawyer-mediator might be wise. If they have the resources, they might be best served by retaining independent counsel and hiring a mediator who then need not be a lawyer. If, however, the parties want to attempt to preserve the marriage relationship, the best mediator might be one with therapeutic training, who could assist them in finding and dealing with the underlying causes of the problems in their relationship. Independent representation for the latter example seems less important. See Folberg & Taylor, (1984: 309-313).

Once the type of professional has been identified, finding a specific qualified individual is somewhat like finding a competent doctor or lawyer or psychiatrist, except that the absence of licensing and generally accepted standards of practice (see pp. 184-206) makes the task even more difficult. Some might want to look at particular indicia of education (such as advanced degrees) or specific experience of a particular individual. Probably a more promising route is to ask some trusted professional for recommendations. Failing that, a call to the local law school, medical school, or social work school might yield reliable results.

8.4   Ethical dilemmas for the mediator. a. This problem presents the basic issue of a serious power imbalance in a divorce negotiation. This issue is discussed in the Folberg excerpt in this chapter, as well as in some of the readings in Chapter 3D. See also Davis and Salem, *Dealing With Power Imbalances in the Mediation of Interpersonal Disputes*, MEDIATION Q., Dec. 1984, at 17; Levine (1984:

137).

A threshold issue for the mediator will be whether he should insist that the wife consult a lawyer, preferably one whose general manner and approach are compatible with mediation. Clearly, there is a great deal of difference between knowingly signing a disadvantageous agreement and stumbling into that same agreement out of impetuosity or simply because the wife wants to get "the whole thing behind her." Obviously, in the latter situation she may have regrets when she comes face-to-face with the financial hardship of having inadequate support, and that is one issue the mediator will want to make sure she is aware of.

If the mediator concludes that the wife is fully aware of the choices she is making, many mediators will be more comfortable in going ahead. But note that Susskind's view (p. 199), if extended to family situations, would argue against the mediator carrying on in the face of such an unfair agreement. See also the dialogue at pp. 198-203 that canvasses the pros and cons of Susskind's view, particularly as applied to family situations.

If, as appears likely, the mediator concludes that the wife is not aware of the court alternatives open to her, then the question arises how she might be made aware. The most obvious possibility, of course, is to suggest that she consult an attorney, but apparently she is not willing to do so. Conceivably, some counseling with her in that connection might be worthwhile; she may simply have a stereotypical picture of lawyers as being necessarily adversarial. But if she persists in her refusal to see a lawyer, then the question will be whether the mediator himself wants to "educate" her. This will be extremely difficult for him to do without losing the trust of the husband.

Thus, there seem various possible solutions, ranging from working with the wife, to facilitating outside legal consultation, to withdrawing from the case altogether. Withdrawal may require considerable self-discipline on the mediator's part, given the mediator's likely reluctance to lose business and his desire to project his self-image as a capable mediator. The solution of going ahead, but telling either both parties or just the wife that the mediator feels the settlement is unfair, seems unsatisfactory. As pointed out above, it will be difficult to keep the trust of both parties once the mediator tilts towards one of them and, of course, if the mediator simply tells this to the wife privately, that may well get back to the husband and exacerbate his resentment. Perhaps, in part due to this resentment and the resulting party perception of the mediator's loss of neutrality, most of the legal opinions on divorce mediation stress that if the lawyer-mediator gives any legal advice, he or she must do so in the presence of both parties.

As indicated in the question, if the mediator tilts towards one of the disputants, that may not only sour this mediation but, when the word gets around, impair the mediator's reputation in the future.

If the wife is "an experienced businesswoman," that might well change some of the considerations above. Since, as pointed out, an initial question is whether the wife knows what she is doing in accepting this unfair settlement, the mediator will certainly have fewer qualms if she is a sophisticated individual. But presumably, under Susskind's view, the mediator would still not be fulfilling responsibilities if he or she went ahead with the mediation.

b. This problem presents an aspect of "mediating in the shadow of the law" (Mnookin and Kornhauser (1979)). That is, most mediations and negotiations take place against the background of a legal system that will be looked to if the parties do not work out a solution themselves. We have already seen an aspect of this in Problem (a) above. As was there indicated, at a minimum most mediators will want to make sure that the parties know their alternatives to a mediated agreement. (Of course that assumes that the mediator also knows what they are.) An important difference between this problem and the previous one is that here both parties seem to be under a misapprehension. Hence, there is perhaps more justification for going ahead, on the theory that so long as there is no question of overreaching and both parties are operating on the same premise, it really makes no difference whether that premise is correct or not.

But that view is arguably short-sighted. It might well be that if the parties knew their BATNAs (see p. 37) they would behave differently. Hence, many family mediators will want to make sure that the parties operate on a correct view of their legal alternatives, most likely by so advising them in the presence of both of them, or conceivably by sending them to separate attorneys.

c. This question presents one of the recurring nightmares of divorce mediators. Most mediators at a minimum insist on a full disclosure clause of the kind suggested in the last sentence of the problem. But even if they do, there may be no way for them to know whether the parties are living up to the agreement.

Often, however, the mediator may get various indirect clues that one of the disputants is playing with a stacked deck. At that point the mediator might raise that question for discussion with both disputants, making reference to the joint agreement to make full disclosure. But if that does not solve the problem, it may well be necessary to refer the parties to independent attorneys, who would then use the normal discovery methods to solve the problem. Some mediators deal with the risk of non-disclosure by suggesting to the independent attorneys that before a final agreement is entered into, each send an interrogatory asking whether the assets disclosed to the mediator include all that party's assets. In that way, any non-disclosure will have taken place under oath, a factor that may encourage full disclosure, particularly if the parties are advised at the commencement of mediation that this is normal practice.

Some mediators insert a clause conditioning the validity of any agreement reached on full disclosure by both parties.

It probably would not make any difference whether the mediator thinks the agreement is fair or not, for, even if the mediator thinks it is, it is difficult to know whether the mediator would still think the same if aware of the unknown, undisclosed assets.

d. Usually, if the mediator has a problem regarding information, the problem is one of not knowing enough. Here, the problem is knowing too much. If the mediator makes a recommendation that is based on the assumption that the husband was the father of only one child, has the mediator indirectly disclosed confidential information? Perhaps the mediator should hold a caucus with the wife and tell her that a recommendation would result in a disclosure. She would probably then withdraw her request for a recommendation by the mediator. If the wife withdraws the request for a recommendation, should the mediator tell the husband that one child is not his? What duty does the mediator have toward the child? Will the child be better off if the information about parentage remains confidential?

e. This problem raises the question presented by the dialogue (p. 199) concerning the obligation of the mediator towards unrepresented parties. Whatever one concludes as an abstract matter on this question, it seems difficult to reach the conclusion that the mediator can proceed without any regard to the interests of the children. To be sure, that is really the duty of the judge who is supposed to review the agreement. But it is well known, as the question points out, that judges tend not to discharge this duty very faithfully. The issue is really one of who can best discharge this responsibility, and both sides of it are forcefully presented in the dialogued referred to above.

A few statutes require the mediator to look out for the best interests of the children. In Kansas, for example, a mediator appointed by the court must "ensure that the parties consider fully the best interests of the children" and must terminate the mediation session if the mediator believes that "continuation of the process would harm or prejudice one or more of the parties or the children...." Kansas Stat. Ann. §§ 23-603, 23-604. The statute raises the issues discussed in the dialogue on pp. 199-203 regarding the accountability of the mediator.

8.5 **Divorce mediation and conventional representation**. Another difficult question in connection with divorce mediation is how traditional partisan lawyers should relate to the divorce mediation process. As pointed out earlier and in some of the materials reproduced in the text, many family mediators now recommend such use of independent lawyers at some point in the mediation proceeding. See also Section VI of the ABA, Standards for Lawyer Mediators in Family Disputes (Appendix E of text).

But the partisan lawyer who has not been a party to the mediation is obviously in a difficult position. How can she give proper legal advice without having been involved in the proceeding that gave rise to the agreement that she is asked to review? This obviously calls for some kind of limited representation. If the client brings the agreement to her lawyer and simply says, "Well what do you think?", the lawyer is bound to point out all the ways in which the agreement is less favorable than what might have been obtained by the traditional process. But that suggests that different ways of involving the traditional lawyer must be utilized. For example, the client should indicate at the outset what led her to use the mediation process. Thus the wife might say something like the following: "I went into divorce mediation because I wanted to try and arrive at an agreement with my husband through use of a more accommodative process than the traditional adversary method. I realize I might have been able to do better in court. Hence, that is not what I want you to tell me. I would like you to look over this agreement which we arrived at after several sessions and after the following information was disclosed by both sides. My main concern is that you tell me whether this agreement is way off base in some respect or whether it omits some essential matter that it ought to deal with." Obviously, the lawyer will want to get the written consent of the client to this kind of limited representation in order to guard herself against subsequent malpractice proceedings.

Sometimes mediators anticipate some of these difficulties by writing a letter to the reviewing attorneys that summarizes the information adduced at the mediation, and the choices made by the parties and the reasons for those choices.

8.6 **Institutionalization of divorce mediation**. The general question of institutionalization of alternative dispute resolution is canvassed in Chapter 11. There are some obvious advantages to publicly provided dispute resolution, primarily the visibility, legitimacy, and public financing that comes with such services. But there are also concomitant disadvantages, such as the danger of increasing bureaucratization and political control. This does not seem to be an "either-or" issue. Divorce mediation ought to be publicly available to those who cannot afford to pay for it privately, as it is in some states (California, for example). At the same time, there is no reason why the public system cannot be supplemented by privately provided mediation. Conceivably the competition between the two systems will act as a healthy stimulus to sound development. For example, publicly provided mediation typically contains some control on the qualifications of mediators. That in turn may have an effect on apprizing the public of appropriate credentials for a divorce mediator.

A key question with either system is who should pay for the mediator, an issue discussed in the SPIDR Report (p. 389). As regards the ethical questions involved in the two types of practice, theoretically they are the same. But as a practical matter ethical questions are unlikely to be raised in connection with public mediation. We are unaware of any cases where the Bar has gone after court-connected employees (such as court clerks) for unauthorized practice. Most likely the mantle of presumptive propriety that clothes the court has been extended also to court employees.

8.7   Practice and policy issues. This raises, in the family context, the issues discussed in Chapter 3D: How does one define a high quality mediation? What types of laws are most effective in enforcing goals for mediation quality? Should there be entry requirements for mediators? Should the mediator be subject to de-certification for failing to encourage the expression of anger? Should there be procedural requirements such as permitting the parties to forego mediation? Despite lawyers' temptation to solve everything with a statute, the goal of encouraging the expression of anger, like others to improve the quality of mediation, may not be achievable through regulation.

8.8   Referral. In this problem, both parties may want to avoid the disclosures likely if the case proceeds through discovery and hearing, and each risks a negative decision on custody. Thus, settlement through mediation seems desirable. If the mother is unfit and counseling will not restore her fitness, the children's interests may not be well served by a compromise that places them with their mother. If, on the other hand, the prospect of losing custody provides the incentive for the mother to undergo treatment and restores her to fitness, their interests may be best served by an early compromise on custody and a settlement that shortens the disruption resulting from bitterly fought litigation over an issue (i.e., her adultery two years ago) that is only of questionable relevance in the current proceeding. This suggests that mediation should be conducted by a mediator with expertise in substance abuse. Further, the court may decide to use a court-employed mediator who will not encourage an agreement that is harmful for the children.

CHAPTER 9 -- PUBLIC DISPUTES

A.   Questions

9.1   The first step would be to identify all those groups with a stake in the issue of shelter for the homeless. Next, you might organize a series of brainstorming sessions, in which representatives of those groups would seek to develop ideas for dealing with the shelter problem. In light of the variety of stakeholders in Middletown, and their common interest in aiding the homeless, such sessions might be quite productive. Thus Susskind and Cruikshank suggest (22-23):

> " ... the mayor, the city council, the various local and state agencies, and the advocacy organizations might have gotten together to invent a solution which took account of each disputant's special needs. For example, a strategy that provided temporary housing in churches or local armories would have gotten the homeless off the street, and thereby would have met their short-term needs. Such a strategy could have been linked to a city or state commitment to convert at least one abandoned building in each neighborhood to longer-term housing for needy residents -- a tactic that would have addressed the welfare and housing agencies' concerns. The advocacy group for the homeless might have been given the task of designing prototype social services for the first rehabilitated housing units. If this was accomplished successfully, RHH then could have been given the long-term assignment of managing similar social services at other sites."

Among the problems that might arise would be the unwillingness of some of the more powerful stakeholders, such as the city council or the state agencies, to participate in the consensus-building effort, or post-agreement judicial challenges by a dissatisfied splinter group from one of the participating organizations. Susskind and Cruikshank discuss these problems at pp. 488-492.

9.2   The issue posed by this question is whether the societal advantages of consensus-building negotiations are sufficiently great that an agreement reached among all concerned groups should be given substantial deference by a court in which that agreement is challenged. If the agreement is patently unlawful, not even close to the line of legality, clearly it would not be saved because it was the product of a consensus-building negotiation. When the legality of the agreement is less clear, so is the effect of its being the product of negotiations in which all affected parties participated and concurred in the result. The best articulation of the competing views is contained in the articles by Judge Wald and Professor Harter cited at pp. 510-511. The most recent development -in the debate is contained in the Negotiated Rulemaking Act of 1990, which provides that regulations which are the product of negotiated rulemaking shall be accorded no greater deference by a court than a rule which is the product of traditional rule-making procedures. While this approach is not binding on courts dealing with consensus-building negotiations in other contexts than rulemaking, it will surely be considered.

Still, one can imagine a judge in this case saying to herself, "If this were a federal neg-reg proceeding, I would probably have to find the agreement illegal. Since, however, it isn't, I'm not bound by the Negotiated Rulemaking Act. Hence, I have a bit more discretion to balance the extent to which the agreement fails to comply with city zoning laws against the extent to which it serves the best interests of the city. Since the agreement will put a thorny issue to rest, and it was a product of full negotiations among all affected parties, I'm inclined to believe that the wisest exercise of my discretion is to sustain the agreement."

9.3   Plaintiff would probably argue that this evidence should be excluded on two grounds -- the "compromise discussion" exclusion and the mediation privilege. Whether the former applies is doubtful.

Initially, it is not clear that these consensus building negotiations can be accurately characterized as negotiations concerning a disputed legal claim. Nor is it clear that defendants seek to introduce the minutes to show the legal invalidity of plaintiff's claim. They may be introducing them solely to show, as Susskind and Cruikshank suggest, that the procedure was fair, and that all parties, including plaintiff, had a full opportunity to be heard.

The validity of the mediation privilege argument will depend initially on whether the state has a mediation statute or common law doctrine regarding mediation privilege, and if so what it provides. Absent controlling law, plaintiff will presumably argue that if consensus-building negotiation can be used against the participants, affected parties will not participate, and the policy of encouraging a negotiated resolution of public disputes will be frustrated. Query whether that argument should prevail if the minutes are introduced solely to demonstrate plaintiff's participation in the consensus-building negotiation, and the fairness of those negotiations.

9.4 The central objection is that ex parte communications to the judge regarding a pending case are inconsistent with the judicial process. Furthermore, the fear that communication between the judge and the mediator might occur, wholly outside the knowledge or control of the parties, might deter their participation in mediation.

On the other hand it can be argued that as long as the mediator does not discuss with the judge the merits of the case, and does not communicate any information likely to influence the judge's decision, the parties are not prejudiced. For example, the mediator could not tell the judge who he thought was being uncooperative, since that might influence the judge's decision on the merits, but might suggest that settlement efforts would be furthered if the judge deferred ruling on a pending motion. The mediator's ability to communicate the latter type of information to the judge could aid substantially in bringing about a settlement without influencing the outcome if a settlement were not achieved. Thus, this type of communication should be allowed.

To be sure, one might respond that the ability to influence the timing of a ruling might affect the outcome, not of the case, but of the settlement negotiations. While that is true, the response would be that many of the mediator's acts might influence the outcome of the negotiations. Yet, as long as the mediator acts for the purpose of encouraging settlement, his acts would seem permissible even though they had the incidental effect of influencing the terms of the settlement.

The State Justice Institute, which is attempting to develop standards for court-connected mediation, dealt with this issue in an April 1992 draft as follows:

COMMUNICATIONS BETWEEN MEDIATORS AND THE COURT

I. During a mediation the court should be informed only of the following:

    (a) the failure of a party to comply with the order to attend mediation;

    (b) any request by the parties for additional time to complete mediation;

    (c) if all parties agree, any procedural action by the court that would facilitate the mediation

    (d) the mediator's assessment that the case is inappropriate for mediation.

9.5   While the concerns expressed by Judge Edwards are real, those concerns do not appear applicable in the case he describes. He is concerned that "environmental standards will be set by private groups without the democratic check of governmental institutions." Yet, in the case of which he writes, the agreement reached by the private parties was presented to government regulators. Presumably, that was not done as a *fait accompli,* but to obtain the approval of the government and ultimately of the court in which the litigation was pending. If that presumption is accurate, this would appear to be a model of successful negotiation of public disputes, in that the private parties negotiated a settlement that met their interests, but that settlement was not final until the relevant public authorities were satisfied that it met the public interest. If that presumption is not accurate, and the private resolution were binding on the government regulators, Judge Edward's concerns are entirely warranted. One might also argue that those concerns are warranted because meaningful government review of a settlement is unlikely if the government does not become involved until the settlement has been fully negotiated.

9.6   The district court (Inmates of the Suffolk County Jail v. Kearney, 734 F. Supp. 561 (D. Mass. 1990)) held that neither the Supreme Court's ruling, nor the increase in the number of detainees, warranted the requested modification in the consent decree. The court stated (734 F. Supp. at 565-6):

> The Sheriff argues that his proposal for double-celling complies with constitutional standards. Even if this were true, which it is not necessary to decide, it does not provide a basis for relief from a consent decree. To permit relief on this basis would make settlements in cases of this type worth very little. It would undermine and discourage settlement efforts in institutional cases if a defendant were permitted to return to court when terms earlier agreed to became more burdensome than expected. It is the very certainty and finality of a consent decree approved by a court that induces participation in it. Defendants' agreement in this case was a firm one, and not merely an agreement to comply with the decree if it was not too difficult to do so, or to comply with the decree until it arguably required more of the defendants than the absolute minimum they would be constitutionally required to provide. It was an agreement by all parties to avoid the risks of litigation involved in pressing for a judicial determination of the issue of constitutionality.

While the district court's decision was affirmed by the First Circuit Court of Appeals (915 F.2d 1557), it was reversed and remanded by the Supreme Court (--U.S.--, 112 S.Ct. 748 (1992)), on the grounds that the district court had applied too strict a standard in deciding whether the consent decree should have been modified. According to the Supreme Court, the growth in institutional litigation, leading to consent decrees that remain in place for extended periods of time, requires that a district court have the flexibility to modify such decrees in response to changed circumstances. Thus, modification of a consent decree may be warranted when: (1) changed factual conditions make compliance with the decree substantially more onerous (2) the statutory or decisional law has changed to make legal what the decree was designed to prevent.

9.7   Phillip Harter has argued that if courts apply a stringent standard of review to negotiated rules, some groups will be tempted to boycott the rulemaking process, preferring an unfettered day in court, and that this will lead to a weakening of negotiated rulemaking. He argues that a negotiated rule should be sustained to the extent it is within the agency's jurisdiction and reflects a consensus among the interested parties. -

Judge Wald disagrees. She raises a number of concerns, all of which are discussed in the cited article. Central among these is her doubt that consensus will always be the functional equivalent of the usual tests of reasonableness or non-arbitrariness used in judicial review. Judge Wald is also concerned about determining whether a consensus actually exists, and whether the appropriate interests were represented in the consensus. On balance, she concludes, it is not clear that adopting Harter's proposed standard of judicial review would reduce judicial involvement in negotiated regulations.

9.8   The argument against attempting negotiated rulemaking in this context is that two of the major players have indicated that they have no flexibility, that they will insist that <u>de minimus</u> must be zero. Thus, fundamental value choices appear to be involved, and in this situation it has been suggested that negotiated rulemaking is unlikely to be useful. Indeed, a proposed rulemaking involving the disposal of low-level radioactive waste was dropped by EPA for essentially this reason (Susskind and MacMahon, 1985:143).

9.9   The argument against participating is that if OMB will not participate, and remains free to advise the President to order the agency to disapprove the resulting rule, the participation of others may be a waste of time. On the other hand, a non-participating group runs the risk that others will proceed without it, and that a consensus will be reached that satisfies OMB, but in which the interests of the non-participating group will not be reflected.

If you did decide to participate, it would be wise to encourage OMB to be vocal in its observer role, explaining the reasons for its concerns with any proposed rule, as well as any changes it would propose. While this might not be technical "participation" by OMB, it would enable the advocates of the proposed rule to respond to OMB's concerns, and might lead OMB to support a proposed rule on which it has been fully heard, and which met its major concerns.

B.   EXERCISES

EXERCISE 9.1:   THE HALFWAY HOUSE

Teaching Instructions

While the General Information for this exercise does not indicate that there will be mediators at the meeting, there are confidential instructions for mediators. Some teachers do the exercise with mediators, others do not use mediators. When mediators are not used, the role of facilitating the negotiations is typically played by the mayor's representatives.

Those teachers who wish to add another role may develop instructions for the Association for Community Mental Health, a group that strongly supports the halfway house as a matter of principle, but, different from the Center for Community Living, has no financial interest in the halfway house.

In order to give this exercise the flavor of a genuine community meeting, we suggest that each group be represented by 2-4 students. To do this exercise properly requires about 3-4 hours. We usually give out the roles at the prior class, along with a master sheet showing who is playing what role so the students can get together in teams before the initial meeting if they wish. Then everyone is supposed to appear at the beginning of class -- say 4:00 p.m. The mayor's meeting might be announced to begin at 4:30 or 4:45, so as to allow for further informal meetings between groups. There are no set ground rules for how the meeting is to run; breaks can be taken, subgroups can caucus at times -- all this is up to the convenors and the group. A terminal time of the meeting is set for, say, 6:15 p.m. Then, following a break, we would undertake a detailed debriefing.

It may be helpful to have name signs for each group, as well as blackboards or flip charts to aid the convenors.

EXERCISE 9.1: THE HALFWAY HOUSE

Confidential Information for Mayor's Representatives

The mayor is quite interested in the proposed halfway house. It presents the city with an opportunity to please the governor and set an example of progressive programming for the rest of the state, while at the same time getting more rent for an old school building than the place is worth. (The State Department of Rehabilitation has indicated that it will approve a budget of $5,000 rental per month; the city would be fortunate to get $1,000 elsewhere.) Unfortunately, rumors have gotten started, and public fears, fueled by misinformation, threaten to scuttle both the halfway house and the mayor's reelection. The empty school building that is to be rented to the halfway house was vandalized last week; you suspect the teenagers, who have been playing basketball and volleyball on the playground and want to keep the small clubhouse they built on the corner of the property.

The school is the only public building available for the halfway house and is easily large enough to house 60 residents.

Your role in these negotiations is quite delicate. While the mayor wants the halfway house, she cannot agree to it if opposition groups are so dissatisfied that her reelection is endangered. The mayor has also told you that the city receives $5,000,000 annually from the State Department of Rehabilitation to support various social services in Northampton (shelters for the homeless, drug and alcohol rehabilitation programs, vocational retraining programs for the unemployed, etc.). This amounts to 75% of the City's budget for these services, and if the Department were to cut off these funds, which it might do if the City will not accept the halfway house, the City would have to eliminate some of these programs and cut others to the bone. The other alternative would be a substantial increase in property taxes. Either of these events would damage the Mayor's popularity and reduce her re-election prospects.

The mayor is willing to be flexible in making concessions to opponents of the project to obtain their support. Unfortunately, this flexibility has no extra money in the budget to back it up. All you have to work with is the mayor's ability to redirect city services, and the rental income from the building (some of which the mayor would like to retain for the general city budget).

If the halfway house does not go through, the mayor will probably sell the property to a private developer to construct an apartment house. One developer, who plans to construct low-income housing units on the property, has already contacted the major. While the major is reluctant to turn public property over to private interests, the city's financial situation requires that in some fashion the property produce income for the city.

EXERCISE 9.1: THE HALFWAY HOUSE

Confidential Information for the Larchmont PTA

The PTA was appalled when the school Board tapped Larchmont for closing two years ago. Some of your members with young children keep hoping against hope that the school will reopen, but there appears to be little chance of that in the near future. To preserve any chance of that, however, you will not agree to any plan that would tear down the building.

You miss the social activity once provided by the school. The playground, while never fancy, used to be a wonderful place for the younger kids to play. That is no longer possible. Not only is the playground overrun by teenagers, but the vacant building seems to attract the worst kind of people.

The neighborhood teenagers say that the playground is the only place around where they can go to play basketball and volleyball. But they admit that they sometimes are frightened by some of the people who hang around the vacant building. The clubhouse they built behind the school keeps getting broken into, and they have found hypodermic needles lying on the ground.

You do not know what the mayor could have been thinking of when she decided on the halfway house idea, though. How she could suggest that the school building should house mental patients, most of whom probably will come from other parts of the state, is beyond you. You do not want your kids traumatized by exposure to exhibitionists. Instead of a halfway house, the mayor should turn a portion of the building into a community recreation center. It is more than large enough for a recreation center; indeed, half the building would be more than ample. She could then turn the playground into a combination public park and playground with room for all the kids to play.

EXERCISE 9.1:   THE HALFWAY HOUSE

Confidential Information for Property Owners' Association

Your organization represents the homeowners in the neighborhood. You are concerned, partially based on horror stories from other cities, that having a large halfway house will reduce property values. Many of you lived through Northampton's worst years. Now that the city seems to be coming back, you do not want to lose everything you have worked for. The last thing you need is a bunch of crazies from all over the state running around and frightening people. Sixty people! You know that the zoning regulations would not permit a halfway house of that size (or any size, for that matter) in a private building.

If the mayor has any political savvy, she will not permit this halfway house. Her reelection chances are not so good to begin with. For years your attempts to attract more police patrols and obtain better street lighting to make the neighborhood safer have fallen on deaf ears. The mayor can ill afford to annoy the property owners further.

The empty building has become a haven for drug dealers and addicts. It should be razed and the land turned into a well-equipped public park if it is not to be a school. You hope the city does not decide to sell the land to private developers, as it did with the other closed schools. Two of those lots now have apartment buildings with low-income housing units in them, and your research has revealed that the zoning rules would permit low-income apartments in your neighborhood as well. Although not as frightening as a halfway house for 60 mental patients, low income housing would not do your property values any good either.

EXERCISE 9.1:   THE HALFWAY HOUSE

Confidential Information for Center for Community Living

This contract with the state is the break your organization has been waiting for. Finally the Department of Rehabilitation seems ready to pay an adequate price for reducing the population at the State Mental Hospital. You want to satisfy the Department that your group can do the job; you also are aware that community opposition could prove a real problem. Halfway houses in other cities that have ignored neighborhood concerns have been forced to close.

You are committed to caring for the mentally ill in the community. You also believe that dumping people back on the street directly from a mental institution makes no sense. Some of the patients may need lifetime care. They may bother the neighbors occasionally, but none of them is the least bit dangerous. In fact, they should improve if permitted some interaction with normal people in the neighborhood.

You believe that the community has been unduly alarmed by the specter of the mentally ill. The National Association of Halfway Houses, of which you are a member, has compiled data which show clearly that the most common grounds for opposition to the introduction of a halfway house -- that crime will increase and property values decline -- has no statistical support. The data show that on a nation-wide basis there are no significant changes in either crime rates or property values after the introduction of a halfway house.

You are a bit apprehensive about having to accept 60 patients, however. This is not a matter of the size of the building; indeed, you could house 60 patients in half to three-quarters of the building. It is rather that it may be difficult to develop a feeling of community within the house and informal contacts with the neighbors with that many people. Nationally recognized standards for the care of the mentally ill suggest that no halfway house should have more than 35 residents. You hope to convince that Department of Rehabilitation to place in the house patients who are residents of Northampton in order to enable the city to care for its own.

You really want this building. The school may be the only possibility in Northampton since the zoning regulations in any neighborhood you could afford do not permit group houses. Because getting this property is so critical, you are willing to be both flexible and creative in responding to the neighbors' legitimate needs and concerns. You also want to impress both city and state officials with your competence and creativity.

One area in which you are prepared to be flexible is in staff-resident ratio. Your normal ratio is 1:8, which is better than the federally approved minimum of 1:10. if it is necessary to assure the neighbors that supervision will be adequate, you can increase the staff-resident ratio to 1:5. That is the highest you can go, however, without raising costs so high that you will incur unacceptable losses in operating the halfway house. Indeed, you should go no further in increasing the ratio of staff to residents than is necessary to meet neighborhood concerns. From a professional perspective, your normal 1:8 ratio is more than adequate, and any increase in supervision cuts into operating revenues.

EXERCISE 9.1:   THE HALFWAY HOUSE

Confidential on for State Department of Rehabilitation

You are in a very difficult situation. After having been neglected for years, the state's program for the mentally ill suddenly is headline news. Your boss, the Director of the Department, was named as a defendant in a successful lawsuit brought on behalf of some of the patients; as a result, the court has given the Department only 60 days to find alternative placements for large numbers of residents. Since you cannot simply dump patients into the street, contracting with private halfway houses must be your primary method of meeting the deadline.

You agreed to attend the meeting called by the mayor of Northampton in an attempt to defuse what appears to be growing opposition to a halfway house from the local community. You had thought that the mayor, who seems to want the revenues, could handle the problems, but she may be too weak. Now you have to keep the opposition from boomeranging and affecting your chances of siting halfway houses in other cities. You also want to make certain this house goes; you cannot afford to lose it. Indeed, you want to place a minimum of 60 former patients in this house. The building is more than large enough to house 60 patients; indeed, half to three-quarters of the space would suffice.

You are willing to lend your ingenuity and whatever power your office has to these negotiations; you have the most to lose if they break down. Unfortunately, the legislature has given you no additional funds to buy off problems; all you have is the money to renovate the school ($150,000) and to contract for the operation of the halfway house ($7,500 per resident per year.) Your boss told the mayor that she could anticipate $5,000 per month for rental of the school, as the state would approve that amount.

You do, however, have one strong card to play in these negotiations. At present, your department is providing $5,000,000 annually to support various social services in Northampton (shelters for the homeless, drug and alcohol rehabilitation programs, vocational retraining programs for the unemployed, etc.). This amounts to 75% of the city's budget for these services, and if the city were to lose these funds it would have to eliminate some of these programs, and cut others to the bone. You have been authorized by the Director of the Department to cut off these funds if the city does not approve the halfway house. You have also been authorized to advise opponents of the halfway house that you have this power, and you will use it if necessary.

EXERCISE 9.1:   THE HALFWAY HOUSE

Confidential Information for the Grey Panthers

You represent an organization that has enrolled a large proportion of the over-65ers in the city, including a strong contingent from the Larchmont area.

Your members are opposed to the proposed halfway house, as well as to any plan to sell, lease, or tear down the school. What they want is to have the school developed into a senior citizens' center. There is absolutely no attention paid to the needs of older folks in this town. At least when the school was open, the grounds were maintained and there was not all of the mess you see now. In those days you could even arrange to use the facilities in the evenings. If you go over to the building at night now, some drug-crazed addict might attack you.

The kids have their schools; you have got nothing. After paying taxes all your lives, it is only fair you now get something for your money.

A halfway house will do nothing to help your fear of crime in the neighborhood or to give you a safe place to meet your friends.

EXERCISE 9.1:   THE HALFWAY HOUSE

Confidential Information for Mediators

You are staff mediators of the Northampton Mediation Service. The Service is a private, non-profit corporation, which trains and supervises both paid staff and volunteers to mediate interpersonal disputes at the municipal court. Over the past five years you and other staff mediators have resolved a small but growing number of disputes in the community over housing and social services. Unfortunately, you still are not well known beyond the courthouse.

Last week you read in the local newspaper about a press conference held by the Larchmont Property Owners Association to announce its opposition, and that of various other community groups, to the location of a halfway house for mental patients in the vacant Larchmont School. You dug around and found out about the upcoming meeting. You believe that you may be able to help the parties resolve what appears to be a ripening dispute and call some attention to the Mediation Service in the process.

EXERCISE 9.1: THE HALFWAY HOUSE

Teaching Notes

Question 9.1 asks the students how a negotiated approach to consensus building should be conducted; the exercise provides them with an opportunity to put their answers to the test in the context of a typical public dispute.

An agreement is possible in this exercise, but it typically does not take place until the groups for and against the halfway house have caucused to reach a consensus on their group interests and options for settlement that are acceptable to all members of the group. The exercise thus demonstrates the importance of coalition formation in the resolution of multi-party multi-issue disputes.

The most difficult roles are played by the mayor's representatives and the mediators. The mayor's representatives must manage the delicate task of persuading the opposition groups to accept the halfway house (or risk the loss of $5,000,000 in state aid, which might lead to her defeat in the next election), while at the same time not pushing the opposition groups so hard that she loses their political support (which could also cost her the next election). The mediators must persuade the others to accept their services when they have not been invited to the meeting. Then they must deal with the representatives of six different groups and guide them to agreement.

One particularly interesting aspect of this exercise is that the representatives of both the State Department of Rehabilitation and the mayor have substantial power to harm the opposition groups if they do not accept the halfway house. The state can cut off $5,000,000 in aid to the city; the mayor can sell the property to a private developer who will use it for low-income housing. Under what circumstances, and how, should the state or the mayor threaten to use their power?

A somewhat simpler version of the problem presented by this exercise -- the siting of an unwanted facility -- is contained in an exercise called <u>Westville: Mediation Strategies in Community Planning</u>. <u>Westville</u> has only three roles, one of which is that of a mediator, and is particularly interesting because the mediator is not wholly neutral; he/she wants the outcome that one of the parties is seeking. <u>Westville</u> is available, as are many other public dispute negotiation exercises, from the Program on Negotiation Clearinghouse, Harvard Law School, Cambridge, MA 02138.

EXERCISE 9.2 CAROLINE'S DONUT SHOP

This problem places the student in the role of a lawyer counseling clients about mediation. The problem is based on a series of disputes in southern California, one of which culminated in an unsuccessful challenge to the ordinance in the California courts. Xiloj-Itzep v. City of Agoura, 24 Cal. App 4th 620,

29 Cal. Rptr. 879 (2d App. Dist. 1994). Professor Lela Love of Yeshiva Law School successfully mediated a similar case arising in Glen Cove, Long Island, through which the laborers and the city agreed to a new location for the job pick-ups, an amendment to the ordinance, and a new system of communication between police and the group presented by the day laborers. Lela P. Love, *Glen Cove: Mediation Achieves What Litigation Cannot*, CONSENSUS, October 1993, at 1. We have included below an excerpt from a recent article analyzing the two cases.

A large class can be divided into groups, each to discuss one of the questions in the exercise and report back its recommendations.

Question 1. The advantages of mediation include an earlier resolution (valued by the laborers who are missing work) and the possibility of settling broader issues of police-laborer communications. Also, since an attempt to secure an injunction was unsuccessful in another such case, settlement may be the only way to secure relief. Disadvantages of mediating include lost time, especially if the clients forego litigation in the interim, and the problem that the settlement will not provide precedent if the issue arises elsewhere. If these clients do not care about the precedent, should their attorneys weigh this as a disadvantage? Also, scarce time may be expended trying to persuade the other parties to mediate. There also may be problems paying a mediator or finding one who is available without a fee. Although the clients may not be experienced negotiators, their lawyers are, so they should not be concerned about bargaining imbalances based on negotiating ability.

Question 2. The city and homeowners may take the case more seriously if litigation is pending and they are facing mounting attorney's fees. Also, if they are reticent to mediate, the court might be willing to mandate their participation. At the same time, the other parties may be more amenable to problem solving if they are not angry about being sued. The publicity accompanying litigation may harden positions. The delay created by filing suit is costly for the laborers. Also, they probably have little need for formal discovery prior to settlement discussions.

Question 3. This is a chance to discuss the advantages and disadvantages of client presence (see Riskin, p.320) and lawyer presence (see Rogers and McEwen, 467). The advantages of client participation include: humanizing the situation for the landowners and city; increasing the number of ideas for settlement; and helping the clients to assess the alternatives to settlement more realistically. The disadvantages include: a more complicated situation, not only because of more participants but also because of language difficulties; and the possibility of highly emotional exchanges that lead to escalation of conflict. A representative group might reduce the complexity without diminishing the other values of client participation. It might also be wise to ask that other parties send only a few representatives. Lawyer participation seems necessary to counter-balance experienced negotiators on behalf of other parties. However, it might be helpful to set ground rules about the participation of parties as well as lawyers. To encourage discussion of broader issues, one might expand the parties to include representatives of the police and other merchants.

Question 4. On the strategy level, one might argue that limits on disclosure will reduce party posturing. At the same time, total secrecy may hurt public confidence in any settlement reached. The partial disclosure strategy discussed in the John Rolfe Parkway case (text, p. 443) might be appropriate. There are legal as well as strategic issues. The open meeting requirements for mediation sessions involving public officials and the legal ramifications of confidentiality agreements are discussed in the text, pp. 421-422, 431-432.

Question 5. This is a chance to discuss the materials in Chapter 3A regarding different goals and styles of mediation, as well as the Chapter 3D materials on mediator qualifications. Should the mediator be a lawyer? fluent in Spanish? experienced with large groups? well-known in the community? Should the clients participate in the process of selecting the mediator?

Question 6. This is an opportunity to discuss the materials in Chapter 5D. How much should be revealed to the mediator? Should the lawyers talk to the clients about a particular negotiation approach? Perhaps the lawyers should explain to the clients that they (the lawyers) may express empathy with the other parties but that this does not mean that they are not also advocating for the clients. The clients should be told about care in not disclosing evidence of crimes, since this may not fall within the mediation privilege, if one exists in this jurisdiction.

The following excerpt from an article by two law professors provides examples of the application of mediation and litigation in similar situations:

Lela P. Love and Cheryl B. McDonald, *A Tale of Two Cities: Day Labor and Conflict Resolution for Communities in Crisis,* Dispute Resolution Mag., Fall 1997, at 8, 8-10.

. . . .

Two Cities, Two Responses

As tensions mounted, the cities stepped up their enforcement of traffic laws. Glen Clove city officials urged the U.S. Immigration and Naturalization Service to round up and detain illegal aliens at the shaping point. In Agoura Hills, city officials worked with local businesses to set up a hiring site in a commercial parking lot. While the site provided public toilets, drinking water and a volunteer coordinator, few men actually got jobs through the facility – although it is not clear why this was the case. It was eventually replaced with a telephone exchange, but the informal hiring practice continued.

In both cities, the workers complained that the law enforcement officers used harassing and abusive tactics, unfairly targeting them as criminals while at the same time ignoring their claims or treating them as perpetrators when in fact they were the victims of criminal activities. Both cities attempted to address the problem by holding public hearings, which only engendered strident debate and a hardening of positions.

In 1990, both cities enacted substantially similar ordinances prohibiting solicitation either to or from occupants of vehicles that are traveling on public streets or from cars parked in unauthorized areas of commercial parking lots. The Glen Cove ordinance more broadly prohibited occupants or stopped or parked vehicles from hiring or attempting to hire a worker.

Seeing these ordinances as unconstitutionally targeted against the Hispanic workers and violating First Amendment rights, civil libertarians and members of the Hispanic community in each city joined to file lawsuits, which in the case of Glen Cove included a class action seeking $3 million from the city. Plaintiffs in both cities sought preliminary injunctions against the enforcement of the new ordinances.

Here the tales of the two cities began to diverge.

Agora Hills

In Agora Hills, representatives of the workers attempted to negotiate with the city, but made no progress. Following the denial of their preliminary injunction, the workers appealed. The California Court of

Appeals denied the appeal in a published decision upholding the ordinance and finding no evidence of its unconstitutional application to the plaintiffs.

Three years later, while crowds of 100 men no longer congregate in one place, the nature of the situation depends on who you ask. The City of Agora Hills contends the problem has gone away. While a few transients still gather to seek work, the "regulars" seem to have moved elsewhere. The Los Angeles County Sheriff's Department, with whom Agora Hills contracts for police services, has assigned a bilingual ordinance enforcement officer in order to improve communication with the day-laborer population. As of July 1, 1997, the telephone exchange was shut down.

Representatives of the day laborers tell a different story, however. They report that 60-80 workers still solicit work each day in Agora Hills, but do so in smaller, geographically scattered groups of 8 to 10 men. With a penalty of $271 per citation, the workers are cautious and disperse when a sheriff's vehicle comes into sight. Moreover, they contend that the sheriff continues to hassle workers and that the presence of a bilingual officer has neither eased the distrust held by the workers toward the city and police officials nor substantially improved communication. In some cases, the sheriff has used back-up units and helicopters to round up workers.

Glen Cove

As with Agora Hills, a state court denied a preliminary injunction against the Glen Cove city ordinance. Facing the prospect of laborious and possibly unsuccessful litigation that would leave broader concerns unaddressed, plaintiff CARECEN (Central American Refugee Center) was receptive to alternatives. The city was also open to alternatives, having hired outside counsel to defend the lawsuit and facing sizeable legal expenses if litigation continued. In early 1992, Hofstra University Law School Professor Baruch Bush suggested mediation and recommended a possible mediator. Both sides agreed to participate.

The mediation was held in April 1992, in a conference room at the Glen Cove Public Library. In two full-day sessions, which were spaced a week apart, the parties raised and addressed a broad range of issues. By the end of the second session, they reached an understanding as to the general substance of an acceptable accord. In December 1992, many drafts and conference calls later, the parties signed a final agreement, which included an amended ordinance.

The structure and timing of the sessions were designed to create an environment that would foster understanding and collaboration, and comport with political realities. In the first session, the parties were invited to describe their perspectives and concerns in an effort to gain – for the entire group – a more comprehensive understanding of the situation. No solutions or proposals were to be put forward at this session.

Many first-session presentations included the sharing of perspectives and stories that may not have been heard in a litigation context. Two day laborers, for example, described the hardship created by the hostile environment. The deputy chief of police and a city council member talked about the situation's impact on the police and town residents. An anthropology professor described how the Salvadorans' historical experience with repressive governments and brutal police tactics made them particularly vulnerable to perceived or actual hostility from the government.

This first session not only educated the participants about each other's realities, but also humanized and connected the parties. This reduced the prior acrimony that the litigation and press coverage had inflamed, and set the stage for tackling the issues.

The week between sessions gave the parties the opportunity to explore with their respective constituents possible proposals to address the issues raised. In the second session, the parties discussed and shaped proposals, and the Glen Cove mayor's visit to the working session enhanced a growing spirit of collaboration.

Notably, the agreement between the parties addressed concerns much broader than those raised by the litigation. These included:

- posting city notices in Spanish as well as English;
- use of the city soccer field by the Salvadoran community;\
- collaboration between the city and advocacy groups to create an alternate site for employers to connect with day workers;
- hosting of community meetings by CARECEN to educate the day laborers about community responsibilities;
- cultural awareness and Spanish language training for members of the police force;
- the institution of a police protocol for interventions in which a party does not speak English; and
- the collaborative drafting of an amended ordinance that both promoted the City's traffic safety concerns and satisfied CARECEN's concerns about discrimination and the protection of constitutional rights.

The agreement became a final judgment of the court in the lawsuit and terminated the litigation. Since many of its provisions required ongoing collaboration between the parties, the dialogue between them continued past the mediation sessions.

Today, Hispanic advocacy groups in Glen Cove report a working "shaping point" with toilet facilities provided by the city and a variety of supportive services for the day laborers. While the shaping point took several years to materialize, the mediation was a component of the change in climate that resulted in the new facility.

. . .

CHAPTER 10 - INTERNATIONAL DISPUTES

A. Questions

10.1 The elements of good mediation practice illustrated by President Carter's activities at Camp David include these:

    a. Careful preparation
- Analysis of Begin and Sadat
- Analysis of U.S. goals and tactics

    b. Ground rules designed to increase prospects of success
- Private negotiations with no communication to others, so that parties would not lose flexibility by posing for constituents

    c. Continuous efforts to build trust and communication between parties and mediator, as well as between parties themselves
- Encourages wives to be present
- Sadat open with Carter at once, so Carter focuses on trying to win Begin's trust
- Encourages direct communication between Begin and Sadat
- Constantly explaining and defending Begin to Sadat, and vice-versa, so that each will respect the other and understand why he takes the positions he does

    d. By judicious communication to each of tactics of other, Carter seeks to avoid d disruptive overreaction to those tactics

    e. Rather than treat each country's delegation as a monolithic whole, Carter r recognizes and makes use of the diversity of interests, skills, and power within each group

    f. Careful listening
- Begin's statement that he will never "personally recommend" dismantling the Sinai settlements appears to lead to the solution of submitting question of withdrawing settlers to the Knesset

    g. Careful focus on language in effort to break deadlocks
- At times, the effort is to find a mutually agreeable definition of a word, or a word that expresses a concept on which the parties agree; at other times, a word or phrase is selected precisely because of its ambiguity, so that each party may subsequently claim the interpretation it prefers. The latter device is commonly used when the parties cannot agree on a particular issue, and neither will concede, but the issue is not sufficiently important to block an over-all agreement.

    h. Discovering vital interests of each, and encouraging them to focus on those issues.
- Because Sadat was more open with Carter, Carter's efforts to discover vital interests were directed at Begin. Carter's efforts to encourage the parties to focus on their long-range interests, however, were directed to both Begin and Sadat.

    i. Use of one-text procedure
- Although Carter never uses the term one-text procedure or single negotiating text (as this procedure is sometimes known), there are suggestions in the narrative that he is using this technique, asking questions to determine each party's interests, drafting a single text, presenting it to each party for comments and changes until a mutually acceptable document is found. Until the document as a whole is accepted by both, neither is bound to any part of it. The use of the one-text procedure at Camp David is discussed and analyzed in Raiffa (1982: 211-214).

10.2   These statutes do not raise the same concerns about the loss of precedent and public access, because the alternative to settlement is another private process – arbitration – rather than adjudication. Also, to the extent that the international tribunals are used primarily by businesses and governments, these statutes do not pose issues of inexperienced negotiators or parties who do not understand the alternatives to settlement. The statutes make a policy contribution not discussed in Chapter 3 because they accommodate the dispute resolution preferences of persons whose disputing cultures favor conciliation over adjudication by placing agreements to conciliate on the same footing as agreements to arbitrate.

10.3   On the positive side, the trend would seem to encourage international business transactions by increasing the chances that disputes would be resolved expeditiously and using predictable standards. On the negative side, the trend reduces the role of courts in disputes that may involve public law issues, such as labor and environmental standards.

10.4   The suggestion that negotiators may be cooperative in approach with other members of their in-group counsels in favor of hiring a negotiator from Hong Kong. If your company prefers you as the negotiator, remember first the admonition of Rubin and Sander that the persons you negotiate with may not fit the generalizations about negotiating culture provided by Brett et al. In case they do not fit the generalizations, you may want to begin with a round of questioning, the most efficient way to get information in order to generate joint gains or advantages for your client. Nonetheless, given the advice in the excerpt, you should be prepared to shift to an indirect approach – what Brett et al. characterize as a "general discussion about the negotiation situation." If this does not result in information sharing, Brett et al. would advise you to proceed to a series of offers and counteroffers, using the effort in part to learn about possible joint gains. It might be important to continue to press for multiple-issue resolution even if the other negotiators want to negotiate one issue at a time, because the former is more likely to generate information and facilitate joint gains. The negotiator should be prepared for (and not be offended by) negotiators who will take forceful negotiating stances. Here the materials in Chapter 2, especially the advice by Lax and Sebenious, may be helpful.

B.   EXERCISES

EXERCISE 10.1   THE MOUSE EXERCISE

Teaching Instructions

Prior to the scheduled negotiations between the mayors, Mouse, and the French National Government, the mayors should caucus for 30-60 minutes in an effort to work out any differences between them, and to arrive at a common negotiation plan. The teacher may also want to encourage a pre-negotiation caucus between the representatives of Mouse and the French National Government, or the teacher may leave it up to them to decide if they want to have such a caucus. (The advantage of the caucus is that it enables them to coordinate their negotiation positions and tactics; the disadvantage is that if the mayors are aware of the caucus, they may view the French National Government representative as allied with Mouse, and so incapable of serving as a trusted mediator between them and Mouse.)

This exercise requires a minimum of 75 minutes (in addition to the prenegotiation caucuses). If you have more time available, you can schedule it to last up to 120 minutes.

(Since the central purpose of this exercise is to demonstrate how different cultural values can affect a negotiation, thus bringing into play the concepts discussed in the articles by Brett and Rubin and Sander that follow the exercise, a teacher may prefer not to assign this exercise until after the students have read those articles.)

EXERCISE 10.1   THE MOUSE EXERCISE

Confidential Instructions to the Mayor of Bailly
General Information

There are a number of concerns regarding EuroMouse that you share with your fellow mayors. You are very upset that the Master Agreement was concluded without your having been consulted, particularly since that your commune is directly impacted by the project.

This impact has already been felt in many ways. Your town lies in a traditionally agricultural rural area, and your constituents are very proud of their farming heritage. Although you recognize that this way of life was already in decline, the arrival of EuroMouse has certainly accelerated the process. Large tracts of the best farmland were expropriated by the national government in return for minimal compensation (FF 4.0/square meter). This exercise of eminent domain is particularly offensive given the fact that the government realized a profit of almost 200% when it sold the land to Mouse, yet made no provisions to aid the communes financially with the problems created for them by the EuroMouse Project.

The land that has remained in local hands has appreciated tremendously in value, which concerns your voters for several reasons. First, as property taxes are levied on appraised values, local residents anticipate seeing their tax burden increase despite the fact that they have not realized any actual benefit from the increased value. Moreover, as most agricultural property has been in the same families for generations, and those families want to remain on their ancestral property, as is the tradition among French farmers, they do not anticipate profiting from selling their land.

The second concern created by the property appreciation is that young residents will no longer be able to afford to purchase land in the area once they seek to establish their own households. They will be forced to move to other areas, thereby severing the family property ties that continue to be very important in France.

There are other issues, both short and long-term, which trouble you. In the immediate term you and your voters are feeling both physically and mentally overwhelmed by the project. The constant construction traffic is degrading the quality of life, and both the traffic and the work itself are raising fears that the environment is being harmed. In a land-oriented farming community such considerations are crucial, as they impact the farmers' very livelihood.

The arrival of Mouse has also created an administrative nightmare for you personally, as you have to deal not only with the concerns of an increasingly upset populace, but also with the myriad of forms, authorizations, licenses, and other documents which accompany a project of this magnitude. Being mayor used to be quite a pleasant, part-time occupation. You now find yourself thrust into a major administrative role for which you have neither the training nor the resources.

From a longer-term perspective you are concerned, both as mayor and as a local resident, about the social impact that Mouse will have on your community. The company recently invited you and your colleagues to visit MouseWorld, and you were absolutely horrified by what you saw. The communities around the park were little more than servicing areas for visitors, and they seemed shallow and artificial. You truly believe that your town represents traditional France and what is best about its values, and you are deeply concerned about the arrival of Mouse, America's ambassador promoting an insidious, fast-food, fast-fun culture, on your doorstep. You do not want your community to become a "quaint" rest stop for visitors on their way to EuroMouse, or for your young people to have to abandon the noble agricultural life to become amusement park workers serving the mindless tourists.

You realize, of course, that the EuroMouse development is here to stay, and you do not harbor any illusions that you will be able to stop the project. What you want is to feel that you have some part in guiding your townspeople's destiny, and that your voice is being heard and respected by both the national government and by Mouse. You are bothered by the lack of respect which you feel has been shown by Mouse in both large and small ways. For example, although you admit that you were very well treated on your trip to Florida, many of the Mouse executives were so presumptuous as to call you by your first name! These people are strangers to you, and you would no more dream of calling them by their given names than you would start discussing their family life with them -- that would simply be disrespectful on your part. You conduct yourself formally during business or political negotiations, and you expect the same conduct in return.

On a larger scale, you have been upset by Mouse's disrespect in going over your head to the national government when dealing with matters such as construction permits, which, by law and tradition, fall within your jurisdiction. The government, moreover, has encouraged such action by responding to Mouse and putting pressure on the mayors to expedite authorizations. Although you know that you are just a local official, you nevertheless represent one of the communities which Mouse is affecting and you feel that the lack of respect is an insult both to you personally and to your community as a whole.

Specific Information - Bailly

Your commune is suffering all of the detrimental effects of the EuroMouse development without anticipating any real gain from it. You feel tremendously betrayed by the national government in all this, as it did not allow you to participate in the original negotiations and then failed to protect your interests. In view of the enormous financial gains realized by the national government from the EuroMouse project, you believe that the national government should provide substantial financial assistance to the towns which are suffering as a result of the EuroMouse project. You also believe that Mouse, which stands to profit so handsomely by this project, should compensate the four towns for the impact of EuroMouse on those towns:

Specific Objectives:

Financial Compensation: You and your fellow mayors have agreed that you should demand total annual payments from Mouse and the national government in the amount of FF 16M per year. The minimum that you will insist on is FF 12M. (How that money would be shared has not been decided, and is discussed below.)

You prefer that all the revenue that the towns receive be in the form of annual payments that are agreed upon in advance, rather than in the form of a payroll tax. Mouse may try to convince you that a payroll tax will bring the towns more money as Mouse hires more employees, but that is too risky for you. Certainty, not risk, is your approach to financial (and other) issues.

Furthermore, an annual payment is not subject to EuroMouse's manipulating their payroll by hiding workers in other companies. EuroMouse is a sophisticated company. They can figure out how to reduce their tax load. You prefer the certainty of knowing that EuroMouse will contribute to the communes directly and annually.

Revenue Sharing. Bailly, like Magny, will play an equal role in the overall success of the park, but would not be entitled to share directly in any significant part of payroll tax revenues, if a payroll tax were imposed. However, you and the mayor of Magny have together insisted that Chessy and Coupvray share with Bailly and Magny all revenues they receive from EuroMouse or the national government, whether in the form of annual payments or payroll tax. (After all, if it were not for the inconvenience to the citizens of Bailly and Magny, whose towns are used as a thoroughfare for trucks, Chessy and Coupvray would receive no benefit at all, as there would be no EuroMouse development.)

Your fellow mayors have not yet agreed to your demands, but you and the mayor of Magny have an ace up your sleeves. Unless Chessy and Coupvray agree to equal revenue-sharing, you will do nothing to discourage local farmers from blocking access to the site. Farmers have successfully blocked roads in various parts of France in recent years to protest low prices and loss of subsidies. There is no reason why they wouldn't do the same to protest the destruction of their traditional way of life. Such an action could bring the Mouse project to a virtual halt, and the negative publicity to Mouse would be terrible. You have not yet told the mayors of Chessy and Coupvray (or Mouse) of your decision in this respect, but you will certainly do so at the appropriate moment.

Press Release. You anticipate that Mouse and the national government will want you to agree to a positive press release, and you are willing to do so if, as part of the total financial package, Bailly receives a guarantee of at least FF 3M per year, either from Mouse, the national government, or both.

Expediting Permits. Your office staff is simply overwhelmed by the volume of permit requests from Mouse. Mouse appears to have no sensitivity to French cultural norms, and expects your staff to give up their traditional August vacations with their families in order to speed up Mouse's project. You have no intention of requiring them to do so. Unless the national government will provide you with additional personnel (at its expense) to expedite the processing of permits, Mouse will just have to calm itself.

Community Planner. You are convinced that the mayors need community planning advice to deal effectively with the enormous changes resulting from the EuroMouse project. Bailly cannot afford to hire a community planner, and certainly wouldn't ask Mouse for one (not after what you saw of the communities around MouseWorld). Thus, you will request community planning assistance from the national government.

EXERCISE 10.1 THE MOUSE EXERCISE

Confidential Instructions to the Mayor of Chessy
General Information

There are a number of concerns regarding EuroMouse that you share with your fellow mayors. You are very upset that the Master Agreement was concluded without your having been consulted, particularly since your commune is directly impacted by the project.

This impact has already been felt in many ways. Your town lies in a traditionally agricultural rural area, and your constituents are very proud of their farming heritage. Although you recognize that this way of life was already in decline, the arrival of EuroMouse has certainly accelerated the process. Large tracts of the best farmland were expropriated by the national government in return for minimal compensation

(FF 4.0/square meter). This exercise of eminent domain is particularly offensive given the fact that the government realized a profit of almost 200% when it sold the land to Mouse, yet made no provisions to aid the communes financially with the problems created for them by the EuroMouse Project.

The land that has remained in local hands has appreciated tremendously in value, which concerns your voters for several reasons. First, as property taxes are levied on appraised values, local residents anticipate seeing their tax burden increase despite the fact that they have not realized any actual benefit from the increased value. Moreover, as most agricultural property has been in the same families for generations, and those families want to remain on their ancestral property, as is the tradition among French farmers, they do not anticipate profiting from selling their land.

The second concern created by the property appreciation is that young residents will no longer be able to afford to purchase land in the area once they seek to establish their own households. They will be forced to move to other areas, thereby severing the family ties that continue to be very important in France.

There are other issues, both short and long-term, which trouble you. In the immediate term you and your voters are feeling both physically and mentally overwhelmed by the project. The constant construction traffic is degrading the quality of life, and both the traffic and the work itself are raising fears that the environment is being harmed. In a land-oriented farming community such considerations are crucial, as they impact the farmers' very livelihood.

The arrival of Mouse has also created an administrative nightmare for you personally, as you have to deal not only with the concerns of an increasingly upset populace, but also with the myriad of forms, authorizations, licenses, and other documents which accompany a project of this magnitude. Being mayor used to be quite a pleasant, part-time occupation. You now find yourself thrust into a major administrative role for which you have neither the training nor the resources.

From a longer-term perspective you are concerned, both as mayor and as a local resident, about the social impact that Mouse will have on your community . The company recently invited you and your colleagues to visit MouseWorld, and you were absolutely horrified by what you saw. The communities around the park were little more than servicing areas for visitors, and they seemed shallow and artificial. You truly believe that your town represents traditional France and what is best about! its values, and you are deeply concerned about the arrival of Mouse, America's ambassador promoting an insidious, fast-food, fast-fun culture, on your doorstep. You do not want your community to become a "quaint" rest stop for visitors on their way to EuroMouse, or for your young people to have to abandon the noble agricultural life to become amusement park workers serving the mindless tourists.

You realize, of course, that the EuroMouse development is here to stay, and you do not harbor any illusions that you will be able to stop the project. What you want is to feel that you have some part in guiding your townspeople's destiny, and that your voice is being heard and respected by both the national government and by Mouse. You are bothered by the lack of respect which you feel has been shown by Mouse in both large and small ways. For example, although you admit that you were very well treated on your trip to Florida, many of the Mouse executives were so presumptuous as to call you by your first name! These people are strangers to you, and you would no more dream of calling them by their given names than you would start discussing their family life with them -- that would simply be disrespectful on your part. You conduct yourself formally during business or political negotiations, and you expect the same conduct in return.

On a larger scale, you have been upset by Mouse's disrespect in going over your head to the national government when dealing with matters such as construction permits, which, by law and tradition, fall within your jurisdiction. The government, moreover, has encouraged such action by responding to Mouse and putting pressure on the mayors to expedite authorizations. Although you know that you are just a local official, you nevertheless represent one of the communities which Mouse is affecting and you feel that the lack of respect is an insult both to you personally and to your community as a whole.

Specific Information - Chessy

You feel tremendously betrayed by the national government in all this, as it did not allow you to participate in the original negotiations and then failed to protect your interests. In view of the enormous financial gains realized by the national government from the EuroMouse project, you believe it should provide substantial financial assistance to the towns which are suffering as a result of that project. You also believe that Mouse, which stand to profit so handsomely by this project, should compensate the four towns for the impact of EuroMouse on those towns:

Special Objectives

Financial Compensation: You and your fellow mayors have agreed that you should demand total annual payments from Mouse and the national government in the amount of FF 16M per year. The minimum that you will insist on is FF 12M. (How that money would be shared has not been decided, and is discussed below.)

You prefer that all the revenue that the towns receive be in the form of annual payments that are agreed upon in advance, rather than in the form of a payroll tax. Mouse may try to convince you that a payroll tax will bring the towns more money as Mouse hires more employees, but that is too risky for you. Certainty, not risk, is your approach to financial (and other) issues.

Furthermore, an annual payment is not subject to the rate at which EuroMouse hires employees. It is also not subject to EuroMouse's manipulating their payroll by hiding workers in other companies. EuroMouse is a sophisticated company. They can figure out how to reduce their tax load. You prefer the certainty of knowing that EuroMouse will contribute to the communes directly and annually.

Revenue Sharing. You are reluctant to share any revenues that you receive from Mouse or the national government with Bailly and Magny. You are not totally inflexible on this point, however, and will ultimately agree to as much revenue-sharing as is necessary to insure that the mayors of Bailly and Magny do not disrupt the EuroMouse project, which will ultimately be of great economic benefit to your town.

Press Release. You anticipate that Mouse and the national government will want you to agree to a positive press release, and you are willing to do so if, as part of the total financial package, Chessy receives a guarantee of at least FF 3M per year, either from Mouse, the national government or both.

Expediting Permits. Your office staff is simply overwhelmed by the volume of permit requests from Mouse. Mouse appears to have no sensitivity to French cultural norms, and expects your staff to give up their traditional August vacations with their families in order to speed up Mouse's project. You have no intention of requiring them to do so. Unless the national government will provide you with additional personnel (at its expense) to expedite the processing of permits, Mouse will just have to calm itself.

Community Planner. You are convinced that the mayors need community planning advice to deal effectively with the enormous changes resulting from the EuroMouse project. Chessy cannot afford to hire a community planner, and certainly wouldn't ask Mouse for one (not after what you saw of the communities around MouseWorld). Thus, you will request community planning assistance from the national government.

EXERCISE 10.1 THE MOUSE EXERCISE

Confidential Instructions to the Mayor of Coupvray
General Information

There are a number of concerns regarding EuroMouse that you share with your fellow mayors. You are very upset that the Master Agreement was concluded without your having been consulted, particularly since your commune is directly impacted by the project.

This impact has already been felt in many ways. Your town lies in a traditionally agricultural rural area, and your constituents are very proud of their farming heritage. Although you recognize that this way of life was already in decline, the arrival of EuroMouse has certainly accelerated the process. Large tracts of the best farmland were expropriated by the national government in return for minimal compensation (FF 4.0/square meter). This exercise of eminent domain is particularly offensive given the fact that the government realized a profit of almost 200% when it sold the land to Mouse, yet made no provisions to aid the communes financially with the problems created for them by the EuroMouse Project.

The land that has remained in local hands has appreciated tremendously in value, which concerns your voters for several reasons. First, as property taxes are levied on appraised values, local residents anticipate seeing their tax burden increase despite the fact that they have not realized any actual benefit from the increased value. Moreover, as most agricultural property has been in the same families for generations, and those families want to remain on their ancestral property, as is the tradition among French farmers, they do not anticipate profiting from selling their land.

The second concern created by the property appreciation is that young residents will no longer be able to afford to purchase land in the area once they seek to establish their own households. They will be forced to move to other areas, thereby severing the family ties that continue to be very important in France.

There are other issues, both short and long-term, which trouble you. In the immediate term you and your voters are feeling both physically and mentally overwhelmed by the project. The constant construction traffic is degrading the quality of life, and both the traffic and the work itself are raising fears that the environment is being harmed. In a land-oriented farming community such considerations are crucial, as they impact the farmers' very livelihood.

The arrival of Mouse has also created an administrative nightmare for you personally, as you have to deal not only with the concerns of an increasingly upset populace, but also with the myriad of forms, authorizations, licenses, and other documents which accompany a project of this magnitude. Being mayor used to be quite a pleasant, part-time occupation. You now find yourself thrust into a major administrative role for which you have neither the training nor the resources.

From a longer-term perspective you are concerned, both as mayor and as a local resident, about the social impact that Mouse will have on your community . The company recently invited you and your colleagues to visit MouseWorld, and you were absolutely horrified by what you saw. The communities around the park were little more than servicing areas for visitors, and they seemed shallow and artificial. You truly believe that your town represents traditional France and what is best about its values, and you are deeply concerned about the arrival of Mouse, America's ambassador promoting an insidious, fast-food, fast-fun culture, on your doorstep. You do not want your community to become a "quaint" rest stop for visitors on their way to EuroMouse, or for your young people to have to abandon the noble agricultural life to become amusement park workers serving the mindless tourists.

You realize, of course, that the EuroMouse development is here to stay, and you do not harbor any illusions that you will be able to stop the project. What you want is to feel that you have some part in guiding your townspeople's destiny, and that your voice is being heard and respected by both the national government and by Mouse. You are bothered by the lack of respect which you feel has been shown by Mouse in both large and small ways. For example, although you admit that you were very well treated on your trip to Florida, many of the Mouse executives were so presumptuous as to call you by your first name! These people are strangers to you, and you would no more dream of calling them by their given names than you would start discussing their family life with them -- that would simply be disrespectful on your part. You conduct yourself formally during business or political negotiations, and you expect the same conduct in return.

On a larger scale, you have been upset by Mouse's disrespect in going over your head to the national government when dealing with matters such as construction permits which, by law and tradition, fall within your jurisdiction. The government, moreover, has encouraged such action by responding to Mouse and putting pressure on the mayors to expedite authorizations. Although you know that you are just a local official, you nevertheless represent one of the communities which Mouse is affecting and you feel that the lack of respect is an insult both to you personally and to your community as a whole.

Specific Information - Coupvray

You feel tremendously betrayed by the national government in all this, as it did not allow you to participate in the original negotiations and then failed to protect your interests. In view of the enormous financial gains realized by the national government from the EuroMouse project, you believe it should provide substantial financial assistance to the towns which are suffering as a result of that project. You also believe that Mouse, which stand to profit so handsomely by this project, should compensate the four towns for the impact of EuroMouse on those towns:

Specific Objectives:

Financial Compensation: You and your fellow mayors have agreed that you should demand total annual payments from Mouse and the national government in the amount of FF 16M per year. The minimum that you will insist on is FF 12M. (How that money would be shared has not been decided, and is discussed below.)

You prefer that all the revenue that the towns receive be in the form of annual payments that are agreed upon in advance, rather than in the form of a payroll tax. Mouse may try to convince you that a payroll tax will bring the towns more money as Mouse hires more employees, but that is too risky for you. Certainty, not risk, is your approach to financial (and other) issues.

Furthermore, an annual payment is not subject to the rate at which EuroMouse hires employees. It is also not subject to EuroMouse's manipulating their payroll by hiding workers in other companies. EuroMouse is a sophisticated company. They can figure out how to reduce their tax load. You prefer the certainty of knowing that EuroMouse will contribute to the communes directly and annually.

Revenue Sharing. You are reluctant to share any revenues that you receive from Mouse or the national government with Bailly and Magny. A payroll tax, if imposed, would go almost entirely to Chessy and

Coupvray. Hence, whether Mouse (or the national government) provide for a payroll tax or annual payments not related to the size of the Mouse payroll, those funds should go solely to Chessy and Coupvray. You are not totally inflexible on this point, however, and will ultimately agree to as much revenue-sharing as is necessary to insure that the mayors of Bailly and Magny do not disrupt the EuroMouse project, which will ultimately be of great economic benefit to your town.

Press Release. You anticipate that Mouse and the national government will want you to agree to a positive press release, and you are willing to do so if, as part of the total financial package, Coupvray receives a guarantee of at least FF 3M per year, either from Mouse, the national government or both.

Expediting Permits. Your office staff is simply overwhelmed by the volume of permit requests from Mouse. Mouse appears to have no sensitivity to French cultural norms, and expects your staff to give up their traditional August vacations with their families in order to speed up Mouse's project. You have no intention of requiring them to do so. Unless the national government will provide you with additional personnel (at its expense) to expedite the processing of permits, Mouse will just have to calm itself.

Community Planner. You are convinced that the mayors need community planning advice to deal effectively with the enormous changes resulting from the EuroMouse project. Coupvray cannot afford to hire a community planner, and certainly wouldn't ask Mouse for one (not after what you saw of the communities around MouseWorld). Thus, you will request community planning assistance from the national government.

EXERCISE 10.1   THE MOUSE EXERCISE

Confidential Instructions to the Mayor of Magny
General Information

There are a number of concerns regarding EuroMouse that you share with your fellow mayors. You are very upset that the Master Agreement was concluded without your having been consulted, particularly since your commune is directly impacted by the project.

This impact has already been felt in many ways. Your town lies in a traditionally agricultural rural area, and your constituents are very proud of their farming heritage. Although you recognize that this way of life was already in decline, the arrival of EuroMouse has certainly accelerated the process. Large tracts of the best farmland were expropriated by the national government in return for minimal compensation (FF 4.0/square meter). This exercise of eminent domain is particularly offensive given the fact that the government realized a profit of almost 200% when it sold the land to Mouse, yet made no provisions to aid the communes financially with the problems created for them by the EuroMouse Project.

The land that has remained in local hands has appreciated tremendously in value, which concerns your voters for several reasons. First, as property taxes are levied on appraised values, local residents anticipate seeing their tax burden increase despite the fact that they have not realized any actual benefit from the increased value. Moreover, as most agricultural property has been in the same families for generations, and those families want to remain on their ancestral property, as is the tradition among French farmers, they do not anticipate profiting from selling their land.

The second concern created by the property appreciation is that young residents will no longer be able to afford to purchase land in the area once they seek to establish their own households. They will be forced to move to other areas, thereby severing the family ties that continue to be very important in France.

There are other issues, both short and long-term, which trouble you. In the immediate term you and your voters are feeling both physically and mentally overwhelmed by the project. The constant construction traffic is degrading the quality of life, and both the traffic and the work itself are raising fears that the environment is being harmed. In a land-oriented farming community such considerations are crucial, as they impact the farmers' very livelihood.

The arrival of Mouse has also created an administrative nightmare for you personally, as you have to deal not only with the concerns of an increasingly upset populace, but also with the myriad of forms, authorizations, licenses, and other documents which accompany a project of this magnitude. Being mayor used to be quite a pleasant, part-time occupation. You now find yourself thrust into a major administrative role for which you have neither the training nor the resources.

From a longer-term perspective you are concerned, both as mayor and as a local resident, about the social impact that Mouse will have on your community . The company recently invited you and your colleagues to visit MouseWorld, and you were absolutely horrified by what you saw. The communities around the park were little more than servicing areas for visitors, and they seemed shallow and artificial. You truly believe that your town represents traditional France and what is best about its values, and you are deeply concerned about the arrival of Mouse, America's ambassador promoting an insidious, fast-food, fast-fun culture, on your doorstep. You do not want your community to become a "quaint" rest stop for visitors on their way to EuroMouse, or for your young people to have to abandon the noble agricultural life to become amusement park workers serving the mindless tourists.

You realize, of course, that the EuroMouse development is here to stay, and you do not harbor any illusions that you will be able to stop the project. What you want is to feel that you have some part in guiding your townspeople's destiny, and that your voice is being heard and respected by both the national government and by Mouse. You are bothered by the lack of respect which you feel has been shown by Mouse in both large and small ways. For example, while you admit that you were very well treated on your trip to Florida, many of the Mouse executives were so presumptuous as to call you by your first name! These people are strangers to you, and you would no more dream of calling them by their given names than you would start discussing their family life with them -- that would simply be disrespectful on your part. You conduct yourself formally during business or political negotiations, and you expect the same conduct in return.

On a larger scale, you have been upset by Mouse's disrespect in going over your head to the national government when dealing with matters such as construction permits, which, by law and tradition, fall within your jurisdiction. The government, moreover, has encouraged such action by responding to Mouse and putting pressure on the mayors to expedite authorizations. Although you know that you are just a local official, you nevertheless represent one of the communities which Mouse is affecting and you feel that the lack of respect is an insult both to you personally and to your community as a whole.

Specific Information - Magny

Your commune is suffering all of the detrimental effects of the EuroMouse development without anticipating any real gain from it. You feel tremendously betrayed by the national government in all this, as it did not allow you to participate in the original negotiations and then failed to protect your interests. In view of the enormous financial gains realized by the national government from the EuroMouse project, you believe that the national government should provide substantial financial assistance to the towns which are suffering as a result of the EuroMouse project. You also believe that Mouse, which stands to profit so handsomely by this project, should compensate the four towns for the impact of EuroMouse on those towns:

Specific Objectives:

Financial Compensation: You and your fellow mayors have agreed that you should demand total annual payments from Mouse and the national government in the amount of FF 16M per year. The minimum that you will insist on is FF 12M. (How that money would be shared has not been decided, and is discussed below.)

You prefer that all the revenue that the towns receive be in the form of annual payments that are agreed upon in advance, rather than in the form of a payroll tax. Mouse may try to convince you that a payroll tax will bring the towns more money as Mouse hires more employees, but that sounds too risky for you. Certainty, not risk, is your approach to financial (and other) issues.

Furthermore, an annual payment is not subject to EuroMouse's manipulating their payroll by hiding workers in other companies. EuroMouse is a sophisticated company. They can figure out how to reduce their tax load. You prefer the certainty of knowing that EuroMouse will contribute to the communes directly and annually.

Revenue Sharing. Magny, like Bailly, will play an equal role in the overall success of the park, but would not be entitled to share directly in any significant part of payroll tax revenues if a payroll tax were imposed. However, you and the mayor of Bailly have together insisted that Chessy and Coupvray share with Bailly and Magny all revenues they receive from EuroMouse or the national government, whether in the form of annual payments or payroll tax. (After all, if it were not for the inconvenience to the citizens of Bailly and Magny, whose towns are used as a thoroughfare for trucks, Chessy and Coupvray would receive no benefit at all, as there would be no EuroMouse development.)

Your fellow mayors have not yet agreed to your demands, but you and the mayor of Bailly have an ace up your sleeves. Unless Chessy and Coupvray agree to equal revenue-sharing, you will do nothing to discourage local farmers from blocking access to the site. Farmers have successfully blocked roads in various parts of France in recent years to protest the destruction of their traditional way of life. Such an action could bring the Mouse project to a virtual halt, and the negative publicity to Mouse would be terrible. You have not yet told the mayors of Chessy and Coupvray (or Mouse) of your decision in this respect, but you will certainly do so at the appropriate moment.

Press Release. You anticipate that Mouse and the national government will want you to agree to a positive press release, and you are willing to do so if Magny receives a guarantee of at least FF 3M per year, either from Mouse, the national government or both.

Expediting Permits. Your office staff is simply overwhelmed by the volume of permit requests from Mouse. Mouse appears to have no sensitivity to French cultural norms, and expects your staff to give up their traditional August vacations with their families in order to speed up Mouse's project. You have no intention of requiring them to do so. Unless the national government will provide you with additional personnel (at its expense) to expedite the processing of permits, Mouse will just have to calm itself.

Community Planner. You are convinced that the mayors need community planning advice to deal effectively with the enormous changes resulting from the EuroMouse project. Magny cannot afford to hire a community planner, and certainly wouldn't ask Mouse for one (not after what you saw of the communities around MouseWorld). Thus, you will request community planning assistance from the national government.

EXERCISE 10.1 THE MOUSE EXERCISE

Confidential Instructions for French National Government Official
General Information

You are an official in the Ministry of International Trade. You joined the Ministry after graduating with a D.E.S.S. from the prestigious Ecole Nationale d'Administration. You have been active in developing the government's new global economic policies, and you were a member of the team negotiating with Mouse over the site for EuroMouse.

You are very proud of the Master Agreement, and believe that it represents one of the first major achievements of a "New France" -- one that is attuned to the realities of international business and is globally competitive. Given the expense and effort, which has been invested in the project to date, it is a political imperative that the development progress as smoothly as possible.

You are quite distressed about the negative press the project has received. France needs to generate new jobs, and foreign investment is an effective way of doing so. The government's global economic strategy was specifically designed to encourage foreign investment in France, such as the EuroMouse project, which is expected to bring jobs and revenue to an area of France where job growth would otherwise be negative.

The mayors are, quite frankly, provincials who do not understand today's economic realities. In view of the rapid development of the European Economic Community and the growth of world trade, preservation of every farm village as it existed 100 years ago is just not feasible. This project will be good for these towns and France, both because of the jobs and revenue that it will create and, more importantly, because of the message it will send to other potential investors. Although there are complaints about higher property values and administrative costs, you feel that change was inevitable in Marne-la-Vallee. At least with Mouse, the towns will reap some financial rewards in terms of jobs and tax revenue.

The mayors are simply not giving the government credit for bringing financial renewal to their communities. Furthermore, as the government is contractually obligated to uphold its agreement with Mouse regardless of how much criticism it garners from the towns, you cannot afford to pacify the mayors to such a degree that Mouse's interests are seriously harmed.

The press has been a problem. The national press ballyhooed American cultural imperialism when the Master Agreement was announced. Now the local mayors are getting national press with their complaints that Mouse is destroying the traditional way of life in their communities. It has also been extremely troublesome to defend the seemingly huge profit the national government made on the sale of the land to Mouse. Finally, although you have not been involved personally, you are aware that Mouse has asked the national government to put pressure on the mayors to expedite approvals and authorizations. The Americans do not understand that provincial France works at its own pace. They want everything done yesterday.

Specific Objectives

When the Assistant Minister for International Trade assigned you to represent the government at this meeting, he told you that he expected you to manage the negotiation so that a satisfactory agreement was reached. He also made it clear that you were being given both the authority and the responsibility for making certain that the outcome satisfied the government's concerns. He also stressed the extreme caution, which should be used during the meeting, given the tightrope the government is walking between its political need to show loyalty to the towns and its desire to promote foreign investment. The government does not under any circumstances wish to be viewed as favoring either Mouse or the towns during the meeting, regardless of its objectives on a given issue. Its specific concerns are as follows:

Press Release: The Government wants the meeting to result in a press release signed by all parties stating that they believe that the project is mutually beneficial, that it is fair to all parties, and that they look forward to working together in a spirit of cooperation. Given the grumblings of the mayors that they were not consulted when the original agreement was reached, it is particularly important that the press release specify that the towns support the government's actions now.

Financial Compensation: You know that the towns want financial compensation from Mouse. You also suspect that Mouse, though opposed in principal to such payments, because they were not provided for in the Master Agreement, will be willing to make some payment, either in the form of a payroll tax or fixed annual payments. The Finance Minister has advised your Minister that he is willing to impose the customary payroll tax up to 2% if your Minister recommends that he do so. You must tread carefully on this issue, as you do not know what positions the parties will take, and the government does not want to be seen as favoring either party.

Sharing of Revenue: As the sharing of payroll tax receipts or annual payments among the towns has no impact on the national government, you are indifferent about the resolution of this issue. Hence, you intend to steer clear of this question unless you believe that involvement could provide you with a significant advantage in another dimension of the negotiation. If you do get involved you must be very sensitive as to how the government's role may be portrayed. The last thing your superiors want is complaints from any towns that they were once again pressured by the government.

Government Compensation: Given the nature of the towns' complaints against the government, you anticipate a request by the mayors for compensation from Paris. Although the government did realize a significant profit from the resale of the land to Mouse, all funds received from that sale, are being used, by prior agreement with Mouse, to build high speed rail and auto routes to EuroMouse. As a result, none of those funds are available to be distributed to the communities.

Once the project becomes profitable and pays off its original investment, the government will, of course, receive a corporate income tax, but that may be years away. Moreover, the government does not want to set a precedent of compensating municipalities for the inevitable negative side effects of government-approved foreign investments. In view of this, the Finance Minister has made it clear that under no circumstances may you agree to any form of monetary compensation to the towns.

Government Assistance: Although the government is unwilling to provide any form of direct monetary compensation to the towns, you are authorized to provide them with community planners and administrative assistants to help them process the extra administrative work generated by the EuroMouse Project. While doing so will impose salary costs on the national government, (unless you can persuade the mayors or Mouse to pay the salaries of any planners or assistants sent by the national government), you are willing to absorb these costs if the mayors will promise: (1) to stop the negative publicity, (2) not to block access to the EuroMouse project site, and (3) to take action to prevent and stop any such efforts by local farmers. The blocking of roads to achieve social or economic goals represents the "old"

France; EuroMouse represents the "new" France, which seeks to attract sophisticated international investors. You cannot allow old ways to block new policies!

EXERCISE 10.1   THE MOUSE EXERCISE

Confidential Instructions for Mouse Representative
General Information

You have recently been transferred from corporate headquarters to manage government and public relations for EuroMouse. You are a rising star in Mouse's strategic planning group, and you see your temporary assignment to the EuroMouse project as proof that your superiors think highly of you. After three years working in public relations and another three years in consumer marketing you returned to school and received an MBA. Five years ago, you joined Mouse. Until a month ago, you were working on a series of projects identifying potential sites for Mouse parks in the U.S. and around the world. You were not involved in the original EuroMouse negotiations with the French government. The Mouse managers who were have moved on to other projects.

Although you have traveled overseas, and worked with foreign nationals to collect information for site assessment studies, this assignment is your first time actually conducting business overseas. Your French language skills are not as good as they might be, but are certainly adequate for this assignment.

Despite the recent problems with the project, you are not too concerned about this meeting. You have done your homework; you believe you have a good grasp of the issues and, after all, you will be dealing with local mayors--it's not as if you're dealing with the Prime Minister. You want to approach the negotiation in a friendly manner. You prefer to break the ice at the beginning of meetings and establish some degree of personal rapport and informality with your counterparts. You detest stuffiness, and like to be on a first-name basis with anyone you deal with. On the issues, however, you intend to do your very best to make sure Mouse achieves its specific objectives.

Objectives

Press Release: You intend to begin the negotiation by pointing out to the mayors how beneficial the EuroMouse project will be for the area. Property values are rising astronomically, and landowners stand to profit handsomely from selling property. Secondly, the French economy has not created jobs in 15 years, and unemployment of French youth age 18-26 is running higher than 20%. Mouse is beginning to recruit locally for permanent jobs, which, you are certain, are far more attractive to the area's residents than is the difficult life of a farmer. The mayors should be delighted that their area was picked as the site for EuroMouse.

You know that Mouse recently took the mayors on a VIP tour of MouseWorld, and are surprised that after seeing how terrific the planned communities surrounding the MouseWorld are, the mayors are still complaining, and in an increasingly public manner. These complaints could hurt Mouse's image and the EuroMouse project. You know that your superiors very much want the public grumbling by the mayors to stop, and therefore one of your principal goals for this negotiation is to get all parties to agree to a press release saying how happy they are that Mouse is
moving into the area, and that they feel that they are being very fairly treated.

You do not anticipate that obtaining this press release will be difficult, as you expect the full cooperation of the French national government representative. This representative is a young, business-oriented person, and you know that the national government has a lot invested in the project, both in terms of prestige and money. In fact, all the profits that the government received on the sale of land to Mouse, is being used, by prior agreement with Mouse, to build high-speed rail and auto routes to EuroMouse.

You think that the government representative should walk into the meeting and order the mayors to cooperate with Mouse. In several instances, Mouse has been able to entirely bypass the relevant local authorities and "go to the top" when things needed doing, and you do not see why it should be any different this time.

Financial Demands: You are astonished at the idea that Mouse, which is bringing tremendous economic benefits to the area, should be expected to provide financial compensation to the towns for the inconveniences and administrative demands of construction. Cities and towns as depressed as these should beg a major employer like Mouse to build in their area, and should offer tax and other financial advantages, not make financial demands!

You recognize that the national government has authority to impose a payroll tax, but you are outraged at the demand for annual payments not related to the Mouse payroll. Mouse is making enormous contributions to both the national and local economies -- increased property values and jobs -- and in view of those contributions should not be required to contribute still further through annual payments. Besides, neither a payroll tax nor an annual payment was included in the Master Agreement between the national government and Mouse.

If this argument is unsuccessful, and Mouse is required to make payments to the towns in some fashion, it much prefers to do so through a payroll tax, rather than through annual payments. (The advantage of a payroll tax to Mouse is that it will diminish in lean economic times, when park employment and revenues are down, while annual payments at a fixed amount would not diminish.) As a result, Mouse is willing to pay <u>more</u> to the towns if that payment is in the form of a tax rather than annual payments. You should point this out to the mayors, as well as the fact that their towns will profit from the growth of EuroMouse <u>only</u> if they receive tax revenues, not if they receive fixed annual payments. (You intend to suggest to the mayors that if they want fixed annual payments, they should obtain them from the national government, which profited so handsomely from the land sale.)

The following chart, which assumes an annual payroll of FF 700M to 1,300M, sets out some parameters of your authority to offer annual payments at differing tax levels, as well as the projected cost to Mouse/revenue to the towns at each level. For example, you are authorized to agree to up to a 2% tax if there are no annual payments, and up to 12 million francs per year in annual payments if there is no payroll tax. You may not agree to annual payments in an amount greater than those indicated in the chart below.. For example, if the agreed-upon tax is 1.5%, you cannot agree to an annual payment of more than $3M.

Tax Rate	Tax Revenue	Annual Payment	Total Cost to Mouse/ Revenue to Towns
0%	FF 0	FF12M	FF 12M
.5%	3.5 - 6.5M	9M	12.5 - 15.5M
1.0%	7 - 13M	6M	13 - 19M
1.5%	10.5 - 19.5M	3M	13.5 - 22.5M
2.0%	14.0 - 26.0	0	14 - 26M

There is one requirement that you must insist on as a condition to any annual payments. Mouse officials have heard rumors that local farmers, particularly those living in Bailly and Magny, may try to block access to the EuroMouse site to protest its encroachment on their agricultural life (which is dying anyway). This would not only cause the project to experience further delays but would also be harmful to the carefully cultivated public image of Mouse. You cannot believe that the government would allow this to occur, but, as a condition to any annual payments you must insist that the mayors agree to discourage such action, and, if it occurs, to request the assistance of the national police ("gendarmerie nationale") to insure access to the site.

Division of Tax and Other Revenues: Whether and how the communes divide up any revenues that they receive is of no concern to you. You have no wish to become involved in this area of discussion, as you do not want to appear to be interfering in the towns' affairs. In fact, if you could, you would not have this issue be a part of the upcoming meeting, as you see it as something that the towns should deal with themselves.

Permits: EuroMouse is behind schedule, and you feel that the towns are largely to blame. The towns have been slow to issue the necessary permits, carry out inspections, and generally have been dragging their feet. In fact, the towns all but closed the commune offices for the entire month of August last year, leaving only a single secretary on duty in each office. You are incredulous at such a lack of business sense. The mayors do not seem at all concerned that they could cost EuroMouse millions of francs. They act as if pacifying their bureaucratic staffs by catering to their every whim is more important than Mouse meeting its deadlines.

It is imperative that you get the towns to speed up the issuance of permits so that the project does not fall further behind schedule. Specifically, you want a commitment that each permit application will be acted on within 30 days of being filed. A permit that is not acted on within that period would be automatically granted.

In order to obtain such a commitment, you are authorized to provide, at no cost to the towns, the services of a consultant from the planning firm that developed the communities around MouseWorld in Florida. Those are beautifully planned, modern, efficient communities, and the mayors would benefit greatly by listening to the advice of the planning firm that developed them. Additionally, with expert advice, the mayors could have a broader vision of the EuroMouse development, and could see how each permit application fits into the over-all scheme. This, you believe, would encourage them to deal promptly with those applications. (You also would be delighted to have a consultant with pre-existing loyalties to Mouse advising the mayors.)

Other than the above, you have no specific guidelines for the meeting. Provided that you believe that Mouse's interests have been satisfied, you are authorized to commit the company to any agreement reached. You also have some latitude to offer low or no-cost inducements to the mayors (e.g. reduced-rate admission to the park for local residents, etc.) if this will assist in achieving a favorable outcome. If you can get the parties to reach a creative agreement, which will both help Mouse's public image and contain costs, you will not only complete this assignment in an extremely positive way, but also secure your position on the fast track. Of course, if you fail, your superiors may decide that you are simply not cut out for international work. In a global firm like Mouse, such a conclusion would not be very helpful for your career.

EXERCISE 10.1   THE MOUSE EXERCISE

Teaching Notes

The questions that follow deal primarily with the cross-cultural issues raised by the negotiation, though we have also found it useful to touch on the concept of BATNA and on one aspect of multi-issue negotiations.

1. What is Mouse's BATNA?
   - Not simply to keep building, because, absent an agreement, the mayors whose villages do not benefit from the payroll tax are likely to encourage demonstrations that will block the roads and impede construction. Such actions will also harm Mouse's public image and perhaps its ultimate gate receipts.

2. But that is nonsense, isn't it? The national government, which wants EuroMouse to succeed as much as Mouse does, will just bring in the police to break up any demonstrations that interfere with construction. So Mouse really has a very good BATNA, right?
   - Wrong. If you know France and French cultural norms, you know that the government is very reluctant to interfere with road blockages or other demonstrations by politically powerful groups. France is a very group-oriented society, in which people accept the right of others to impose inconvenience on all to obtain their group's goals. "I'll support your group today; you support my group tomorrow" And this view strongly discourages government intervention to block demonstrations
     - For Mouse to know its BATNA, it must know French cultural norms

3. How do cultural differences affect the parties' positions on the issues involved in this negotiation?
   - Payment of financial compensation to communities
     - Mouse – Should be no payment. Mouse is bringing jobs and economic development, and its presence increases property values. A U.S. community would give Mouse tax breaks, development grants, etc., to attract it. These towns are nuts to think that Mouse should pay them for reviving their economies!
     - Mayors - Putting on Mouse ears to amuse American tourists is demeaning. The influx of tourists and foreign (American) workers will play havoc with our traditional life style. Increased property values are a curse not a blessing, since we don't want to sell land that has been in our families for centuries. The effect of higher land values for us is simply that we must pay higher taxes, and see our children move away because they cannot find affordable housing here.
   - Expediting permits
     - Mouse – These people don't seem to understand that time is money. How can they possibly shut down in August when we have permits that must be processed so that we can get on with our business?
     - Mayors – The Americans have no respect for the quality of life or for tradition. We have always taken August vacations; that's when the family gets together. Surely, issuing the permits a few days earlier does not warrant the destruction of French family life and tradition
   - Community planner
     - Mouse – Our community planners are highly skilled. Look at the great job they did with Mouse World on Florida
     - Mayors - Mouse World is totally tacky. We would not want anything to do with a planner involved with Mouse World

- Payroll tax vs. fixed payments
    - Mouse – We can offer you more with a payroll tax than with fixed payments because it is tied to our success. The risk is minimal and the potential gains are great.
    - Mayors – We are more comfortable with a fixed payment, even if it is less, because we do not like risk. We also do not trust Mouse to report its payroll accurately because it is not French, but a multi-national conglomerate.
        - Are the different perspectives of Mouse and the Mayors on this issue a result of their different nationalities? If not, what is the basis for their differing perspectives?
            - This is less a matter of national differences than of conservative, unsophisticated small-town mayors on one side and sophisticated business people on the other side. This same dynamic – rural conservatism and distrust of big city shenanigans could play out in a purely internal negotiation in either France or the U.S.
        - What that teaches is that all cultural differences are not necessarily trans-national differences. You can do a cross-cultural negotiation within your own country as well, and must take this into account in your negotiation preparation – Are there any cultural differences between us and the folks we are to negotiate with that could impact on the negotiations?

3. Apart from the cultural differences which we tried to build into this negotiation, we also tried to make the negotiation still more complex by presenting you with multiple issues and multiple parties: 4 mayors, Mouse, and the French national government. I assume that in order to be most efficient, you dealt with one issue at a time, resolving it before you went on to the next one. Am I right about that?
    - Shouldn't be. If you negotiate one issue at a time, you deprive yourself of the opportunity to trade high priority items for low priority items. Particularly if you start with the easy issues, on which agreement is not difficult, you may find yourself at the end with issues that are high priority for you, and you've nothing to trade to get them. So you should not negotiate one issue at a time, but negotiate issues in blocks, or, even better, negotiate all issues at the same time.
        - How can you negotiate all issues at the same time and make any progress? How can you keep 15 issues in play at the same time?
            - The key is to enter into tentative agreements, ideally involving blocks of issues, but with the explicit understanding that nothing is final until everything is final. In that way, if you do get to the end, and are stuck for trade-offs, you can always go back and renegotiate a few items, trading what you care less about for what you care more about.

3. Getting back to cultural issues, what should you do to minimize the likelihood that cultural differences of the sort we saw in Mouse will interfere with reaching agreement?
    - Prepare for cultural differences. Learn all you can about the culture of the people you will be negotiating with. . .not just national cultural differences, but also regional (do Texans come from the same culture as New Yorkers?), and even contextual (what do business people from the south of France think about this issue?)
        - The best way to prepare for cultural differences is to engage someone who knows the culture in question

3. Finally, as important as it is to be prepared for cultural differences, don't get so fixated on cultural differences that you forget that you will be dealing with individuals who are themselves, not merely representatives of their culture.
    - Pretty obvious. If somebody from Japan hired an expert on the United States, even on the Midwest, approach to center city redevelopment, would he be fully prepared to negotiate with you on that subject?
- As important as it is to understand the culture from which the other negotiator comes, it is also important to know the other negotiator.

EXERCISE 10.2   ALPHA BETA ROBOTICS NEGOTIATION

Teaching Instructions

While Mouse sought to demonstrate how different cultural values can affect a cross-cultural negotiation, Alpha Beta seeks to demonstrate the effect of culturally based differences in negotiation style. The exercise is most likely to be successful in that respect if the students can stay in role during the exercise. Thus, you may want to instruct them to read and follow the advice about their negotiating style that is contained in their confidential information.

We recommend teams of 2-4 students for this exercise, and a time limit of 60-75 minutes.

EXERCISE 10.2   ALPHA BETA ROBOTICS NEGOTIATIONS

Confidential Information for Alpha, Inc.

Five months ago, your firm approached and held preliminary discussions with local representatives of Beta, Inc. on a possible robot manufacturing and marketing relationship. Some tentative understandings have been reached regarding the general nature of a collaborative arrangement, but a number of specific details still need to be worked out. Your bargaining team will be going to Beta to discuss these points with Beta Inc. You would like, if possible, to wrap up the deal on this trip.

In preparing for your trip to the country of Beta, which none of you have previously visited, you read a number of articles and guidebooks on Beta. While Beta is a large country, with some regional variations, it appears that Betans generally exhibit behaviors, which are characterized as "formal", "unemotional", "passive", "indirect", or "patient". They also tend to behave collectively, and have a strong sense of group loyalty.

Your long-range strategic objective is to become a profitable, innovative, global, full-service supplier of automation equipment and systems. You believe leadership in equipping the "factory of the future" will come by putting more pieces of the automation puzzle together than any other firm. Even in the robotics portion of this business you believe that the key to success lies in having a broad range of models to offer industrial customers. You have also determined that you must get into the market now, not five years from now. You must first accumulate experience and establish yourself as the first and favored supplier of those companies turning to automation to boost their quality and productivity.

Top management has considered a variety of options with respect to achieving these goals. It has concluded, for example, that the company robotics program is developing too slowly. Exciting things will definitely be pouring out of the labs and into production in about 3 to 4 years, but at the moment, the company cannot rely just on in-house capabilities. In order to establish an initial market presence, to learn the business and to bridge the transitional R & D gap, Alpha must acquire and exploit the leading edge robotics technology of other firms as an interim move.

Licensing high quality technology from leading foreign firms seems to be the best strategy. Alpha Inc.'s unique strategic advantage is its large industrial sales, distribution and service network, in addition to its experience installing factory automation packages. These qualifications have made Alpha an attractive potential partner in the eyes of a number of foreign robotics producers, including Beta Inc., a leader in the field. Beta Inc. is producing a variety of types of robots. Their robotics are both high quality and cost competitive.

In preliminary talks with Beta Inc., it was tentatively agreed that 1) the relationship will be for 7 years; 2) initially Alpha Inc. will receive fully assembled Beta Inc. robots from Beta Inc.'s current model lines to be sold under the Alpha Inc. name; 3) later on Alpha Inc. will begin to assemble robots using Beta Inc. technology and components; 4) the agreement will be non-exclusive, meaning that Beta Inc. can enter Alpha Inc.'s markets directly at any time and can also enter into relationships with other firms in Alpha.

Five issues that still need to be decided include:

1) <u>The number of different models involved.</u> You would like the number to be 8; you will take 6 only as a last resort.

Your interest in so many models is in line with Alpha's "supermarket of automation" strategy. Fewer models will mean that several different manufacturers' robots may be needed to automate a factory. This will increase the transaction costs of putting together a deal as well as the costs to service and maintain equipment supplied by many different manufacturers.

2) <u>The number of Beta Inc. units to be imported and/or produced under license by Alpha each year.</u> You would like that number to be 150 of each model, a total of 1200.

While you believe that Alpha Inc.'s share of the market will be at least 1200 robots a year, you do not want to be overextended and have to maintain Beta Inc.'s expensive robots in inventory. You know that Beta has a commitment to vastly increase its manufacturing capacity and you are confident that as your sales volume increases, Beta Inc. will be able to increase production. Thus, while you do not want to commit to more than 1200 robots per year initially, you anticipate being able to sell perhaps as many as 900 more than that after the first year.

3) <u>The matter of technology sharing.</u> Beta Inc. is aware of your research related to artificial vision for robots, though they do not know that you anticipate that at least 4 more years of development will be necessary before robots with artificial vision will be ready for commercial use. You do not want to share this technology with Beta Inc. because you think that it may be Alpha Inc.'s unique technological contribution to robotics.

However, if Alpha Inc. is to develop its own robotics manufacturing capacity, assistance from a company like Beta Inc. which is already manufacturing robots in volume will greatly reduce the learning curve. Beta Inc. has already agreed in principle to assist Alpha Inc. in developing the capacity to assemble Beta Inc. robots during the latter part of the licensing agreement. You want a firm commitment as to when this transfer of technology will occur.

You may have to provide access to the artificial vision technology in order to get access to the assembly technology.

4) **The royalty rate.** You are willing to pay a 3% royalty on gross sales of Beta Inc.'s robots. If necessary, you can go as high as 7% if Beta Inc. comes through substantially on your demands on items 1, 2 and 3 above.

5) **The dispute resolution clause.** In your preliminary talks with Beta Inc., you indicated that you wanted a contract provision that all disputes would be resolved by final and binding arbitration. You think such a clause is highly desirable, because some disputes are inevitable in any long-term relationship, and you don't want to get involved in litigation in the Betan courts or in attempting to enforce an Alphan judgment in Beta. The Betans were initially resistant to arbitration, however, and you do not want to see the deal fail on this issue. Thus while you should try once again to persuade Beta Inc. to accept an arbitration clause, if necessary you will settle for a mediation provision, since you have great faith in the capacity of mediation to resolve most disputes.

While there are other robotics manufacturers, Beta Inc. is the only producer with a full product line. If no agreement can be reached with Beta Inc. you will have to negotiate with at least two other producers in order to have a full product line. This will cause delay in the implementation of Alpha Inc.'s strategy to be the premier provider of factory automation.

THE ALPHAN NEGOTIATING STYLE

Negotiators from the Alpha culture typically employ a style (i.e., set of behaviors) which is *individual, informal, impatient, direct, emotional and aggressive*. It is vitally important that your team exhibit this "style" in your bargaining with Beta Inc. today. Guidelines on how to do so are provided below. You should discuss each guideline as a group and plan how each will be followed in the negotiating session. A little practice may be useful in regard to some of the prescribed behaviors. In your negotiations you must:

1. **BEHAVE INDIVIDUALLY**--Initiative is characteristic of your "can do" culture, and is expected from each of you; you each have individual responsibilities and can make individual contributions. The words "I" and "you" should be prominent in your discussion at the bargaining table. Decisions by your side can be made either by voting or independently by the appointed group leader.

2. **BEHAVE INFORMALLY**--Alphans don't attach much importance or significance to ceremony, tradition or formalized social rules. You consider formality, style and protocol as pompous and arrogant. Alphans are easy-going, casual, relaxed and friendly people; they love to kid and joke around. Greet people with vigorous handshakes and slaps on the back. You want to get on a first name basis as soon as possible.

3. **BEHAVE IMPATIENTLY**--To be idle is wasteful and non-productive in the Alphan culture--"time is money." You feel annoyance when confronted with delay or opposition. You want to get right down to business--no "pussy-footing" around. You are willing to make concessions throughout a negotiation. The idea is to settle one issue and move on to the next. What you want is an effective total package obtained in the most efficient manner possible.

4. BEHAVE DIRECTLY--In the Alphan culture it is a matter of honor to "get the cards on the table." The assumption is that no matter how much it hurts, the "truth" is good for you and it is a sign of strength and maturity to give and receive negative feedback. So today you'll "tell it like it is" and minimize ambiguity and uncertainty by complete openness, explicitness and frankness. You won't hesitate to "clear the air" if it needs it.

5. BEHAVE EMOTIONALLY--Alphans tend to be extroverts and show emotion easily, exuberantly and rapidly. Alphans also tend to be confident and optimistic; be sure to enter the negotiation room confidently and to talk assertively. But convey sincerity and warmth since that is also a big part of your character.

6. BEHAVE AGGRESSIVELY—Taking risks, being active, and intelligently using power are all virtues in the Alpha culture. You are full of enterprise and initiative. You are ready and willing to take issue or engage in direct action. Your tool kit of persuasive tactics includes threats and warnings.

EXERCISE 10.2   ALPHA BETA ROBOTICS NEGOTIATIONS

Confidential Information for Beta Inc.

Five months ago, your firm was approached by and held preliminary discussions with local representatives of Alpha Inc. on a possible robotics manufacturing and marketing relationship. Some tentative understandings have been reached regarding the general nature of a collaborative arrangement, but a number of specific details still need to be worked out. The Alpha Inc. bargaining team will be arriving in Beta to discuss these points with you.

In preparing for your meetings with the Alpha negotiating team, you have read all you can find on Alphan culture. While Alpha is a large country, with substantial regional variations, it appears that Alphans generally exhibit behaviors which are characterized as "individual", "informal", "impatient", "direct", "emotional", and "aggressive".

Beta Inc.'s strategic plan calls for significantly boosting overseas sales of robots so as to attain greater scale economies in production. You especially want to develop a presence in the currently small but rapidly growing Alphan market. This implies, of course, the need for a high quality industrial sales, distribution and service network. You have considered the options of exporting directly to, or establishing a joint venture or wholly-owned subsidiary in Alpha. However, given the large cultural differences between Alpha and Beta, the difficulties of servicing robots overseas, and the rapid technological changes in robotics, Beta Inc. has decided (as have other Betan robot producers) that the Alphan market at this time can probably best be served via a licensing arrangement with a local Alphan company. You can offer that company proven, high quality robotics, either in the form of fully assembled units or the technology and components needed to produce them.

Alpha Inc. looks like an ideal candidate to become your licensee--it has the desired technical competence, industrial marketing expertise, service network, quality control, distribution system, general management and business reputation. You are a bit concerned, however, that by helping Alpha Inc. you may create a competitive monster that may come back to haunt you in the future.

In preliminary talks with Alpha Inc., it was tentatively agreed that 1) the relationship will be for 7 years; 2) initially Alpha Inc. will receive fully assembled Beta Inc. robots from Beta Inc.'s current model lines to be sold under Alpha Inc.'s name; 3) later on Alpha Inc. will begin to assemble robots using Beta Inc.

technology and components; 4) the agreement will be non-exclusive, meaning that Beta Inc. can enter Alpha Inc.'s markets directly at any time and can also enter into relationships with other firms in Alpha.

Five issues that still need to be decided include:

1) <u>The number of different models to provide to Alpha Inc.</u> You currently have eight models in production. You would like to provide Alpha with only four of them, and will under no circumstances provide more than six models. If you must go to six, you would still prefer to provide only four models in the first year or two. Supplying Alpha Inc. with robots will require increasing production capacity. You would like to control capital expenditures by phasing in the increased capacity.

2) <u>The number of Beta Inc. units to be imported and/or produced under license by Alpha during each year.</u> You would like the number to be as close to 400 per model as possible, since your strategic goal is deep penetration of the Alphan market. As with the number of models, however, you prefer to move up to the desired number gradually.

3) <u>The matter of technology sharing.</u> You very much want access to Alpha Inc.'s R & D technology related to artificial vision. You are certain that with your manufacturing expertise and your line of universal assembly robots that together you and Alpha Inc. could be the first to market the low cost universal robots with vision. This <u>is the most important issue for you.</u>

You reluctantly agreed to help Alpha develop its own robotics manufacturing processes. Just when this transfer of technology will occur was left open. You will only make a firm commitment regarding the transfer of manufacturing technology if you get access to their artificial vision technology.

4) <u>The royalty rate.</u> You believe a rate of 5% on gross sales is just and reasonable. If absolutely necessary you might consider a royalty rate as low as 3% in order to get access to the artificial vision technology.

5) <u>The dispute resolution clause.</u> In your preliminary talks with Alpha Inc., they indicated their desire for a contract clause to provide that all disputes would be resolved by binding arbitration pursuant to the rules of the International Chamber of Commerce. Betans generally perceive arbitration as too adversarial a process for parties to a long term relationship, and you share this distaste for arbitration. You would rather have no provision at all for disputes, counting on the strength of the relationship and the parties' need for each other to lead to a negotiated resolution of any difficulties. Thus, the most you will agree to is a   clause requiring each party to negotiate in good faith to resolve any misunderstandings, as well as a provision for outside assistance, such as mediation, for the negotiators.

While there are other firms distributing robotics, no other organization in the world has adopted Alpha Inc.'s strategy of being a full-service supplier of automation equipment. If no agreement with Alpha Inc. is forthcoming, you will have to negotiate with several other distributors in order to have the distribution capacity that your strategy requires. This will cause a delay in the implementation of Beta Inc.'s strategy since there have been no negotiations with other distributors.

THE BETAN NEGOTIATING STYLE

Negotiators from the Beta culture typically employ a style (i.e., a set of behaviors) which is <u>collective, formal, patient, indirect, unemotional</u> and <u>passive</u>. It is vitally important that your team exhibit this "style" in your bargaining with Alpha Inc. Guidelines on how to do so are provided below. You should discuss each guideline as a group and plan how each will be followed in the negotiating session. A little practice may be useful in regard to some of the prescribed behaviors. In your negotiations you must:

1. **BEHAVE COLLECTIVELY**—Loyalty to the group is essential and takes precedence over personal feelings. "We" is more important than "I" (the word "I" should not be used today). Any decisions by your side must be reached via group consensus. If all of you cannot agree, than defer making the decision.

2. **BEHAVE FORMALLY**—Betans are "polite to a fault." They attach considerable importance to fixed customs, rules and ceremonies. Betans frequently open negotiations by giving gifts to opposing negotiators. (This is a ceremony intended to show that the negotiations are only part of a broader relationship.) Betans bow when greeting others, and use last names only (using first names is embarrassing for you), exchange calling cards if available, and often sit throughout negotiations with erect posture.

3. **BEHAVE PATIENTLY**—Patience and endurance are cardinal Betan virtues. As noted above, the negotiations are only part, though an important part, of a long-term relationship that will be established if the negotiations are successful. Thus, it would not be out of character for you to start the negotiation session with a discussion of something completely unrelated to the licensing deal.

Stick with your demands as long as you can; you have faith in the righteousness of your bargaining goals--they are just, proper and fair. Betans seldom make piecemeal concessions; make any concessions only at the very end of the bargaining session.

4. **BEHAVE INDIRECTLY**--In Beta, tentativeness, vagueness and playing hard to read are standard behaviors. Don't look members of the Alpha team in the eye when you are talking to them, look down instead (facial gazing is considered aggressive and individualistic). Use the word "yes" when you mean "I hear you talking" or "I'm trying to understand." The word "no" is hardly ever employed in Beta. Answering in the complete negative would lead to embarrassment and loss of face. So instead of "no", substitute "that would be very difficult" instead.

5. **BEHAVE UNEMOTIONALLY**—Betans do not show emotion easily or quickly. They go to great lengths to hide their inner feelings. You do not laugh easily with strangers. Emphasize reserve and modesty, and limit your facial expressions. Do not openly disagree or lose your temper in a negotiation session.

6. **BEHAVE PASSIVELY**--Betans dislike crude or Machiavellian bargaining tactics such as bluffs, threats or escalating demands-- "crude tactics cause great injuries." You dislike bold use of power and excessively logical or pushy people. If pressed or challenged, try to change the subject or just remain quiet. You know how to pause and wait in silence for long periods before proceeding with further talk.

EXERCISE 10.2   ALPHA BETA ROBOTICS NEGOTIATIONS

Teaching Notes

Apart from the difficulties caused by the different negotiating styles, this is not a difficult negotiation, since there is a zone of agreement on each issue. A typical agreement will follow this pattern: Beta agrees to provide Alpha with six models (perhaps only four the first year), and Alpha agrees to take 200-300 of each model in the first year, 300-350 of each model in succeeding years (since Alpha expects total sales after year one to rise to 2100 per year). The parties agree to technology sharing at a fixed date in the future, and to a royalty rate between 3-5%. They further agree to mediate future disputes, sometimes adding a "negotiate in good faith" requirement.

While this is representative of a typical agreement, it is equally, if not more typical that the parties do not reach agreement. The slow, passive Betan negotiating style often infuriates the Alphans, who sometimes do not believe the Betans genuinely want a deal. As a result, the Alphans may stop searching for creative means to break initial deadlocks, leading to impasse, or may simply announce that an impasse exists. other negotiations may move too slowly to reach agreement within the allotted time. In any event, a negotiation that could lead to an agreement often ends in deadlock. Even for those groups that do reach agreement, there is apt to have been considerable frustration and occasional anger (usually suppressed) during the negotiation.

In discussing this negotiation, students will often say that if they had not been required by their instructions to remain in role, they would have modified their negotiating style in order to be more accommodating to the style of the other team. They may suggest that the exercise is flawed because it does not allow them to make such accommodations.

From our perspective, this suggestion ought not be followed. As the exercise now stands, it is a powerful demonstration of the negative impact of not accommodating one's style to adapt to cross-cultural differences between negotiators. The students are likely to remember that lesson longer after a frustrating negotiation in which none of the negotiation teams did accommodate to the different cultural norms of the other team.

Among the questions that might be raised in discussing this negotiation are: What behavioral difficulties did you encounter? Were you adequately prepared for those difficulties? How would you prepare for these negotiations in the real world (raising and discussing the different perspectives of Brett (pp. 555-557) and Rubin and Sander (pp. 557-560))? If you hadn't been required to stay in role, how would you have dealt with the other team's different negotiating style?

CHAPTER 11. THE FUTURE OF ADR

11.1 Both the approaches advanced by the committee members have shortcomings. The "separate department" approach may compartmentalize the disputing process into litigation and settlement sectors, to a client's tactical and economic disadvantage when, in fact, it is an organic whole. Transaction costs are likely to be increased as more lawyers are involved in a case. And there is no reason to suppose that many of the best litigators are not also excellent negotiators and dispute resolution practitioners. On the other hand, in a large law firm, there is likely to be a wide variation in sensitivity to and knowledge of alternatives. In a busy firm lawyers may not feel that they have the time to explore alternatives and will resort to the most familiar patterns of disputing even if in the long run they take more time and cost more.

A middle approach is to educate all lawyers in the firm in alternatives so that they can incorporate these concepts into their daily practice, but also to designate one or more persons in the litigation department as the alternative dispute resolution experts. These persons would be responsible for 1) screening each dispute or group of disputes on intake and periodically thereafter, and 2) with the attorney in charge of the dispute, thinking about the best settlement strategy and process for the dispute. They would also be responsible for keeping abreast of developments in the alternatives field and would be available as a resource to the other lawyers in the firm.

11.2 The general notion that parties should attempt to resolve their dispute by ADR prior to bringing suit is a sensible one. It can be seen as a counterpart to the duty to apprise clients of ADR options (p. 290) and the CPR pledge (p. 567). The problem comes in the enforcement. Requiring the moving party to give notice to the other party prior to bringing suit presents no particular problem. But what is meant by the requirement "that the parties have attempted, and failed, to resolve their dispute" ? Compare the response to question 6.11 dealing with a "good faith" duty to mediate.

The sanctions provision of the proposal raises questions similar to those presented in many arbitration programs. See p. 389 for a discussion of this issue in the SPIDR Report. But note that sanctions for refusal to better an arbitration award are different from sanctions for refusal to accept an offer from the other side. In the former situation there has been some independent determination of the value of the claim and hence the case for sanctions if the loser does not better his position in court is more tenable. The issue here would be very similar to that presented by Federal Rule 68 which presently permits such sanctions for offers by the defendant. But a proposal to permit both parties to make offers, and, more important, to include attorney's fees, has met strong opposition, particularly from the civil rights community which is concerned about using this type of sanction to discourage innovative claims.

11.3 In theory the proposal seems like a good idea. First, it would lead a knowledgeable and responsible group to seek to define – hopefully with wide input – the key ingredients of an effective dispute resolution process. Compare the analogous grant to the Federal Trade Commission under the Magnuson-Moss Warranty Act of 1975 of the power to determine what constitutes the elements of a fair dispute resolution procedure that a consumer must first exhaust before bringing suit. See Goldberg, Green and Sander, Dispute Resolution 389-396 (1985). Unlike the situation in the Magnuson-Moss Warranty Act, here, as in the Good Housekeeping Seal of Approval, the stamp of approval would not be related to access to court, but would be simply for the guidance of the consumer.

Second, as pointed out in the question, the criteria established might serve as useful guides to organizations that had dispute resolution mechanisms of various kinds.

One problem might be that the task would be an immense one. First, as indicated, there would be the critical job of drawing up the basic guidelines, and then there would be the job of applying them to "providers." Does this include courts? Does it include government agencies or only private organizations? Suppose a provider disagrees with the evaluation given by NIDR to its dispute resolution process. What remedies are there for review?

11.4   There is a basic initial question whether court-annexed ADR should be financed by the disputants or by the public fisc. Although the incremental ADR costs for litigants are likely to be a small amount vis à vis the amount at issue in larger cases, some believe (see, e.g., Sander, 1992) that as a matter of public policy courts should pay all the dispute processing costs, no matter what process is used. Otherwise there is a perverse incentive to use court adjudication just because the neutral is provided free. If public funds are to be used, then a choice arises between general court funds or a special add-on filing fee. The former seems right in principle, but in a time of tight budgets, the latter may be a viable alternative. It can also be defended on the ground that the costs are thus allocated to the group that will directly benefit from more efficient case processing - a kind of user fee.

As regards the volunteer alternative now used in some community programs and a few other settings, there is an obvious benefit to the court as well as the volunteers. And if there is adequate training and careful screening, there will be a valuable byproduct - the development of a knowledgeable and concerned cadre of dispute resolvers who will help to "spread the word" and utilize ADR in other situations (e.g., volunteer lawyers performing a court-annexed mediation may use mediation in their other cases). But what do we say to our talented young graduates who want to make a career of helping others resolve their disputes? That they should find some other work to support themselves and do dispute resolution in their spare time? Compare Chapter 11B.

11.5   The cited Zeughauser article, which deserves reading in full, raises some important questions about changing the incentive structures at law firms. Under his proposal, there would be an incentive for the lawyers to settle early, as he says. But ADR work is not rewarded unless there is a settlement, which may have its own perverse effects. And unless the client gets a significant discount from the litigation budget (which is used to determine the fee due on settlement), there may not be adequate incentive for the client to push towards ADR. But an approach like that suggested seems worth further investigation and testing.

11.6   One general counsel said that his directives to his lawyers to increase mediation use were unavailing until, to combat tradition, he required lawyers in his office to provide a written explanation whenever engaging in discovery before trying mediation. This "forced diet" concerning the lawyers' information needs resulted in the company shifting to mediation in 40 percent of their business cases (Rogers & McEwen 1998:843). As regards the general relation of discovery to settlement, see the Answer to Question 5.12.

11.7   Stuart G. Webb, a Minneapolis lawyer who has practiced collaborative law full-time since 1990 argues that the collaborative lawyer's withdrawal if the parties go to litigation is the "governor" of the concept. "We lawyers drift to court," he warns. "If the negotiating lawyer is also preparing to litigate, litigation will be part of the mindset. Conversely, a lawyer who cannot threaten litigation must learn to negotiate more effectively."

CHAPTER 12 - DISPUTE RESOLUTION PROBLEMS

12.1: Irving Weston v. Lawyer's Press, Inc.

Litigation does not appear an attractive procedure for this case. The issues of under-promotion and misrepresentation present difficult legal issues, likely to be quite costly to try. In view of the lost records, the royalties issue may also require considerable proof, adding further to trial costs. Also cutting against litigation will be Lawyer's desire not to have a dispute between it and one of its authors public knowledge, as that might tarnish its reputation with other writers. Finally, the parties have an ongoing relationship with respect to the sessions law project, and litigation is likely to damage that relationship still more, to the mutual harm of the parties.

In a case like this, the optimum approach would appear to be mediation, in which the primary focus would be on maximizing future sales and establishing a better system for royalty reporting, both issues on which the parties have common interests. Focusing on these issues may take some of the emotional steam out of the disputes as to past under-promotion and underpayment of royalties, and so make those issues easier to resolve. If not, arbitration of these issues would be appropriate, though not inexpensive because of the previously mentioned difficulties of proof. Arbitration might also be necessary on the misappropriation issue, unless Lawyer's is willing to negotiate, as part of the overall mediation, a financial settlement of that claim.

A final issue is whether mediation would be appropriate for the fraud and misrepresenta- tion counts. If the participants in mediation are the alleged wrong-doers, it may be difficult to achieve a successful resolution in light of the face-saving considerations that will likely be involved. However, even if others (who were not involved in the alleged fraud) are present at the mediation, questions of credibility are likely to be an issue. This raises the question of whether credibility issues can be adequately dealt with in mediation. Typically, they are dealt with by putting them to the side and working out a settlement without attempting to resolve them. If a resolution is necessary, or a formal means for at least testing credibility is desirable, a mini-trial can be convened, limited to taking the testimony of the key witness, with opportunity for cross-examination. That will provide the parties with common information about likely determinations of credibility at trial, and so may spur a negotiated settlement.

12.2: Casey's Fee

Since the admissions procedure issue appears to be the most complex (most of the negotiating time was devoted to it), and an intricate, but mutually satisfactory settlement of that issue has been reached, an initial suggestion might be to split that issue off from the financial issues, and regard the former as settled. The mediator might point out to the defendant that splitting this issue off does not put it in a position in which it will necessarily pay more than it has already agreed. For, if both the damages and the fee issue are litigated, defendant may be successful in reducing the damages to the individual plaintiffs sufficiently that its total costs will be less than the $750,000 it had agreed to pay ($500,000 to the individual plaintiffs, plus its $250,000 offer to Casey). If, for example, defendant succeeds in reducing damages to $250,000, it could be found liable to Casey in the amount of $400,000, and still come out ahead. Of course, whether all financial issues are litigated or only the fee issue, the costs of litigation will be substantial. The mediator should point that out in seeking to obtain a settlement of the financial issues.

If the financial issues are to be litigated, in what forum should this litigation take place? One possibility is the federal court in which the case is pending, but that has disadvantages. There is apt to be considerable delay in getting to trial (this case has been pending for seven years, and both parties may now wish to end it as soon as possible), and the judge, who is the fourth judge assigned to this case, will have to be educated in all its complexities, promising a lengthy and expensive trial.

Another possibility is to appoint the mediator to serve as an arbitrator, and to try the financial issues before him in an arbitration forum. This is likely to be faster than court adjudication (unless the mediator has a greater backlog of cases than the district court), and less expensive, since the mediator's extensive involvement in the case will make it unnecessary to spend time educating him. (Some of that saving, however, will be lost by the need to compensate the arbitrator, a need that would not arise if the case were tried in court.) A provision for final offer arbitration might even break the log jam and lead to a negotiated settlement.

The central disadvantage of trying the financial issues to the mediator turned arbitrator is that he is likely to have learned things in attempting to bring about a settlement that should have no bearing on his decision as an adjudicator, but will be difficult for him to block out in reaching a decision. It will be particularly difficult for him to do so in this case, where he has spent over 150 hours with the parties, mostly in separate meetings.

One might, to avoid this problem, suggest that the parties appoint a different person as arbitrator. If they do, however, they will be faced with the same expensive proposition of educating him as of educating the district judge if they tried it before him. Indeed, in financial terms this would give them the worst of both worlds -- they would be required both to pay the adjudicator and to spend time educating him.

In sum, there is no wholly satisfactory way to resolve this dispute by adjudication. Hence, the best course might be for the mediator to point this out to the parties, and to encourage them to make further efforts to reach a negotiated settlement. (In fact the mediator did so, but with only limited success. The parties appointed the mediator to serve as arbitrator, and tried the fee issue before him.)

12.3:   American Can Co. v. Wisconsin Electric Power Co.

The costs of litigating this case would be enormous, and the likely outcome, in view of the technical issues, would be very difficult to predict. Additionally, the time necessary to achieve a resolution through litigation would be substantial, and during that time the recycling facility and two WEPCO boilers would probably remain unused. Thus, it is to both parties' advantage to resolve this dispute promptly. Still, the difficulties in doing so are likely to be great.

This is the kind of case in which individuals on each side are likely to be heavily invested in the case, especially if they were involved in the project originally. They made decisions and actions which they now are defending; careers may hinge on the outcome. For these reasons, despite the business context, disputes of this sort can be just as emotional as a marriage dissolution, taking on the quality of "good vs. evil" in the eyes of the individuals involved.

The parties' emotional positions are often reinforced by their one-sided views of the facts and law. In this case, the issues are so complex legally and factually that each side can find somewhere in the contract or the events of the previous years ample support for its position. In this situation, negative information may be undervalued, ignored or disbelieved, even by the attorneys. Thus, it is not unusual in cases of this sort for both sides sincerely to predict that they have a 75 per cent or better chance of winning in court.

If the conditions which create this gap persist, it is highly unlikely that the parties will be able to negotiate a settlement. Thus, to overcome the barriers to a negotiated settlement in this case, the conditions which create this gap must be altered. Emotionalism must be reduced by bringing in individuals who were not involved in the project originally and thus do not have a direct personal stake in the outcome. The gap between the parties' estimates of likely outcome must be narrowed by developing and sharing in a neutral setting the relevant factual information and the parties' characterizations of the legal implications of that data. Finally, the parties must be made to appreciate the huge risks of a total loss if the case goes to trial and of the steps they can take to eliminate those risks by developing a businesslike solution. .

The mini-trial seems ideally suited for this kind of dispute because of its involvement of top business managers who were not involved in the underlying decisions regarding the recycling project and thus do not have any personal stake in the dispute, but who have the authority and the perspective to try to resolve the dispute on a business-like basis. The mini-trial also seems well-suited to this dispute because it affords an opportunity for a reasoned dialogue on the merits of the legal dispute before these managers. This enables them to get a realistic view of the strengths and weaknesses of their case, and thus to form a realistic judgment of their best alternative to a negotiated agreement. Armed with this information, and with the detached perspective of the manager facing the decision whether to invest in this dispute, the managers on each side may be able to bridge the gap between them by conceiving some use for the idle facilities.

(The case on which this problem is based was actually settled through use of a mini-trial. See Gorske, "Wisconsin Electric, American Can Settle a 4.1 Million Suit Through Mini-trial," 1 Alternatives 23 (Nov., 1983)).

12.4:   The HAL 2001 Computer

From both sides' perspective, the optimal strategy is to resolve the disputes over past events and accounts as quickly as possible and resume leasing to third party users, assuming a viable market still exists. After all, it is in the parties' mutual interest to keep the stream of revenue from the users running. If the parties are unable to negotiate directly the adjustments to the original agreement that must be made to make the arrangement acceptable to both sides, a mediator may be able to assist them.

A mini-trial also seems like a good approach in this case for two reasons: (1) the involvement of "fresh" managers at a higher level of authority (and, possibly broader vision) than those previously involved; (2) its truncated but focused exchange of information about the underlying dispute. The first factor should increase the likelihood of finding an integrative solution. The second addresses the problem of lack of information, as well as giving each side its "day in court."

The new information the mini-trial business participants receive about likely trial outcomes may narrow the gap between the parties created by overly optimistic estimations of success. Once this gap is narrowed, the business people should be able to find a solution that bridges whatever gap remains.

Two caveats: (1) If Leasco is serious about the antitrust counterclaim, genuinely believing it may recover $150 million, and HAL believes that claim is frivolous, it will be very difficult to find a settlement until one of those views changes. A $150 million gap is unlikely to be changed without new information, such as the views of a neutral expert. Thus, the parties should consider, as a first step to settlement, obtaining the advice of a neutral through either an advisory arbitration limited to the anti-trust issue, or a mini-trial similarly limited. (2) Another caveat is that if Leasco is on the verge of insolvency, HAL may want to avail itself of whatever speedy, pre-judgment processes it can use to recover possession of the processors. Of course, taking such action may well precipitate exactly what HAL fears most -- Leasco going under in possession of the processors.

12.5: Cincinnati Foods

One view is that there should be no dispute resolution clause whatsoever. There is an ample supply of farm operators to meet your client's needs, and the transaction costs of changing suppliers when there is a dispute may be less than the transaction costs of attempting to resolve such disputes. A competent dispute systems designer will always weigh the transaction costs of changing an existing system against those of continuing with the current system.

In this case, the transaction costs of the current system are substantial, and the client appears to have determined that some changes are necessary. At a minimum, then, the form contracts should set out a simple negotiation procedure, consisting of one or two steps, followed by mediation. Ideally, this would be accompanied by a one-day training session in interest-based negotiation for both Cincinnati Foods personnel who are likely to be involved in disputes with the farm operators and the operators themselves.

A more difficult question is whether there should be a provision for binding arbitration. It can be argued that Cincinnati Foods should not make such a clause available, since to do so would likely make it financially possible for the farm operators to enforce their contracts, a capacity which they now lack. Whether that argument is persuasive will depend on whether Cincinnati Foods believes that its interests in better relations with the farmers, and perhaps a better image in the community, justify making available an accessible forum that can bind it where none now exists.

12.6: Dyna-Mo Company

This question is intended to encourage the student to think about the varying possible effects of mediation in a situation of power imbalance. Having done so, the student is better equipped to decide whether she wishes to provide mediation services in such a situation.

One possible effect of the availability of mediation here is that the company, clearly the more powerful party in any dispute with one of its employees, will refuse to grant any of its employees' claims regardless of the mediator's suggestions to the contrary. In that event, mediation would be useless. Another possibility is that when an employee has a "just" claim, the mediator will use her powers of persuasion to encourage the company to grant that claim. To the extent that were to occur, mediation would serve to reduce the consequences of the power imbalance.

On the other hand, if the mediator persuades the company to grant the most "just" claims of the employees, those which it would be most egregious not to grant, that may reduce the incentive for the employees to seek structural changes (in this case, unionization) that would alter the power imbalance. To the extent that were to occur, the major effect of mediation would be to preserve the existing power disparity, albeit ameliorating some of its more egregious consequences.

Each student (and mediator) must decide for herself whether, under these circumstances, she would agree to provide mediation services for Dyna-Mo.

12.7: Neighborhood Care. Inc.

There are a number of reasons why this dispute will be difficult to resolve:

1. Although there are two immediate parties to the dispute -- the church and the neighborhood -- Neighborhood Care, Inc. (NCI) is an absent party whose track record and capacity to respond to the neighbors' concerns will be of critical importance.

2. The neighborhood is a diffuse aggregation of individuals. Who is authorized to speak for it? How can the church be sure that if it agrees to certain concessions demanded by the current spokespersons for the neighbors, others will not come forward later and make different demands. Compare the discussion of this issue in Chapter 9.

3. There are many vital facts that need to be ascertained before a viable settlement can be reached. Among these are the precise plans of NCI and their past record in similar situations, as well as the provisions of the governing zoning ordinance. Nonetheless the neighbors and the Church have many interests that overlap, and many of their apparent differences seem to be based on possibly incorrect assumptions about the other, or grievances concerning unrelated prior events. Thus, the dispute seems well-suited for mediation. Accordingly perhaps the best that can be achieved in the initial mediation session is to allow some airing of each side's grievances, with a view to separating their asserted positions (e.g., "we don't want a bunch of loonies running around our neighborhood") from their underlying concerns ("how can we be assured there will be adequate supervision of these individuals"). In addition it may be possible to agree on a process for future dealings between the parties and for finding out the facts about NCI's track record and present plans.

Thus a mediator may wish to begin by seeking to ascertain each side's interests which any acceptable solution must address. Some of the neighbors' fears may be quite unfounded (e.g., that NCI's activities will increase crime and reduce their property values). But their underlying concerns must be carefully considered. Some of these appear to be:

1. Noise;

2. Parking;

3. Defining the precise boundaries of the NCI operation (in terms of hours per day, number of patients etc.);

4. Assuring adequate supervision;

The Church will also need to be made aware of the basis for some of the neighbors' concerns (i.e., the Church's past failure to consult with the neighborhood re day care and Sunday school activities).

On the other side, the neighbors need to be made to understand that the church has its own needs (e.g. to help ex-mental patients make a safe transition to normal life and to supplement its waning income), and that it is not oblivious to the neighbors' legitimate concerns.

The upshot of this initial meeting might be a better understanding by each side of the legitimate concerns of the other, and the establishment of a small working group with representatives of all the interested parties whose task will be to work through some of the above issues and come up with specific proposals for the principals to consider. In addition, there is the question whether any half-way house activities will be permitted pending the attempt to work out a formal agreement.

In addition to addressing some of the substantive issues listed above, any agreement should also contain a grievance procedure to aid in the implementation of the agreement.

12.8: <u>Wittamore v. Fairview Clinic</u>

1. Reference to the factors impeding a negotiated outcome that are listed at the end of Chapter 2 (pp. 98-99) suggests that many of them are present here.

    a. <u>Emotionalism and Failure of Effective Communication</u>

Whittamore and Singson are both in high dudgeon, each convinced of the correctness of his own position. Neither seems to have engaged in an interest analysis, with a view to discovering the many common interests they have (such as effectively serving the medical needs of the community, being fair to the remaining physicians at Fairview Clinic, setting a good precedent for similar such cases in the future etc.).

    b. <u>Linkages and Absent Parties</u>

There is an important linkage of the Whittamore-Singson dispute to the marital conflict between Andrew and Jane. Indeed the latter has created the present controversy, yet Jane is not even a party to the present dispute.

Singson is also aware that the present case may create an important precedent for future cases arising under the non-competition clause. This may make him reluctant to enter into a "special deal" with Whittamore.

    c. <u>BATNA</u>

It does not appear that the parties have made any careful assessment of their legal positions (e.g., the validity of the non-competition clause in these circumstances and the likelihood of the high damages being claimed by Singson being upheld by a court). Hence their present claims are extreme.

2. At first glance it might appear that the present dispute centers largely around an unsettled legal issue (i.e., the validity of the non-competition clause), and that therefore arbitration might be the preferred ADR process. That is certainly one possibility. There are few, if any, factual disputes. Hence an arbitration award could be quickly obtained.

But at bottom this case represents a paradigm case for mediation. It involves potentially long-term relationships. The interests of the various parties - some at the table, some not - need to be fully explored if an integrative solution is to be worked out. It is particularly important in this type of situation to avoid a winner and a loser, and rather to seek an accommodative resolution that will leave all the major players feeling as if they have been heard and their concerns fairly addressed. For example Whittamore and Singson might conclude that it was in everyone's interest for Whittamore to leave, but that by way of compensating Fairview for the lost business, Whittamore would pay it 10% of all fees earned within the first two years from individuals who were previously Fairview patients, and that Whittamore in turn would refer to Fairview any patients whose health care needs he could not handle.

Conceivably med-arb might be used if the parties wanted to use mediation but also wanted to be assured of a definite resolution.

A minitrial might be less suitable here because it would not be likely to give enough opportunity to air the parties' concerns, and because there are no uninvolved absent principals here who might be able to take a new look at the case for the purpose of settlement. The key players here are also the principals.

12.9: University Housing Disputes

The landlords' conditional support suggests that arbitration which is binding on landlords will not be acceptable. Similarly, the tenants' interest in fairness indicates that they will not accept an arbitration process which is binding on tenants but not landlords. Thus, a non-binding process such as mediation may be the only process acceptable to both sets of parties. Given the lack of negotiating experience by tenants, it may be better to begin with mediation, rather than using a multi-step process beginning with negotiation, because initial negotiations by tenants and landlords may create antagonisms that will complicate mediation.

The clause should address the choice of the mediator (probably those working in the University program), the agreement regarding confidentiality, the timing, the fees, the efforts required to comply with the clause, and the consequences of noncompliance. The SPIDR Report (Chapter 6) suggests by way of analogy that clear compliance requirements (attend for at least two hours, bring copy of the lease) and mild sanctions (later court action will be dismissed subject to re-filing for non-compliance, for example) will provide an incentive to attend in most cases and that it is not worth the extra costs, in terms of stimulating litigation, for sanctions to secure universal compliance.

(a) Providing Legal Advice Some related issues were considered in Chapter 7. Some options include:

(1) mediation by lawyers, provided that it is clear in this jurisdiction that lawyer-mediators are not acting unethically if they provide legal information to unrepresented mediation parties.

(2) referrals to pro bono or legal services lawyers.

(3) provision of summaries or videotapes of legal issues related to landlord-tenant relationships.

(4) provision of non-lawyer advocates for the tenants (though if they are really providing legal information, there may be unauthorized practice of law issues).

(b) Need For Statute. The student should ask whether a mediation privilege statute covers mediation by this program. If not, review the arguments for and against privilege in Chapter 3D. Another issue is whether a statute is needed to toll any filing deadlines. If immunity is sought, a statute providing for immunity is probably required.

(c) Confidentiality Issues. As discussed in Chapter 3D, a confidentiality clause may be unenforceable against a court subpoena. At the same time, its provisions regarding return or destruction of written records may make the subpoena unproductive. Further, parties will often comply with something they have promised to do.

Given the inexperience of the tenants, the program may want to make a detailed written description about the limits of confidentiality. Otherwise, the tenants may rely to their detriment on the confidentiality clause. The issues involved are discussed in Question 3.30.

(d) <u>Qualifications of Neutrals</u>. This raises the issues discussed in the SPIDR Qualifications Report in Chapter 3C. One issue may be of overriding importance such as the desire to get legal information to the parties by providing lawyer-mediators. If not, there is no indication that entry requirements beyond aptitude and training will serve the program's goals. Depending on the experience and level of distrust, the program may wish to consider joint mediation by landlords and tenants.

12.10 <u>Griswold v. Langdell</u>

This case is typical of many public sector disputes where each party runs off in a different direction, expending vast energy and resources, rather than sitting down and exploring with the other interested parties a solution that might benefit all the parties. See Chapter 9. Hence, this would seem to be a promising case for the Director of the State Office of Dispute Resolution (see pp. 495-496) to become involved in.

The Director might first meet separately with each of the interested parties (the appropriate officials from Langdell, Griswold, EPI and DNR) to explore more fully their respective concerns. That in turn may reveal other parties who should be involved in the proceeding. Although Langdell and Griswold are presently the primary antagonists, it appears that their interests may well be compatible in that Griswold, too, is running out of room for its solid waste, and is experiencing rising citizen opposition to the increasing cost of protracted litigation. Hence this may be a good opportunity for collaborative problem solving.

But there are also some potential obstacles:

1. This type of case is likely to raise many of the problems discussed in Chapter 9, such as the role of the press and persuading the principals who stand behind the agents at the table. Another problem involves who will pay for the mediation process. Even though it may be demonstrable that the costs of mediation would be much less than the costs of litigation, litigation costs are often part of standard operating costs while mediation costs have to come out of special budgets. This is one of the anomalies of ADR practice. The State Office of ADR may have some funds for this type of proceeding, at least funds sufficient to get the process started.

2. Although Langdell's and Griswold's interests are fairly apparent, EPI's and DNR's are less so. EPI may see in this case a good opportunity to get publicity for its work. This goal may conflict with the attempts of the mediator to work out a quiet compromise. Hence at a minimum any mediation effort would need to address that concern (e.g., by giving EPI appropriate credit for any solution worked out).

3. Conceivably EPI will want more than publicity, namely a public declaration that DNR's procedures are inadequate and perhaps even illegal. Such a goal may be difficult to attain in mediation, though it is always open to the parties to agree not only on a mutually acceptable solution to this case but also agreed procedures for handling similar cases in the future.

12.11: <u>Citizens v. Western Nuclear Corporation</u>

The vastly different outcome predictions which have led to the negotiation impasse are unlikely to be affected without new information. The most useful new information would be a credible neutral opinion regarding outcome. The issue here presented is how best to obtain such information.

One possible means of doing so is through a minitrial. The central weakness of the minitrial in this situation, however, is that it will be exceedingly difficult for the neutral advisor to provide a credible prediction of likely outcome because this is such an unusual case. It is unlikely that there have been enough similar cases to enable a neutral advisor to predict with any certainty how a jury is likely to respond to this one.

The best means of dealing with this situation is to conduct a summary jury trial, in which actual jurors can respond to the plaintiffs' theory of damages. To be sure, one advisory jury may not be representative of all potential juries. Still, the opinion of even one such jury is likely to be more persuasive to the litigants than is the opinion of a former judge or lawyer concerning what a jury is likely to do.

In the actual case from which this problem is derived, Judge Richard Enslen, U.S. District Court, Western District of Michigan, conducted a summary jury trial using two advisory juries. One jury found no liability, the other came in with a $2.8 million verdict in the plaintiffs' favor. The confidence of both parties was shaken by the disparate outcomes, and they reached a settlement promptly after the summary jury trial. (The summary jury trial in this case is described and re-enacted in a videotape entitled "Summary Jury Trial", distributed by the National Institute for Dispute Resolution.)

12.12   Satcom, Inc. v. Telecom

If you represented Satcom, your chief concern might be to get a neutral opinion in support of Satcom's position that the reimbursement clause applied in this situation, since this would aid Satcom in its settlement negotiations with Telecom. Under these circumstances, one of the evaluative procedures would be best. If a significant objective were to obtain a precedent, going to court would be necessary, since none of the private procedures establish binding precedents. But obtaining such a precedent would be an unlikely objective in this one-shot situation, with no apparent linkage to other disputes. Moreover, court does not appear to be an attractive option for Satcom, since a trial is at least two years away.

Let us assume, however, that Satcom is primarily interested in restoring its relationship with Telecom, perhaps because it hopes to use the technology it has developed here in another project with Telecom. If that is so, mediation would appear to be the preferred procedure. The minitrial, the summary jury trial, and neutral evaluation are not generally as effective as mediation in maintaining a relationship (see Table 1, p. 295), but, depending on the nature of the barriers to settlement, one of them may be preferable for your client.

One of the barriers to settlement appears to be the current poor relationship of the parties, leading to ineffective communication. Another is that they have different interpretations of their agreement. Multiple parties will also be a factor if there are significant differences among the three corporations that compose Telecom. Under these circumstances, Table 2 (p. 297) suggests that mediation may be the best choice, because it is the most effective in dealing with both poor communication and multiple parties. The minitrial, the summary jury trial, and neutral evaluation are preferable to mediation only in their capacity to deal with the issues of contract interpretation.

From both perspectives, then, mediation appears to be the procedure of choice. It best satisfies your client's objectives and is probably most likely to lead to a settlement. If, however, the dispute between the parties as to their contractual obligations makes settlement through mediation impossible, one of the evaluative procedures -- the minitrial, the summary jury trial, or neutral evaluation - will be required. One possible course of action is to propose to opposing counsel that the parties attempt to resolve the dispute through mediation, but shift to one of the evaluative processes if the mediation reaches an impasse on the legal issues. Another possibility is to consult further with your client and opposing counsel about the significance and difficulty of the legal issues, with a view to recommending that the parties use one of the evaluative procedures initially, followed by mediation if necessary.

If you decide to choose one of the evaluative procedures, you should determine whether neutral evaluation and the summary jury trial are offered by the courts in your jurisdiction. (To be sure, if neutral evaluation is not judicially offered, you can still set it up privately, as a form of advisory arbitration). If both are available, you must then decide which format is most likely to lead to a settlement, and to satisfy your clients goals: the involvement of both clients and a mock jury (summary jury trial), the ruling of a retired judge or other presider (minitrial); or the relatively speedy and inexpensive analysis of an experienced attorney (neutral evaluation).

In the Telecom-Satcom case, considerable evidence concerning the parties' intent may be required; hence the comparatively superficial analysis of neutral evaluation may have little appeal. As between the summary jury trial and the minitrial, the latter may be preferable, since your client wants to maintain a good relationship with Telecom, and in the minitrial top-ranking executives of both companies would hear evidence and argument in a less formal setting than in the summary jury trial.

12.13   A Neighborhood Dispute

The principal question for the prosecutor is whether the public interest would be better served by a public disposition (court adjudication or a plea bargain between the defendant and the prosecutor's office) or by a private settlement. If the defendant's behavior indicates that he is a threat to the public, the public interest calls for a public disposition and the imposition of criminal sanctions. If the defendant's behavior is an outgrowth of this particular dispute with his neighbor, and does not present a threat to others, then the public interest is well served by private resolution. In this driveway dispute, the prosecutor would surely conclude that the defendant's conduct, absent any evidence of a pattern of violence in other contexts, was an outgrowth of the dispute with his neighbor, and hence that a private settlement would be appropriate.

If the prosecutor allowed a private settlement of this matter, the procedure of choice from the public perspective would undoubtedly be mediation, with its focus on relationship issues. Of course, the alleged victim (Smith) would have to be willing to participate in such a proceeding. But he would probably be willing to do so, unless he wanted public vindication, since mediation is more likely than a criminal proceeding to settle the underlying dispute about the driveway. In addition, in mediation Jones might agree to reimburse Smith for his medical expenses and any lost wages.

12.14   Thomas v. Eagle Rifle Co.

Your clients' primary objectives in selecting a dispute resolution procedure would appear to be privacy (in the sense that they do not want a trial) and maximizing their recovery. They might also have interest in keeping costs down and obtaining a speedy resolution, but these would not likely be as important as privacy and maximizing recovery. Unfortunately, the procedures that are likely to maximize recovery, at least if your clients are successful, are arbitration and court, both of which would involve a trial. Thus, if your clients genuinely want to avoid a trial of any kind, mediation looks like the best bet for them.

Your clients do want a settlement of this matter. The impediments to settlement appear to be the parties' different views of the legal outcome if the case is tried, and the linkage of this dispute to other disputes involving Eagle. Mediation is often used in overcoming both impediments. Thus, the combined analysis of client objectives and impediments to settlement support the general presumption in favor of mediation.

It is quite unlikely, however, that Eagle will agree to mediation. Its primary objectives in selecting a dispute resolution procedure would be vindication, a favorable precedent, and minimizing recovery. These objectives each point in the direction of a binding procedure, probably court, and Eagle has been quite successful in court.

There is no indication in the facts that Eagle has settled similar suits against it. To the contrary, its strategy (like that of the tobacco companies) appears to be that of litigating to impress other potential claimants with its firmness. Thus, unless Eagle perceives some weakness in its litigation position in this case, it will probably have little interest in settlement.

If, however, Eagle does see some risk in litigation, it may be quite willing to engage in secret mediation, coupled with a confidentiality clause attached to any settlement. If however, such a provision would prevent your clients from carrying out their publicity objectives, the likelihood of reaching agreement on either a settlement procedure or settlement terms is quite slim.

Still, you will lose nothing by proposing mediation to Eagle, and should certainly do so.

12.15 <u>The Virginia Medical Group</u>

One possibility would be for Ross to enter into an agreement with the physicians that he would not sell his stock without their approval. That might reassure the physicians that control of VMG would not pass to a third party, and so encourage them to remain part of VMG.

In the dispute from which this problem was developed, Ross offered to enter into such an agreement, but that offer was not accepted. Initially, the physicians did not completely trust Ross to abide by his agreement. Furthermore, such an agreement would leave Lane and Shawn as 50% stockholders, and the physicians wanted them gone.

Another possibility would be for Ross to offer to sell his 50% interest to the physicians for $ 1,000,000 (which he did in the real case). While this offer has the seeming defect of moving Ross out of VMG, which he does not want, and keeping Lane and Shawn in VMG, which the physicians do not want, Ross' purpose was not to get the physicians to accept his offer, but to put pressure on Lane and Shawn to sell their stock for the $1,000,000 the physicians had offered them. The pressure is created because Ross' offer dramatically weakens the Lane-Shawn BATNA, while at the same time strengthening the physicians' BATNA.

If the physicians can buy Ross' 50% interest for $1M, they don't need the Lane-Shawn 500/o interest to block the possibility of a sale of VMG. Conversely, if the physicians own a 50/o interest in VMG, the hope of Lane and Shawn that they might some day persuade Ross to join with them to sell a controlling interest to a third party is gone. Thus, the effect of Ross' offer to sell his 50% interest for $1M was to present Lane and Shawn with the choice of accepting the physicians' offer of $ 1 M or be left holding unsalable, essentially valueless stock. Faced with that choice, Lane and Shawn accepted the physicians' offer.

One might think that Ross ran some risk that his offer would be accepted, but that risk was easily nullified. Initially, Ross knew that the physicians would rather buy out Lane and Shawn than buy him out. Furthermore, Ross told the physicians, prior to making the offer, what his strategy was, and they agreed that they would not accept his offer without first advising Lane and Shawn that it had been made, and that it would be accepted unless Lane and Shawn matched it. They further agreed that if Lane and Shawn did not offer to sell their interest, and the physicians bought Ross' interest, Ross would receive a long-term agreement to serve as Executive Director of VMG. Thus, no matter what happened, Ross would remain an integral part of VMG.

12.16 Due Process for Mediation Cases?

This question requires the student in the first place to compare and contrast the goals of litigation and mediation. The adjudication process looks to the past, seeks to determine facts and then apply rules of law to them. Many, if not all, of the cited protections are designed to further those goals.

A mediator, on the other hand, helps the disputants to come to a mutually acceptable settlement. It is future-directed, and does not entail factual determinations. Hence procedures like pleadings, evidentiary rules, discovery, and sanctions for perjury are not germane. (One might also note in passing that since "evidence" in a mediation is not given under oath, a sanction for perjury would be difficult to apply. Of course it is part of the flexibility of mediation that many of these "protections" could be built into a particular proceeding on an ad hoc basis, but one would presumably do this only after carefully weighing the benefits against the costs (such as inhibited disclosures). For example, one might insert a clause into a separation agreement that was the result of a divorce mediation to the effect that the agreement will be void if it turns out that either of the parties had assets significantly different from those listed in the agreement.

Aside from these general observations, it may be instructive to look in more detail at some of the specific procedures. For example, given the custom-made nature of mediation agreements a compilation of past settlements seems of dubious value. But in light of the pervasive concern about the fairness of mediated agreements - particularly in situations of serious power imbalance - some kind of court review might be worth considering. This already occurs in divorce agreements involving children or in certain regulatory situations. Whether it would make sense to require such court approval on a pervasive basis seems open to question.